Death of a Selfish Altruist
(Tales & Poems from a Minor League Culture Worker)

CHRIS STROFFOLINO

Iniquity Press/Vendetta Books

Also By Chris Stroffolino

Notes to a MFA in Non-Poetry (Spuyten Duyvil, 2017)

AnTi-GeNtRiFiCaTiOn WaR dRuM rAdIo (Boog City, 2016)

Life In A Tin-Can (e-book, 2015)

Single-Sided Doubles CD/LP (Pop 3Snob, 2010)

Speculative Primitive (Tougher Disguises, 2005)

Scratch Vocals (Potato Clock (2003)

Spin Cycle (Spuyten Duyvil 2001)

Shakespeare's 12the Night, with David Rosenthal (IDG Books, 2000)

Stealer's Wheel (Hard Press, 1999)

Light As A Fetter (Situations, 1997)

Cusps (Aerial/Edge, 1995)

Oops (backyard press, 1991; Pavement Saw, 1994)

Incidents (Iniquity Press, 1991)

Copyright 2018, Chris Stroffolino
Iniquity Press/Vendetta Books, Seaside Heights, NJ

Cover: "Swamp Deal," Brian Lucas. http://brianlucas-art.com/paintings/

Chris.stroffolino@gmail.com

TABLE OF CONTENTS

1. PREFACE (or Afterword)
2. WORKING CLASS FOOLE OR WORKING CLASS TRAITOR?
3. 70S DECAY IN READING, PENNSYLVANIA..................................21
4. Think Tank 1968
   A) Trying to Make Sense of The Ruins of My Childhood….
   B) Radio As Parent
   C) My Mother, Grandparents, & The White Working Class
   D) Muddled Thoughts On What a GSH Song Meant To Me @17
   E) The Rise Of The CD…
   F) Meanwhile, Back In "What Do You Want to Be When You Grow Up?"

5. THE 1980s: CAN COLLEGE MAKE-UP FOR THE LOSS OF A WALKING CITY AND HELP MAKE AMERICA GREAT AGAIN? (or why meeting John Yau was better than winning the poetry prize)..43

6. A CULTURE WORKER AMONG SPECIALISTS: THE PHILLY YEARS 47
   A) Double (or Triple) Life?
   B) Graffiti Bridge
   C) Grace To Live As Variously As Possible
   D) Attempts At Synthesis: Lorri Jackson

7. THE 90S: CROSSOVER OR SELLOUT?..82
   A) Another Academic Attempt At Straddling Specializations
   B) "Underground Classic"—A Reading Of One Of My Poems From The 90s
   C) Meanwhile, "Outside The Poem."
   D) New York City
   E) Volksboutique
   F) Poetry Wars and Poetry Détente
   G) In The Shallow End Of *American Water*
   H) I know I shouldn't be too harsh on myself, but…
   I) "Some of My Friends Love Le Roi Jones, But….."
   J) Notes To A Sideman Manifesto

8. MINING THE FAULTLINE: Oakland In The 21st Century Technocracy...123
   A) January Term
   B) The Crash of 2004
   C) The Lost Years (or Help Me!)

- D) Ghost Town
- E) Bay Area Radio
- F) The "Great Recession" and Obamamania
- G) Train & Boat Tour (Forgive Me, I Get Carried Away)
- H) Meanwhile, Back In My Professional Life
- I) Meanwhile, Back In My Disability
- J) Meanwhile, Back At The Warehouse
- K) Leonard Cohen Digression
- L) Save KSUF and Occupy Radio
- M) The World Is Not Conclusion (Or Making Fun of Tragedy)

9. Between Poetry And Prose 164

10. APPENDICES
    - A) What Can Be Learned From Rwanda About Battling Depression 167
    - B) "Underground Classic" (poem) 172
    - C) What, If Anything, Can David Lowery or Steve Albini Teach Us About The State of Music Today? 173
    - D) What Can It Mean To Start A Record Label In The New Tech Economy? 179

Preface (or Afterword)

Once upon a time for some
Basic needs were sacred
And the sacred was a basic need

Should we start with a text
that doesn't know
what genre it should be—?
Oh, I could go in many directions
but it depends on who is listening
and in solitude it's easy to forget
till you remember you gotta compartmentalize for a job

Still, you believe in that fertile pre-genre place
where characters might be words (and vice versa)
& dramatic monologue poetry
is at least as dialogic as plays and novels,
where argument essays need not be edited out
of creative writing assignments
nor poetic effusions edited out of the comp class

Can I get music back without a home?
Can I get a home back without music?
If it must be both, do I ask for too much?

++++++++++++

Between Music and Meaning

Meet me, menial mendacious munificent mumblecore murmurers!
Mesh, merciful merchant mommies menstruating men.
Merge Middlemarch mud, mourn muscular museum mummy.
Metaphysical metatarsus molecules molest misty mountains,
Mink mind muse!
        Menace morning's mobile mobocracy memorial
Most modern multi-syllabic mores moderate midway mushroom mirrors.
Motorize misery mischief melopoetic moralist
Monstruosuly mugging middleclass mushy meddle.
Mouth mouse, moose moth, mousse melded meliorists.
Muckrake military's Mocha, monkey monk.
Multiply meek monopoly misfortune moans, mercenary merchandise.
Motivate microphone, mild Millenial mojo.
Mistrust messianic metonymy missives.

Mimic Moloch megaphone, melodic mildew
Mince metal mosquito music, meaty meltdown memoirs,
Model moral Megadeath moochers, metropolitan Metallica miasma.
Mllk monogamy, mechanistic meteor metaphor.
Mingle, minor minister mistress,
Melt melancholy, megalomaniacal meter.
Mollify money's moody modulations,
Mix mucus multi-media murrain,
monotonous Monterey messy Montana.
Musty mothery Mediterranean, medley
Mercurial multi-vitamin mellow membrane muro
Measured midwife minstrel motion morpheme
Melomaniac municipal mumbo-jumbo miscegenation molded moon.

"Are We Instruments?"

Did I believe that poetry could transcend or at least suspend dualisms, take the low road and the A train, code switch, live in two worlds, create communities? It was kind of in between song, on the one hand, and the op-ed essay on the other (news that stays news like an execution). And, when I say between, I meant a bridge more than a wall, between two social scenes, two people, two moods, two "sides of myself" (being born on the cusp of watery Pisces and fiery Aries), I meant able to synthesize, or at least cancel each other out in a way leaving visionary transcendence or holy 20th century commercial secular materialist society "nothing" perhaps stripped of its Elizabethan associations with a female body portal through which the vast majority enter this life, and a majority of men wish to enter again….. the (w)hole peace (piece), or at least the possibility of a continuous present, and/or debates about the relationship between hobby and lobby, busyness and business, and yes, silence to compliment the sound of music, to help give it an edge, to pay back the debt more than a mere rock critic could, as if, indeed, people are the best part of nature and I'd rather be played like a flute than be read like book until I get to dress up like a flute that can also pass for a drumstick so you can play the drums with me and tickling a woman is like beating a drum and tickling the ivories like a drum is not beating a woman and at some point I have to draw a line though you may know how to veto it and the sound we make together is the music in the poem of your eyes and I love the music of the word "Synesthesia" and I like the way it sounds better than the way it looks (just like a lot of my favorite musicians) and I loved the idea of poetry as a kind of mood lit room you may call a closing of the eyes beneath a big droopy tree in summer they'll probably say is overgrown, but that won't stop them from taking selfies of it as they chop….

Enter The Knives; Enter Second Person

The press found you homeless & disabled in the belly of the Hollywood car beast & was fascinated by the story of how you had made it to the top of your profession with award winning books and a stint in a well-beloved semi-famous band, before crashing and burning. They love riches to rags stories and perhaps believe that they have enough culture cache to stir reader sympathy and serve as an ambassador to help get you on your feet again, and they buy you meals so you'll talk with the digital replacement of the tape recorder running and they seem interested as you wax poetic on that worker-owned collective you tried to get going before the slum lord decided he'd get in on the lucrative gentrification craze, and evict you (and the City of Oakland has used the tragedy of 36 who died in the Warehouse fire as an excuse to evict people ostensibly on the grounds of "safety!")--- but when the stories come out they edit out all mention of community centers and the advantages to warehouses and co-ops ("atavistic Motown factory"), and cast you in the role of the quirky, albeit charming, 'self-contained' and/or 'mentally unstable" authentic individual. Homeless with no safety net and (ironically) forced to act like a "bourgeois individual" at least as much as when you were one, maybe more. More seen than seeing, an animal. Is a zoo a jail? Is homelessness more of a circus? And, concerning cats, is it true what they say: "when you cut off his balls/ he tries to do with his claws/ what other cats get to do with balls." And maybe then you wonder about propaganda and the "free press," and you want to scream, but you lost your band, so, contextless, they call it raving....

+ + + + + + + + +

"Even in the era of higher pollution and smoking, more Americans were healthier when there were more local dance clubs." In the land of love, it's said, watch out for argument spies to come and infiltrate to get you feel the need for evidence to sew up the holes in your claims which you didn't think of us claims but as lyrics in a song, phonemes used so your voice can be pleasing, beyond or before meaning if not morality. Yet, I've been studying and want to learn the ways of the arguers (even though I spent years trying to break them). I can't scold them as "deplorables" or "normative discourse," but maybe I've been kidnapped and placed in a courtroom and I'm not even the defendant but the perfunctory court-hired defense attorney who frankly doesn't understand the defendant pronounced guilty for not being from this land....

"America would be healthier, happier, more democratic, and less racist if it hadn't become less musical."

"Well, first you have to prove your descriptive assumption that it is less musical...."
.........As if we traffic more deeply in facts than beliefs...
(and "as if"
        is a great poetic
                        cop-
out   from one angle)
Of course, my evidence is insufficient
    But some of my best friends are more interested in arguing against argument itself...

absentminded baby calls daddy death every fragrant grouchy horizon island jogs kinesiology light music night ooh ooh paradise queen romance smoke talk under vituperative walking xanoxious yesmen zamazons

"Oh, give me a fact that topples my belief, or marry me!"
Indeed, "substantial support for my claim"
May wither with the simplest blooming flower
"Let's Rock" (or whatever you call it)
"I'm so rusty on trumpet, I blow into it and words come out!"
"The summer flower to America is sweet
It grows from the drone like Pinocchio's nose.
I mean soil, if only Earth Wind and Fire
Hadn't forgotten Water!..."
On trial, I defend their most watery moments...
And try out some syllogisms for the students.
"#WaterisLife" (Standing Rock)
"Water Is A Privilege, Not A Right" (Nestles CEO),
Therefore, Life Is A Privilege, Not A Right!
Poetic logic!
Music used to flow more like public water fountains,
But now both are more bottled, more barren
(even if the MP3 isn't strictly a thing,
Google still makes a lot of money off the adverts)
And for the poets who scorn my third rate
Logopiea heavy, *phanopiea* deficient,
Earnest political Brecht didactic calls to collective action,
Wanna jam?

All bad conclusions dethrone everything for gallant hovercrafts imperially judging kleptocratic lifers mandated neighborly plantation owner quack recovering systemic torture uncle violet wisteria. Xerasia, you're zealous.

For Some Of Us, "I" Is A Trigger Word

They try to put me in a self again
"There's a knot in your head you can't untie
You're the town crier in search of a cry,
Make yourself miserable, lost all your friends,"
They scold, then ask me if I hear voices.
"I hear yours loud and clear, and heard (and cried)
about a movie called Alive Inside.
A senior center offered more choices
To Alzheimer's patients. Expensive pills
Proved futile, but music revitalized
Like a fountain of love. The staff was wise
And knew expanding this program cures ills
But couldn't get the funds they applied for
Though they got grants for pills. Your peace is war."

++++++

Arthur Blythe constant decree elevates fetishism's garage hobby in jazz's lost marketshare? No! Open party queue relocates slowly to undercut visionary weightless xray yeoman zone!

So, after 20 years in the lyric land of poetry and song---
Unless lyric be called not land as much as water—
Or until I realize that concrete calls itself land
So that the water the lyric identifies with
Is really the real, living, land,
Do I find some mooring on narrative story architectures
And do they devalue the kind of reading that focuses on the worlds
That can be found or made from the juxtaposition of two words or phrases?

"Yeah, but that doesn't mean you can't read it as poetry....slowly."

analog belt chamber draft emissions
festive glossy hydrogenated
intrinsicate jury knits lace mittens
notable opaque passivity
questions Rolling Stones turning
uniquely variable waste xenon young zibaldone!

And coming from the lyric land, I've tended to downplay the difference between creative non-fiction, and fiction. They sometimes form a unified front against poets; I've heard novelists and autobiographical writers scorn poets for lacking attention span, and for needing immediate gratification, and lacking their discipline (or their paid year-long sabbatical). And from the lyric land or sea, the differences between these narrative prose genres seem like 2 clouds on the horizon that look contiguous, but when they get over head, space between them opens up and that's probably how those under the space between those clouds see us lyric folks on their horizon (of course all song is poetry; all poetry is song). The term "creative non-fiction" is contrasted with "fiction" (since fiction, by definition, is creative), but that doesn't necessarily mean, in the final analysis (if there is such a thing), that this "non-fiction" is more truthful than fiction is, especially when I have lived long enough to tell the same story over and over again in different ways, from different angles, or thematic portals, to tell different truths that complement rather than contradict each other.

Do two negatives make a positive? Does non-fiction equal truth? As I see it, any truth any "non-fiction" account of my past can give is probably going to tell more about the present in which I'm writing this than the past. So, this makes no pretenses of being definitive, and the sequel (which may seem to be about something entirely other than 'my life' outside of, or in a crack in, the space-time continuum), will no doubt be better....

Even with these qualifications, however, as I embark on writing that seems to fit in the genre of "memoir," I get scared by one big hazard: it's been said by many that a contributing factor in the death of Dave Eggers' sister is the way he portrayed her in his non-fiction book, so readers looking for that kind of memoir that digs deep into the family romance will probably be disappointed with (most of) what follows in this collection (though there may be some crumbs, or grains of sand, which you can see a world in), like spending much more time on the role of radio in my upbringing or raising than on my biological parents (both of whom are now deceased). I know that seems disrespectful to some,....but it may be more accurate, given the dominance of the electronic babysitter in the last half-century (The original title of the memoir back in 2004 was *Radio Orphan*, and much of that spirit still informs this version).

Yet when I say this book aspires to the quality of "non-fiction," I do not only mean the "creative non-fiction" taught in MFA programs that is based on a story, but also the kind of "non-fiction" that is more like an essay, that is less interested in stories than in ideas, or the dance of the intellect, argument, or at least the imagination (even if in the 21st century you have to downsize it to Attention-Deficit-Disorder), whether more like an Op-Ed piece or an academic essay or record review or even sermon. Some call it "Non-Creative Non-Fiction" which seems safer than calling it "Truth," or at least "The Telling," as difficult an art to master as the art of losing.

While many poets still cling to the "show, don't tell" taboo, and novelists can show the telling by framing it as spoken by a character, I like to think the genre of memoir can permit "telling" at least a little more (a right often denied homeless people)—not that telling is necessarily more authentic or "absolutely naked" (it's theatrical, right? as I am gladly presenting my narrator self as a clearly flawed character, who perhaps can be forgiven his tendency to want to preach to the choir, because at least he's kinda funny about it, no?).

And, besides, perhaps in a memoir, like in the Ancient Epic from a less specialized time that could also include instruction manuals and business proposals, we can make room for little personal vignettes that might seem patronizing and self-congratulating, and HAVE NO LITERARY VALUE, like:

"I hear a woman singing a very rhythmical melody as she's pushing a shopping cart down the sidewalk of the block across from the Y that used to be lined with auto-shops and mechanics, but is now the Artisan Bakery and the store that sells $500 jeans made by prison labor (proudly claiming "made on the inside to be worn on the outside"), while I'm parked parallel to the sidewalk, sitting in the backseat of my car, grading papers. As the sound of her voice fades I realize how incredibly beautiful it is and I have one $2 bill left, and I have to limp after her and give it her, and she smiled and my only regret (aside from underpaying her) is that I didn't do it right in front of the café so people who make more money than me would see it so they can give themselves permission to notice unexpected beauty, and let the street be hers as much as they think it's theirs....."

Or, Just Coz It's In Sonnet Form Doesn't Mean It's Literary:

Some homeless people make very good street
patrol, pushing with a swagger and smile
a shopping cart up a new rezoned mile
of "Do Not Enter" shops. Dressed smart, sings sweet,
strong slow walk, homo erectus. He owns
these sidewalks in motion still. His function,
to guard, to breathe safety plus religion
into the tight fitting pants and the loans
of the nouns of the "proper perspective."
He'll probably circle back in an hour
just to make sure, as jobless as a flower
trading for money, knowing it can't live.
He don't wear a gun and tensions decrease.
Useless, or our soon deputized police?

And the broets go:
Aid branded corporatism Dionysian empathy faith ghost highshool independence juts Kardishian limelight mental neoimperialist pinches querulous racist statement trilateral. Vacate western xenophones, yengles zaftig!

At its worst, then, this book will be "not narrative enough for those who value creative non-fiction, but not intellectually rigorous enough for those who value cultural argument" (and certainly not lean enough to stand with the best didactic poetry)! I may mix them up in a mushy middle! For instance, I do not reprint my Ph.D dissertation, but I do try to some of its main points in "folksy language." But I think it's necessary to not just try to show the way I was acting, or what I was acting against, but also to show (to try to remember) what I think I was thinking, since, I found, in over 20 years as a culture worker, that thoughts don't always "lose the name of action" (as Hamlet put it), and the faultline between thought and action remains elusive in the white-collar world (as grading is an "inexact" science).

Of course, there's often (if not always) going to be a discrepancy between what you think is happening and what *is* happening, but the homeless are not 'just homeless.' And, if like Emily Dickinson, I "dwell in possibility, a fairer house than prose," as much as I do in what prose calls reality, it's easy to say that much of what I'm nostalgic for about say the 80s and 90s is as much the possibilities, or promises (too oft, alas, unrealized) of those times as it is the actualities. Is it my heart that asks "Were things really better then? Or were they just easier for me? Or was I just stronger? Or very lucky?"

Nonetheless, as I'm writing this while others are preparing for a Conference on Poetics of The 90s in Orono, ME, and I watch others of my generation, and younger, give their cultural versions or personal perspectives of what Mark E. Smith once called "US 80s/90s" and grapple with the immense paradigm shifts that have transformed American culture in the 21st century, I feel a need to weigh in, and, in the final analysis, I cannot yet tell if the goal is more to "tell my story," or "the story of those I love who are unjustly marginalized in this increasingly impersonal technocracy" or to "make an important cultural point," in this the year of our Lord 2017, when many people who called me a catastrophist back in 2001 and 2004, now themselves have joined a mass (yet fragmented) hysteria asking "what went wrong, what went wrong? What to do, to do, to do? *Don't wanna die at 50....*

Enter The Catastrophist

Regardless of whether the autobiographical writer is a famous cultural producer whose life, in one way or another has changed the course of history or culture (say James Brown or Donald Trump), or a seemingly more "minor league" player like myself, I often read autobiographies or memoirs for insight into the cultural and historical "ground" at least as much as the "figure" (can the Mona Lisa Smile while the Land behind her frowns, etc?). So, with that in mind, what does what one journalist referred to as the "rags to riches to rags" story of what used to be called (by whites at least) a generation Xer, now crippled, homeless, and 50 in an ableist, classist, anti-collectivist society (to say nothing of white supremacy) have to do with what Scott Timberg called the *Culture Crash* and Robert Reich and Joseph Stiglitz and the like call the increasing wealth gap?

So, in this book should memory be constrained by the burning cultural question of what can we do to make America better than it is not, and than it's ever been, in a way that is as non-partisan as possible? Or would that be setting myself up to be a cranky curmudgeon? Can it really escape the zeitgeist? How do YOU do it? Can a working class white male write a book that could be useful to my multi-cultural students (not that I would force them to read it). Can I write about my personal eating disorder without writing about our culture's eating disorder?

Almost brutal, cake, donuts, ecoli! Festive gorge hungry indigestion juice kiwi lacquer minimalist nothing or publicized quantities resource stomach's toxic uvula valiantly warning x-men yodeling "Zipcar!"

What does what some shrinks call my personal anxiety (and/or PTSD) have to do with the "nation's ailing infrastructure" and "frayed social safety net" (and the perma-temp economy and the 21st century technocracy)? What does what other shrinks call my depression have to do with what spin doctors call "The Great Recession" coz they don't want to alarm anybody into collectivism, but rather privatize the word depression coz who needs Government New Deal programs if you got Big Pharma to stabilize moods for an inflated price.

The Great Recession got famous just as coincidentally my life was falling apart. They didn't seem to have anything to do with each other at first (certainly Goldman Sachs wasn't driving the car that hit me). After all, it was primarily about housing, right? And I was not a home owner, mortgage holder, and pretty much had given up hope & accepted my renter lot. I wasn't even a renter, but I sublet from renters—but soon the dots found a way to connect themselves though not without great loss of negative capability, and "irritable groping" for (un)certainties...

Dream Sequence Digression: One Small Depression For Me; One Great Recession For (American) Mankind.[1]

There are some things concerning which we must always be maladjusted if we are to be people of good will. We must never adjust ourselves to racial discrimination and racial segregation....We must never adjust ourselves to economic conditions that take necessities from the many to give luxuries to the few. We must never adjust ourselves to the madness of militarism.... Thus, it may well be that our world is in dire need of a new organization, The International Association for the Advancement of Creative Maladjustment." Martin Luther King, at the American Psychological Association's 1967 conference

[1] See Appendix one: What Can Be Learned From Rwanda About Battling Depression

The cultural argument goes something like this:

"By 2012, many however had already given up hope. The savings of those who had lost jobs in 2008 or 2009 had been spent. Unemployment checks had run out. Middle aged people, once confident of a swift return to the workforce, came to realize they were, in fact, forcibly retired. Young people, fresh out of college, with tens of thousands of dollars in debt, couldn't find any work at all. People who had moved in with friends and relatives at the start of the crisis had become homeless....Full-time employment declined by 8.7 million from November 2007 to November 2011...an increase in the true jobs deficit of 15 million" (young people stayed in schools coz they couldn't find a job, thus devaluing the PhD)....Not surprisingly, more than half of the unemployed had experienced emotional or health problems as a result of being jobless, but could not get treatment, since more than half of the unemployed had no health insurance coverage." Joseph Stiglitz

"But let's talk about you."
Meanwhile, the shrink has diagnosed you with depression & her professional reputation depends upon being able to convince you (or at least the state) that she is solving it, but you can see she's struggling & want to help her out a little:
"Dear Alexa, I mean, oh shrink, are you really interested in solving my depression, or just in solving "behavior associated with depression?"
"One person's depression may be primarily caused by some biological dysfunction while another person's may be primarily caused by a very stressful life experience, and in your case I'd say it's a combination of the two."
"How do you measure my depression? Are you measuring it against the times when I wasn't (called) depressed, or the times I'm manic...."
"We try not to say manic anymore...."
"Or are you comparing my mood to some Urban Spaceman norm that maybe doesn't exist?"
"I think you're in denial about being depressed, or at least that it's a disabling condition...."
"I think Moses would be diagnosed bipolar if he were alive today...and I think you're in denial about environmental factors.......(long pause).... Do you believe the personal is the political?"
"Why do you ask?"
I mean, if we want to solve my depression, I think we have to work toward solving the depression."
"What depression?"
"The crash of 2008. Surely, you've heard of it."
"Oh, that's just economic; this is psychology....(aside to audience: "He's not just depressed but also suffers delusions")
"But why do we use the same word for the psyche that we do for the economy?
"We don't; you're depressed, but the economy's just going through a recession. The Great Recession...."
You (aside to audience, "ah, like Jumbo Shrimp"): Dammit! Dammit! Dammit! I'm so sick of the phrase "Great Recession." "Non-partisan," my ass. It reeks of spin, like you're not in as much pain as you think you are...Kids love recess. Rich congressmen take them. The Great Vacation!" But as Stiglitz says, the last time inequality approached the

glaring level we see today was in the years before the great depression. So why not call it a depression?"
"I'm just a psychiatrist. I have no power over that. Why does that matter to you?
"When people suffered from depression in 1929, they weren't considered particularly abnormal. After all, it was The Great Depression, a collective depression, and thus could only be solved by social means. I mean if a Great Depression comes, so can the threat of a worker's revolution (and a racist New Deal appeasement program that was still too democratic for the corporations) be far behind? I think that could cure my depression....
"You're only mildly depressed compared to some, and this has nothing to do with electoral politics."
"Yes, but if a person is diagnosed with depression during the great Recession, they're called abnormal, and this can only be solved individually, through pills so expensive, it actually makes the Great Recession worse......They've privatized depression to prevent a collective movement!"
"Yes, I misdiagnosed you, you're not just depressed, you...."
"I'm Greatly Recessed!"
"What?"
"If a Great Recession comes, can a bank bailout be far behind?"
"Your psyche is not the economy....(Aside to audience: okay, I'll humor him). Besides, we're in the recovery now!"
"So they say...."
"Wall Street is Up!"
"But the standard of living—is down...for most blacks, despite Obama, ...and even for whites as the 99% movement figured out...The economy that's recovering doesn't include us....."
"You don't need to carry the weight of the world on your shoulders...."
"Why not?.....Or, (Aside to audience: I'll humor her) I can do the same thing to recover The Economy is; I can just deny that the swelling lumpen-proletariat ranks IN ME are really part of the economy, and say, yes, MY Economy is getting better even if everything's falling apart around me, but that's not really part of me....and this is what anti-depressants can do! A little shot of that plutocrat feeling for us peasants at the homeless clinic! Yes, I can be a self-contained individual, just like those libertarian technocrats!........Still......I can't help but feel this growing mass insecurity in an era of homeland security. Too much distrust! I worry!"
"It's not worry, it's Anxiety™. Sounds to me like you need Anxiety medication as well as anti-depressants. You're more talkative now, certainly less depressed, but increased anxiety can be a side effect of anti-depressants."
"So, why not just wean me off the anti-depressants."
"You'll take an anti-depressant in the morning, and an anti-anxiety at night!"
"So, 2008 is not just The Great Recession, but also The Great Anxiety! Depression is just part of being Bipolar; and 2008 was a very bipolar year for America as "The Great Recession" warred with "ObamaMANIA, and Obama himself tried to be the Goldilocks "Just right" Aristotlean Golden Mean between them, and there was a contemporary country song called "I Think The World Needs A Drink" (not necessarily sung by a

Climate Change Denier)....
"Do you feel better? We have 1 minute left."
"One more question: Do you think less people would be depressed if we removed economic incentives for doctors to diagnose it?
"We'll talk about that next time."
"Well, I guess you earned your money. I do feel less depressed. Now I feel angry."
"The anti-anxiety pills will help. Let's talk about that next time."
"Ah, next time. Can I bring an out of work drummer & we'll pay her with half your salary?"
Shrink laughs…
"Watch out, laughing is a kind of counter-transference."
"Well, be glad you're privileged enough for the talking cure; some only get pills."
"Aren't you afraid that Google Home or Alexa may replace your job, and you'll join all the cut-priced poets, and journalists, and musicians, dancers and teachers, and sing "Song Of The Cut-Priced Shrink?"
"We'll talk about that next time." **Curtain; end dream sequence digression**

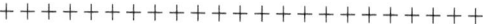

While looking for a cultural analogue to my own trauma may be a way of failing to confront my own mistakes, my intention is more to connect my personal trauma to a wider cause, as if we can't be truly selfish unless we are altruistic, for, yes, I am prejudiced toward the naive belief that if you really did what you think you're best at (as long as it doesn't hurt anyone else) that the economy, and the ecology, would benefit.

I'm just an example, a test case, a sideman, a minor-league culture worker, or Working-Class Foole,[2] but even in my life I've seen the personal (my own little story) intersect with the political and the cultural (if not quite like Forrest Gump), and, yes, I'm egomaniacal enough to appreciate, if not quite demand, hecklers and pause buttons, as if, in writing (as in the water walking therapy pool) I can still be that wide eyed forward looking 20 something rather than the backward looking 75 year old retiree passing on her hard-gained wisdom and knowledge of the old days, the ground that made her and that she helped make, and of course the mistakes…..the discrepancies between hopes and dreams and ways and means…..

And, aye, there's the rub of the retrospective glace at my age, and perhaps at my age we're required to take responsibility for the failure of our generation. Certainly, there's ample precedent for it, as we were born in the shadow of the baby boomers who witnessed (or felt helpless) in the great 1968-1980 backlash.[3] For years, I've listened to the Baby Boomers' regrets; they're big business. Many of us Generation Xers found ourselves defensively blaming the baby boomers since

---

[2] Yes, I'm spelling it just like Robert Armin did.
[3] The subject of chapter one, "70s Decay"

they were blaming us, but even if they blamed us unfairly, the question remains: Were we to blame for some of the negative changes in society in the last 20, or even 30, years?[4] Despite my attempts to dig myself out of being raised (or razed) by Hollywood, was I just a product of my age? Was "the mind" willing but "the flesh weak," or vice versa?

I've been asking these questions (perhaps a little too) relentlessly since 2004, when I became bedridden and disabled from a near-fatal car accident, and fell into a kind of void or pit in which the zeitgeist, as well as any sense, of place, community, drifted away in a Vicodin haze, and I lost my sense of sublime futurity for a retrospective glance, asking like Curtis Mayfield after he was paralyzed from the neck down when a rack of stage lights fell on him while playing an outdoor show in Brooklyn, "what in the world have I ever done wrong?[5]" and wondering if I've ever really done anything right?

Questioning karma, feeling increased empathy (if it'd be called shy of sympathy) with soldiers coming back addicted to morphine, and disillusioned, and "bent and paralyzed" after the war, even if I had once called him sexist for identifying with the speaker to "Ruby Don't Take Your Love To Town." ("If I could move I'd get my gun and put her on the ground." "But, the whole point is, he can't move, and if he could move, she wouldn't be cheating on him." "Yeah, but I still ain't gonna bring it up with a woman, unless she brings it up first.")

I'll try to blame myself so as not to presume to blame others, but I know I can't really live up to that standard (after all, I know you probably want some drama, and I can always blame the past self who wanted to blame others in this writing), but mostly I blame hostile systemic external obstacles rather than any individual I've known, and this may allow some mercy to save us from self-blame.

But, yes, I am haunted (the shrinks say traumatized), not only by the specter of Betsy Devos, but by a relentless feeling of Devo, de-evolution, so I grope for some sign of hope, and progress (if my mom were alive today, it would be easier for her to go to college than she could as a working- class woman in the 60s). And if I'm trying to unburden myself of some of my biggest mistakes in this book (and minimalize braggadocio), perhaps it can make the goals (including the non-teleological goal) clearer… …..and when nostalgia is mixed up with regrets, perhaps the result (or progeny) can be "learning from mistakes," or "starting again with an open mind,"…..and, damn, I need a shot of futurity…

Zal Yanovsky xenogamy weighs vertebrae underwater. Truth successes! Rapid Quiz Pale omnicrawl, nausea mouth lingers like legal kickbacks injuring hundreds. Good Friday existence essence dumps chocolate crosses, Bruce Andrews

---

[4] Not that you have to agree with me that they're worse; the shrink can say I'm just projecing…
[5] https://www.youtube.com/watch?v=-AFglJAORxs

And yes, we 50 year olds fragmented and scattered, with little or no social safety net, can regroup and learn from our (I mean my) mistakes, or at least I can use this writing to bring into dialogue a few of my overlapping "WEs," the first person plurals one can identify with, even in solitude, or sitting in limbo, or protracted winter hibernation though it's already May: the working class we, the AM-Top 40 radio we, the college radio activist we, the anti-Hollywood we, the introvert we, the poet we, the session musician we, the sideman sideshow we, the conceptual artist we, the Shakespearean we, the teacher we, the Oral Culture we, the written culture we, the Oakland Warehouse Coalition We, the anti-gentrification we, the "we need a black arts district we," the anti-tech-revolution revolutionary we, the amphibious pragmatist we, the dancer we, disabled we, the depressed we, the homeless we (though I could never really feel comfortable "speaking" for that one, because in my experience the homeless "we" is as varied as the non-homeless "we," if at present in the USA, still lesser in numbers), but screw the "white male we," and if you ever catch me acting like my ideology is that of the white male we, heckle me please. And it's never too early to plan for that Punk/Funk Retirement Home, or at least a Funeral Party (why wait till after you're dead)....oh, and when I die please second line.....

Ah, the music, and cultural and lit crit we, curator we, the DJ we, the peasant and bourgeois editorial we, the New York School we, the Philly Oakland underground we, the sweeping-up-the-condoms-in-the-porn-section-of–a-video-store-we, while the stereo blares a warm slow song from the 90s not released until 2010 when the meaning of "released" had changed, and I can't tell if it's sad or not, but Suzanne said it's a breakup song:

We're building this puzzle, it seems that it's taking too long
It's hard to find my face in that mess
You're doing pretty good out trying to shuck impatience away
But it's kinda hard to cut it off at the root....

And then the chorus---

I forgot the things that made you love me
I forgot the things that made you want to hold my hand
I forgot the things that made you love me
And if you give me the chance I'll forget them again."

But to do that he has to remember them again, no? If a woman sang that to me, would I run away in horror, saying screw your on-again, off-again love? *Abolish boyfriend? Code divorce? Enquirers flock garbage headlines. I just kindled Lucky magazine's natural opiate precondition. Quickly, really suddenly. Tediously. Undulating victory xanthines your Zoogle...*

But generally, those looking for insights into my private love life will be disappointed, unless you see the relentless tug of possibility against desperation as another form of testosterone OD, or that Freudian ID some say branded my celebrated poetry of the 90s. And, indeed, as you might already be able to tell, whatever calm there is here is mostly between the lines; a restless, speedy, agitated tone appears often in this writing, and perhaps that's from trying to cram 30 or 40 years of experiences, and thought-actions or action-thoughts into so few pages…..like a fish out of lyric water….gasping for air as if it's not a right but a privilege, and mimicking much of what I hate about the imperialist 1% oppressor!

Argue! Brutalize! Cuddle danger's eager fibrillation!
Guess his "I" just kicks lazy Mediterranean
No, only poetry quells radio's sadness.
Tundra underbids Vatican Whitehouse's
Xanthous Yulelog zip-drives.

++++++++++++++++

"The Elephant in The Room" or "The Marriage of Artist & Activist" (trailer)

"I don't really care about politics except when it affects the ability to make art; the problem is, it always does…..".----Dion De Arroganto

"But if you really want to do something, y'all need to mix a little politics with your love of entertainment,"--- Louis Jordan, New Orleans, 1948

For the past 20 years, when asked what my occupation is by the government for taxes, the most accurate thing an accountant told me to say is "Writer/Teacher/Musician." Each of them have various sub-specializations, but they all seem like the same job to me: culture worker. So perhaps it's best just to sum all these WEs up in the phrase "Culture Worker We," as in "Culture Workers Of The World Unite!" And, as a culture worker I'm torn. In the musician role, I've seen many of my collaborators and friends, who used to make a living doing music now, in this 21st century Tech-dominated economy and culture, have to change their profession, or downsize to hobby what was once a job. But in the poet role, I see many poets seeming or acting more immune to these economic and cultural paradigm shifts, because the assumption that poetry—at essence doesn't (and even shouldn't) pay has been so naturalized in the 90 years since Bertolt Brecht wrote "Song Of The Cut Priced Poet (for the first third of the 20th century when poetry no longer paid)."

Brecht's poem is a mock-lament for the death of the aristocratic patronage system that benefitted Wordsworth and others.   The poem presents the poet as civic servant, and since many poets I know, in their day jobs, are civil servants (teachers, social workers, journalists, etc), even if their civil service is to refuse the right of the "system" to exist, what he says may be relevant today. The poem asks us to put ourselves in the shoes of the recently downsized, so I'm pre-disposed to sympathize or at least empathize with the plight of the poet who was abandoned by the ruling class due to a variety of factors you could place under the umbrella of Modernity, but it also invites us to ask: do socio-economic conditions always affect content as well as aesthetic style ("the politics of poetic form")?

In the early 20th century electric mass culture (radio, records, Hollywood), such poets had lost their role as propagandists for what today we could call the military industrial complex, or the social order (the same was happening in painting, as photography was replacing it, and, religion in many ways was being replaced by scientists and psychologists). Economically and culturally, the 20th century capitalist got more bang for their buck if he hired psychologists and advertisers. Yet it's hard to feel sympathy for the poet in this mock-lament because Brecht is clearly satirizing the speaker of the poem, as a literary whore to the oppressive bloodthirsty machinations of Euro-American imperialism, even as he himself is being exploited, for instance:

On the forms you sent to us demanding taxes
We painted the most astonishing pictures for you.
Bellowing in chorus our hortatory verses
The people, as always, paid the taxes you claimed were due.

For Brecht, this crisis presented an opportunity for the cut-priced poet to recognize himself or herself as a fellow proletarian in the collective class struggle, working on the level of the cultural superstructure. It suggested the need for a mass-art, an art that took advantage of the tools of the new mass culture then in its infancy (but already reified into a one-way-street controlled by the rich), even if he had to go outside the parameters of what's called poetry, in America at least, to do it, to create a more collaborative art that could be sold cheaper, like a Threepenny Opera, and in America, even today, he's mostly known for "Mack The Knife" and "Whiskey Bar" (or maybe that meme about dancing in the dark times). Yet despite the groundbreaking achievements of Harlem Renaissance writers during this time, and writers like Henry Hart, and the American Writers' Congress (1935), "during the 1930s there occurred a power struggle within the American left that resulted in the ascendency of literary elitism (represented by New York City's Partisan Review) over that of working-class populism (which found a voice in Chicago's The Anvil). The populists lost." (Reed 349).

For a little sliver in the 50s and 60s and early 70s, the Beats and the Black Arts Movement may have been able to use mass culture (just as TV was using them to lure people to it) to be populists, but coming to poetry in the 80s and 90s, populism was kind of taboo, and we didn't expect to make poetry pay. The negative of not getting paid had become a positive, "to liberty not to banishment," or "it's not worthless; it's priceless," and I couldn't help but find attractive its promise of a minimal economy that seemed to operate outside the cash nexus.

In this 20th century poetic transvaluation, the rise of the cut-priced poet parallels the rise of free verse, but I knew that even though poetry didn't pay, it still had its rules and/or taboos, and even though it didn't pay, I still got $300 for my first feature reading at the age of 24 (which could pay for 3 months rent where I lived, at the time!), and I wouldn't have been able to get my teaching job without it; and even though it didn't pay as much as music, it was certainly cheaper to make. Poetry had cultural capital, and because it was no longer a profession in the economic sense (unless you're Billy Collins), it became a kind of "recession proof activity." Perhaps.

Zonthic, yesterday's xylophones want Velvet Underground trumpet silence. Raiders quench petroleum osteoarthritis no more! Lawrence, Koch Joke Industries hail grail, fallopian employees' downsized clean breath art.

In the 21st century, we are facing a paradigm shift that seems greater than the one that Brecht and other modernists faced a century ago: the so-called Tech Revolution (the drastic social changes Schumpeter calls "Creative Destruction") and it must be remembered that one of the stated goals of the new technocracy is to increase the wealth gap; it's not an "unfortunate side-effect." Most blatantly, perhaps, Amazon has severely cut into profits from small publishers, putting many of them, as well as bookstores, out of business. This was not an accident. Amazon founder Jeff Bezos' intention was to "totally disrupt the local bookstore business," (Taplin, 79) as public space becomes increasingly privatized (they're working on supermarkets now).

We're told the consumer benefits from this loss to the producer, but even though your book prices seem cheaper, make sure to factor in the additional money you pay to Big Tech every month. In this 21st century "sharing economy," we now pay for many things we used to get for free (or at least for cheap); bottled water is perhaps the best example, but I could also invoke Oakland's Cat Town, a café where you can adopt cats, which seems like a cool idea until I went in only to find that you have to pay a $5 fee to be let into the room with the cats (thank god there are still traditional cat shelters and "ghetto alley cats" as the beautiful graffiti on the shelter's billboard reminds us). Another example is Oakland's Impact Hub, where you pay a monthly fee for the privilege of getting to sit at a desk with your laptop and network with other people willing to pay a monthly fee to network. Back in the 20th century, we used to be able to do that at coffee shops, for free (well, for the price of a cup of coffee). So, I don't see many consumer benefits, especially since most of us consumers are also producers (only the super rich get to be consumers without having to be producers).

Zuckerberg does Zumba. Yes, and yearns for xenophobic Xeroxes of white walls vaunted and valued united ugly to trump trickle down serial selfies religiously rehearsed quarreling proud putative operatives only negative Nazi music movement love landscape kiss kicks jewelry janitors in between Islams' hedgefund hope gringo-fundme gentrified forgotten forage effervescent ecstatic deadbeat donor crisis calm beyond boogaloo algebra angels!

Now this Amazonification may not matter that much to poets who have already resigned themselves to, or even embraced, the fact that they're not going to make a living from book sales, but since many of the now shuttered bookstores had once held readings and literary performances, this affects the literary scenes culturally as much as economically. Furthermore, many poets are still struggling with the ways social media has changed their writing. Social media has clearly led to the 21st century "Cut Priced Journalist," with 50% fewer journalists able to make a living today than a decade ago. "What seems obvious….is to produce more content at a lower price" (Taplin, 164). And, certainly, in music, as many have shown, since the rise of Napster and Youtube (and the Google—Facebook nexus), musicians who were able to make a living a decade ago from record sales, no longer can (and not just baby boomers, but generation Xers like The Silver Jews). As a result, many produce more glut because quantity matters more than quality—not that the two always have to be opposed; what's needed is better distribution (and curation) in which the artists have at least as much say as the techies.

And Anschutz browbeats Berman & Company, cries "China Cheats Consumers," Divestment Dead End English Empire forsaking foreign fiends gerrymandering globally hurriedly hating idealistic intercommunalism jettisoned ku klux luxury liberals market rate moderate minstrels not negating off stage "obsolete" privatization pundits queasily quarantined quiet radio remembers sequestered swinging seventies think tank unsung understated understanding violent violin victual wah wah xylophone yapping zeppelins….

So even though some poets may look at some of these other culture workers with a kind of "welcome to the cut-priced club" diffidence, I can't turn away when I hear the other culture workers sing their sad, angry, or even funny, "Song of The Cut-Priced Journalist," "Song of The Cut-Priced Musician," and "Song of The Priced Out Bookstore," and since many of the poets have day jobs as professors, we might want to get working on that collaborative "Song Of The Cut Priced Professor," once the MOOCS get the bots replacing teachers so critical thinking essays can turn into standardized tests, to deprive our students who learn best in face to face collaboration. The rise of online classrooms is at least as much a threat to education as No Child Left Behind and Betsy De Vos' privatization plans (Zuckerberg is a big supporter of charter schools). And, it may not be long before Alexa and Google Home replaces the Cut-Priced Psychiatrist!

And this shared fate is why I feel a need for artists to unite more than ever (despite our aesthetic differences), and I may not have activist skills per say, but maybe together we can yet form an alternative economy based on time honored values of thrift and community before America's inflationary economy began its way of demoting us even while it pretended to promote us. For even if more of us are Depressed, or Greatly Recessed, than ever, together, we could pool our depression and it can add up to a Great Proactive Collective Anger, just like in the old cartoons when they surround the mansions of the rich with blowtorches and such!

Sometimes you have to laugh at yourself, ...and I purposely juxtapose the earnest cultural arguments with the theatrically ridiculous cultural argument, such as Chapter 5s in which a self-proclaimed New York Snob engages in a little compare contrast with Bay Area (white) Culture. Perhaps it's kind of a frivolous prose poem, or "comic relief." Yet, this book is not merely a cultural argument, especially after you get through the first chapter which explores the decay, and cultural ruins that I (and many of us generation Xers) grew up in. It's a personal purging as well as a provisional poetics! (with a shattered fourth wall for the lovely question mark).

I have divided the body of this book into 4 chapters; loosely speaking, it's 4 decades and 4 Cities: Reading, Pennsylvania in the 70s, Philadelphia in the 80s, NYC in the 90s, and Oakland in the 21st Century. You could say the book traces a narrative, where personal and the political break-up and make-up again and again. The personal (the so-called "meat" assuming you're not a vegetarian) doesn't really make its prosaic entrance until Chapter 2, while chapter 1 explores shaping influences, the backdrop of cultural decay.

I readily admit that readers looking for more than a few hints of my childhood in a family context could become disappointed or exasperated by the half-baked cultural analysis they'll find in Chapter One ("Class Traitor? 70s Decay in Reading"), but these ruminations on radio, the Reagan Republican and a reading of a Gil Scott Heron lyric in help set up, and even ground, the vision or perspective that informs the subsequent chapters (on the 80s, 90s, and 00s), and provide some continuity amidst the many disruptions of time and place.

By the beginning of Chapter two ("Can College Make Up For The Loss of A Walking City And Help Make America Great Again"), a fledging sense of self (as figure) emerges (if it hasn't already emerged in this preface), on the verge of entering college, trying to skirt around consumerism and the need to specialize while yet "nostalgic for a time before he was even born." If "the figure" gets lost in "the ground" (the themes, the cultural relevance) in Chapter one, in Chapters 2, 3 and 4, conversely, the cultural arguments may get lost in the rush of life experiences and artist communities, and the symbiotic relationship between solitude and social life, whether in the 80s punk and poetry scenes in Philly, or finding "the grace to live as variously as possible," and getting to collaborate with Grace Hartigan (and others), in NYC in the 90s (and, yes, as we get closer to the present, the chapters get longer....)

Thematically, the battle with (over)-specialization and segregation is a central thread throughout...both aesthetically, and ethically....as is the theme of widening mind/body dualism in the 21st Century Tech culture, and my ever-changing relationship with radio. Disability Rights Activists, Educational Reform and Adjunct-Teacher Rights, and Homeless/Housing activists, might find some common ground with the polemical digressions in Chapter 5. Along the way, some incidental cross-generational analogies can be made (the 70s is to the 60s what the 90s is to the 80s for instance), as the final chapter sometimes circles back to the earlier one, if on a more minor scale (the second time as farce?).

And while offering a 6 page "reading" of one my poems from the 90s may seem self-indulgently frivolous (who cares what I think about the American institution of breakfast?), it may also get as close to what I was feeling/thinking at the time, as any "kiss and tell" story about the Silver Jews or the poetry wars herein included. Like my life, this book tends to "err on one side and then another," in hopes of finding balance and wholeness that can't be personal if it's not also social, and perhaps that's why the word "meanwhile" is used to transition between paragraphs or sentences (as a feeble attempt of invoking the simultaneity of living a double, or even triple, life in a specialized society). And Chapter 5 shows how I have lost that balance in the 21st Century, yet asks: can a boat/train tour help fix America's ailing infrastructure (Obama) and Make America Great Again (Reagan, Trump) —and I hope you dig the soundtrack in the footnotes!

Since I write this during a great period of cultural upheaval in America, and in Oakland, however, witnessing Big Tech's Cultural and Economic Take Over as a disabled teacher from a box seat in the belly of a city being colonized by Silicon Valley in the 21st Century, that sense of desperation obviously distorts my recollections of the past (just like, in 1992, while many were saying "we won," I had a hard time seeing it because my mother had just died), but I am more than willing to acknowledge that, ultimately, writing a memoir is like wandering through the night "as a figure in the distance even in my own eyes," (as Silver Jews would put it) or perhaps it's an attempt at clearing space for a gathering.

This book is also an attempt at a tribute to all the amazing culture workers I've had the pleasure to meet or work with (some of whom are still alive), including Gil Scott Heron, Gary Adelstein, George McGovern, John Yau, Candace Kaucher, Lamont Steptoe, Jerome Robinson, Ellen Tiberino, Hugh Wattles, Lorri Jackson, WKDU RADIO, David Roskos, Ken Greenley, Cheryl Dunye, Linh Dinh, Chris Funkhouser, Paul Hoover, Maxine Chernoff, Robert Creeley, Peter Gizzi, Michael and Barbieo Gizzi, James Tate, Grace Hartigan, Pat Steir, Christine Hill (Volksboutique), Adrienne Shelley, David Rosenthal, John Ashbery, Jennifer Moxley, Carla Harryman, David Bromige, Anselm Berrigan, Alissa Quart, Joe Pernice, David Berman, Steve Malkmus, Steve Albini, Brett Ralph, Amiri Baraka, Caroline Crumpacker, Rebecca Wolff, Brenda Hillman, Miriam Jacobson, Ernie K.

Doe, The New Brutalists, Greil Marcus, Vanessa Beggs, Brett Evans and Janine Hayes, Jolie Holland, Kitchen Sink Magazine, The Graves Brothers Deluxe, Greg Ashley, Rachel Thoele, Rocky Yazzie, Nehemiah St. Danger, Barrett Avner, BEME The Rapper, KUSF RADIO, Delia Tramontina, Sylvie Simmons, Bettina Hubby, Tif Sigfrids, Oba T'Shaka, Ishmael Reed, D. Scot Miller, KPOO RADIO, Judy Juanita, David Mullen, Khafre Jay, Malik Diamond, and many other culture workers who have let me work with them, and who have done more than I against tremendous odds.

And I have no idea if this book is ultimately more *Agitated bored cautious depressed enervated flailing generous homeless individual judged kvetching la la melodic neutrality omniscient possibility quips recorded secretly televised under-represented volunteer wounded xylem yearning zippers*, or does it *Accept balance courage diet entertainment fertile galvanizing heartbeat illuminating jazzy kind local mature natural opulent proletarian questioning resonant severe temperate unified vigilant warm xenogamous yoga ziggurat*?

(and if you actually like this preface, you may be disappointed by how prosaic the "body" is......)

CHAPTER 1: WORKING-CLASS FOOLE OR WORKING-CLASS TRAITOR?---70S DECAY IN READING, PENNSYLVANIA

In recent years (and especially in the wake of the Trump election), many of the loudest pundits in the corporate media have made much of a distinction (and division) between a demographic termed "the white working class" (in the fly over or "rust belt" states) and the white (coastal) elite. In broad brushstrokes, it's geographical, and one may picture an electoral landlocked sea of red in the heartland surrounded by thin coastal borders of blue (though the reality is much more complex county by county). There's a debate whether this blue is being pushed by the red into a rising sea (that has nothing to do with climate change), or whether the blue has the poor red surrounded, but though this distinction overlaps with the old "City" (blue) over "country" or, these days, more likely "exurb" distinction, this cold civil war allegedly has as much to do with whether you went to college (and mind-body dualism) as where you live.

There's also an implication (promulgated by writers such as J.D. Vance of *Hillbilly Lullaby*) that these college educated white collar coastal elite types generally make more money, and have a tendency to look down on the white working class even if the white working class may make more money in real terms, since it generally costs much more to live in the 'blue' zones. But regardless of the actual income, I'm one of these "blue state whites" who feels very uneasy when a fellow "blue state white" (like Thomas Frank) provocatively titles a book, *What's The Matter With Kansas?* And I feel disgusted when a northern (or San Francisco) white condemns southern segregation while supporting—in less overt ways--redlining, gentrification and the prison industrial complex. And when some Californians wax wistfully about the possibility of CAL-exit, I can't help but think of the displacement of the black (and even white) working class in LA, Oakland, and San Francisco in recent years (just because it's called a sanctuary city doesn't mean you can afford to live here on the exploitative underpaying wages many undocumented workers get).

Knowing that any separate California government would have to give an even louder voice to this state's two largest multi-national industries: Hollywood, and Silicon Valley, makes me want to identify more with "the white working class" against these elites, but only if I can also side with the *black* working class too. It makes me want to scream: *just because I'm white collar doesn't mean I'm not working class*, and yes, a working-class hero is something to be, and I got a long way to go, but even though I got a Ph.D., and left a red (dying) factory town (well, actually purple) and ended up in the blue coastal cities (Philly, NYC, Oakland), I plead my case in this court, I am not the coastal elite (though I could really use a raise)![6]

So when Trump voters are asked when was it that America was great, quite a few refer to that period American economists refer to as "the great compression," roughly the 30 years after World War 2 (20 of which overlap with Jim Crow), and many economists and pundits tend to trace the roots of today's economic and cultural crises to the 70s, and I must admit, growing up in the 70s, and catching the tail end of this time, I can attest to a strong visceral decay both in my home town (which I used to say died giving birth to me), as well as in the music mass media was pushing, and the ways they pushed it. This was the backdrop I "came of age" in.

However, just as many Trump supporters tend to place the primary blame for the decay, and the decline of the middle, and working, class not on the 1% who control the economic and cultural means of production, but rather on "illegal immigration" (the influx of undocumented workers and refugees), Islam and even #BlackLivesMatter, so back in the late 70s, the corporatists spent millions on think tanks to create a massive public relations (propaganda) campaign to get many white working class folks to place the blame on the few government

---

[6] In the 21st century economy and culture dominated by the techno-determinists, the 17th century "rationalist" doctrine of mind/body dualism that has been used to justify racism, slavery, sexism and classism is as alive, and destructive, as ever. Not only does Google's chief technologist proudly claim that technology will 'allow us to transcend the limitations of our biological bodies and brains," but, according to Peter Thiel, only "the scientist, the entrepreneur, or Venture Capitalist" can be properly called mind: the rest of us (even with a Ph.D in the "liberal arts" or "humanities"), or anyone who believes that *democracy* is more important than capitalism, are considered "the unthinking demos," which sounds suspiciously like "the unwashed rabble" or "surplus population," whether you're a trucker replaced by a driverless truck, a heart surgeon replaced by a machine, or a Culture Worker.

attempts made in the 60s and 70s to address systematic racism ("affirmative action" etc).[7] Since these (racist and classist) myths still hold much sway in the cultural imaginary, I think it's important to consider some theories of what lead to "The Reagan Backlash" to make sense not only of my childhood, but also how America got in the mess it's in today.

Think Tank 1968 (for Joy Karega)

"People are starting to get too free, free
enough to say how they want to be free
& it's being heard, taken seriously
We can't just beat them down physically
Though we'll do that in case of emergency.
More effective to change the economy
Since 'the military and the monetary
[hook up] when they think it's necessary'[8]
It might take 2 decades, or maybe 3.
But we'll rob their little slice of autonomy
And even fool some in to thinking we—
I mean they-- are more free," Ah to be free
Free enough to say it's just a theory
--a fairy tale--   of true conspiracy......

Trying To Make Sense Of The Ruins Of My Childhood Without Mentioning My Biological Father

Part 3 of Adam Curtis' BBC Documentary, *The Century of The Self* (2002) argues that the radical (white) "countercultural" left of the '60s who had largely rejected the American consumer society got roped back in through "New Age" or "Me Decade" self-actualization psychology which Reagan appealed to in order to help win the election. The advertising industry shrewdly began to focus more on "lifestyle" marketing (or what others call niche marketing or market segmentation) around the same time John Lennon was following (but also helping to set) the fashion, primal screaming his way to the freedom of the new music industry standard of the 1970s "solo artist" (though to his credit, he never quite could get into those Superstar Arena Rock ambitions that McCartney had).

Lennon at least was prescient enough to warn:

keep you doped on religion and sex and TV
and you think you're so clever and classless and free
but you're still fucking peasants as far as I can see.

---

[7] The Powell Memo, The Tri-Lateral Commission, etc
[8] Quote from Gil Scott Heron's "Work For Peace." (1994)

And, indeed, *The Century of The Self* (2002) tends to reduce the baby boomer "hippie" generation to a caricature of such hippie peasants, and many of us punks and generation Xers could applaud, as we could place much of the blame on that generation while ours tended to be ignored or blocked by theirs.

As we watched videos of those Esalen and EST clothed or nude encounter groups, it's hard not to think of the Monty Python skit in *Life of Brian*, when Brian, fed up that he's being followed and taken as the messiah, shouts "you're all individuals" and the crowd shouts (in unison), "Yes, we're all individuals" and one guy in the back corner says "I'm not." Yet, Curtis, obviously, is painting in Broad Brushstrokes; not every Yippie! or Weatherwoman became a stockbroker like Jerry Rubin. Curtis also seems to over-emphasize the role of the (white) hippie/new-age "fringe," who collectively decided, after government crackdowns on their activism, to drink the koolaid that the deeper, truer, revolution, must be inner and individual (perhaps gotten from Bobby Dylan or a reductive misreading of the feminist battlecry, "the personal is the political").

Nonetheless, Curtis does make a strong case that part of Reagan's appeal, to white voters at least, is that he would get the government "off their backs" and set these "self-actualized" people loose to do what they want. This may seem odd to those of us who experienced the Reagan years as an era of repression, known for its union-busting, and bloody crackdowns on Central America, and of course "Just Say No" and stepping up Nixon's "war on drugs" and the mass incarceration industry. But think, for instance, of his (largely symbolic) promise to do away with the federal 55MPH speed limit! This could win over the Easy (and uneasy) riders, or Hell's Angels and perhaps some disaffected Vietnam veterans ("there's a hole in daddy's arm where all the money goes").

Like the skinny "supermodel" on the cover of *Cosmopolitan* with chocolate cake in her hands, Reagan was selling mixed messages, not just because he preached "Family Values" (while being the first president to be divorced). His appeal to the word "freedom" was a form of dog-whistle politics, but it must be remembered that it wasn't just the right wing southern strategy backlash to Great Society and Affirmative Action programs that cast government itself as a more repressive force than when it was enforcing Jim Crow laws more, but it was also that many of the white radicals in the anti-war movement had largely turned their back on labor (as Ishmael Reed, and others have pointed out).

When I read things like the Powell Memo, I can understand why some of the right wing think tanks of the 70s and the Tri-Lateral Commission could smile, "those hippies want the government off their backs; great! That's what we, the corporatists, want. We'll get rid of the draft and dismantle social programs and regulations that have kept us from rising higher since those pesky New Deal regulations in the 30s! (and this can break their rather superficial alliance with, say, The Black Panthers)."[9] But, obviously, there were other factors beyond the

---

[9] And, almost 40 years later, we still see the Republicans selling the word "freedom" to the same effect (the freedom caucus).

psychological and advertising industry that contributed to this transformation of American culture in the 70s.

Radio (as well as the record industry) is a field in which we can see the cultural superstructure intersect with the material base more clearly than in many other fields (poetry, for instance).

What was happening to U.S. commercial music radio and musicians throughout the 70s, to me, is at least as profound a cause for what lead to the "Swing To The Right" the election of Reagan signified and effected, and was clearly as much a part of the system Nixon sought to devise....to crush 60s liberation movements...."without seeming to" as the War on Drugs was: to use so-called mere entertainment to effect a cultural (counter) revolution that was a necessary pre-condition for the "Reagan Revolution."

Radio-As-Parent
"We've been raised on replicas of fake and winding roads," David Berman, Silver Jews

If it "takes a village" to raise a child, I was raised as much by TV's "global village," and even more by radio, as I was by my parents or the Catholic church.[10] Growing up in the 1970s, I caught the tail end (though I didn't know it at the time) of the great American means and mode of cultural (re)production known as AM-Top 40 radio, which most historians say began around the time of the controversial "desegregation" craze circa 1954 (Jackie Robinson, Brown V. The Board of Education, for instance). Although the rise of this form of radio accompanied controversy, racist backlash, and the unfortunate birth of "youth culture," it offered hope for (and a portal to) a less segregated America (without having to pay the price of total loss of culture through assimilation). Even if it was merely symbolic as the same radio station playing new hits by James Brown, Frank Sinatra, The Beatles, Dionne Warwick, and Ramsey Lewis in one 15 minute stretch between commercials (or, in terms of political lyrics, playing both "Eve Of Destruction" and "Ballad of The Green Berets"), there was at least a vibrant cultural dialogue going on....

This, however, was starting to change as I was given my first radio (which only had an AM dial on it) as a six-year old. In the late 1960s, and most crucially in the years 1969-1974, much of the power (or muscle) of the American music industry was consolidating and centralizing in L.A. (the death of NYC's Brill Building, Allen Toussaint's New Orleans studios and labels, and Motown's Detroit based operations are just three examples). Smaller record labels in cities and towns throughout the country were being outmuscled by increasingly multi-national conglomerates. Back in the 50s and 60s, the major labels had tried to crush these

---

[10] And as long as the field of psychology is stuck in its emphasis on the "family romance" (when it's not merely a biochemical determinist), ignoring the role of media (and today social media) in child rearing, it will continue to misdiagnose.

labels with the payola scandal, but when that didn't work, they realized they could have more success by cutting out their economic base from under them.

Sometimes all the multi-national media conglomerates had to do was wait for an old regional label owner to die of old age (like when Syd Nathan of King Records died, and Polydor could buy James Brown); other times labels like Columbia/CBS/Sony paid Harvard to help it devise ways to lure artists away from black labels or white-owned R&B labels like Atlantic would largely abandon their R&B rosters to sign Led Zeppelin and Yes for their more lucrative white audiences. Other times, they just had to wait for another inner-city nightlife district to get bulldozed to make way for a freeway. In short, the centralization of the music industry to LA circa 1970 not only made the industry a more impenetrable monolith, a larger than life ("too big to fail") entity than previously, but it also accompanied (or even caused) a re-segregation of the music industry, and not just between blacks and whites but between a proliferation of niches, between blacks and blacks, and whites and whites, as well as the overhyped few who liked the trickle down "integration" of disco).

If we view the process of what happened to the American music industry in the 70s in light of what the psychological and advertising industries were doing (as seen in *The Century of the Self*), we can see that radio was beginning to be marketed more (and music was more distributed) as lifestyle choices too, but since radio reached more people, and can reach kids at a younger age (not too many 5 year old kids want or need Esalen or EST, but will become devotees of contemporary pop music) as well as adults who wouldn't go to a shrink even if they could afford it (some call a jukebox the poor man's psychologist), it's not at all unreasonable to conclude that if we're looking for causes for the fragmentation of the left and the "Reagan democrat," it's not just a cut and dry blatant case of watching an "outlaw" biker like Charlie Daniels singing a hippie anthem like "Uneasy Rider" in 1973, but by 1980 singing the pro-Reagan "In America" in 1980, but we can also see it in bands like (the more "apolitical" and "escapist") Foreigner and Styx!

In the new system, or music industry mandate, there would be more division, and more "mind/body dualism" (a return to "normalcy") albeit under a different name. Just as the mind is placed "above" the body, the new FM music stations were placed "above" the "lower limit" AM stations; FM was sold as "upward mobility." AM played short cheaper top 40 7" singles, FM played longer more expensive Album-Oriented Rock (AOR) 12" LPS. AM Music was great on little transistor radios when you're walking; FM was allegedly better on giant speakers when you're driving, or chilling with some 420. AM was more about thrift; FM was more about inflation, and less bang for your buck. AM went more with a small intimate *Soul Train* dance floor (back when every town had at least 5) while FM was larger than life arena rock, baby![11]

---

[11] Graphic/ Chart provided upon request....

AM was more eclectic, more multi-ethnic or multi-cultural; FM became more exclusively white. FM was bigger and more "progressive," and allegedly sounded better ("no static at all") to more refined ears, more Euro-Anglo, more watered down California "C&W" (think The Eagles). FM fancied itself more thinking man's music. Sure, both had their share of schlock: AM had its John Denver cheeseball as much as FM had its Styx, but in general it was more danceable (even the white songs were more danceable, say "Little Willie") and more black. AM Top 40 was more like a downtown (as even Greil Marcus of the Baby Boomer orthodoxy admits), while FM was more like the new Malls on the outskirts. AM was more the hope of a desegregated city, FM was white flight to the suburbs…(this was almost analogous to the civil war between my "blue" working class mother and my "red" working class father; oops I said it!).

I still think it's even debatable that FM sounds better. Yes, perhaps I got a chip on my shoulder about this because, as one of the poorer kids at my 99% white school, the allegedly cooler, taller, more waspy Jones' kids who had color TVS and basements and stuff not only picked on Italians (coz the Puerto Rican kids were too busy working slave labor jobs in the mushroom houses), but also scorned me because I was "backwards" because I was more into The Detroit Emeralds or Joe Tex's "I Gotcha" than *Led Zeppelin IV* (though I loved "Whole Lotta Love"), and this of course was years before I had any "hip" Lester Bangs or Nelson George or punk and hip hop scene to help me feel less alone…

But it wasn't like there was much of a choice by the end of the 70s; I was only a teenager and everything in all genres (with the rare exception) seemed like a watered-down version of the early 70s and 60s (I hadn't yet dug back to the 50s, but I could understand why some people said I was too retro, and I didn't care for Bob Seger's "That Old Time Rock And Roll" either, even if I agreed with that message, the sound of the song contradicted it). There were less edgy sounds, less political lyrics (whether left-wing, or blatantly right wing, like there used to be). More importantly, the playlists were reifying, becoming more rigid. Sure, I liked the Rolling Stones, but "Sympathy For The Devil" is overplayed.

Music was becoming more and more specialized and sub-specialized, and all this niche marketing and segregation, and increased aversion to "risk taking" accompanied the rise of the "rock t-shirt," a precursor to Facebook branding. The corporations were doing their best to usher us like cattle into a commodified lifestyle choice. Hard Rock? Soft rock? Funk? Quiet Storm? Etc. Etc. Surely, you fit in to one of these. You must! C'mon if you really had to choose, you'd be this kind of thing. Music is part of your identity! Hell, even those weirdos over there, the *eclectic kids*, are a niche (and today's Facebook algorithm and data-miners rely on this kind of thinking). Nah, I still gotta stand up for the eclectic kids, and I wonder would Styx have gotten so lame, so damn "white" sounding had they had James Brown to keep it in check.

By 1980, even though the percentage of Americans listening to commercial music radio was at least as high as it was in 1960, job opportunities for DJS, or others who wanted to work in that field were far less available due, in large part, to automation and the rise of syndicated national chains which has accelerated further in the 30 plus years since.

Furthermore, by 1980, more DJS were fired, and the ones who remained had less autonomy and personal interaction with their local audiences than they had in 1965. In short, radio was becoming more like TV, and on a much deeper, more structural level than MTV. Because TV had always cost so much more than radio, TV was always dominated by national networks (like NBC as a front for General Electric, one of the biggest players in the military-industrial complex) than by local programming. Radio, at least between 1947 and 1977 (not coincidentally the years in which America had more of a middle class than ever before, or since) was primarily local in emphasis, and the national playlists like *Billboard* or *Cashbox* had significant grass-roots input from the local DJS, so that regional hits had more of a chance to be national hits, rather than merely consuming the "trickle-down" playlists determined by corporate headquarters (the model that has dominated the music industry since the late 1970s).[12]

In retrospect, the 70s were less fragmenting than today, yet that ain't saying much. If you happen to be one of the few blessed who fit in a niche, more power to you. But I think market segmentation helped create more social separation and alienation, as if the medium that had once been a bridge between human consumer (or listener) and producer had become more of a wall. Like increased globalism, culture was getting further and further away. In the early and mid 20th century, the northern corporate music culture (NYC, before it went LA) had kind of swooped down to the south to get more "raw" talent from poorer blacks, and poorer whites, to hook more consumers, but now they were ascending to that great northern cold sky heaven again (though they dressed it up as sunny Hollywood with palm trees, yachts, and everything). [13]

It was not market-segmentation alone that could effect this transformation, then, but the increasing marginalization of the local. Mass cultural music was becoming

---

[12] In the 1960s, according to Jonathan Taplin, "movie attendance continued to drop...and by 1969 most of the studios were teetering on the edge of bankruptcy." (Move Fast and Break Things, 235). This was partially due to the rising audience for TV, but it was also because of the increased popularity of music radio during the 60s. Quite a few people were rejecting the formulaic Hollywood movies, and the sedentary passive attention required for a two hour movie when they could find a more efficient and deeper engagement with life through music being disseminated largely through radio. Yet Hollywood was not only able to redefine itself after the success of Easy Rider (which piggybacked on 60s music), but also by taking over its rival, the more decentralized music industry. http://www.radiosurvivor.com/2011/06/09/a-history-of-radio-and-content-part-iii-the-rise-of-fm-music-radio/
[13] http://dispatchespoetry.com/articles/commentary/2016/12/931

more like McDonalds colonizing every town with a narrowing range of options, but making a mountain out of the molehill of the difference between it and Burger King, or Snickers and Milky Way, for even though there were more music formats, even taken together, there was less variety than there had been when the local economies had at least a little more say in America's national music culture and/or industry. But this isn't just about music, but about the difference between what had happened to my working-class hometown since its heyday and the ruins it was when I was growing up in the 70s.

My Mother, Grandparents & The White Working Class

My mother was white and part of the working class, if not "the white working class," and even though she died young in 1992, I just can't imagine her voting for Trump, just as she didn't vote for Reagan or Bush.

My mom was born on the exact same day/year as Paul McCartney and Roger Ebert. This, by some definitions, makes her too early for the post-war baby boom, as Pearl Harbor was attacked while she was in the womb, and, by the time she was born, her father was in the army in the "European theatre" and her "Rosie-the-Riveter" mother was working in a textile factory. She thus was more accurately a working-class *war baby* in contrast to her baby-boomer brother born after my grandpop came back from the war to work as a U.S. mailman, by day, and a hunter/environmentalist/scoutmaster by night while my grandmom, when she could steal time away from her other duties, was a semi-professional/hobby singer in a woman's secular choir.

Perhaps they were the classic nuclear white middle class family of the 1950s and 60s. They were starting to call Poles white in those years, and, besides, "white" was more German than WASP in my town where thick "Pennsylvania Dutch" accents were common, certainly my Grandpa had one. Furthermore, I always thought the term "middle class" was a way to obfuscate the working class identity that was more common in the 30s and 40s when my grandparents "came of age." Indeed, both worked manual labor in our small industrial town. I remember them telling me they bought the row-house my mother grew up in (with a basement and attic, a porch and a little back yard with a bird-bath) for like $3000 in that era of "The Great Compression."

Neither went to college. College was out of the question and not really as necessary in those days as it[14] would be for her grandchildren's generation, and TV didn't enter their lives until they were in their 30s and my grandpa was approaching 40. My grandma was born the same year that the first radio station in Pittsburgh was broadcast, and didn't get a radio until she was 9 or 10 during the great depression (when the repeal of prohibition allowed her father's bar to reopen again legally). My grandma told me that when she decided to get a TV in the mid 50s, the other women at the factory said, "be careful, it could make you fat,[15]" to which she replied, "no, I'm going to smoke" (and indeed she stayed thin until she quit smoking in 1989 after my grandpa died of lung cancer). Mass culture manufactured "youth culture," and generation gaps and other forms of ageism weren't as dominant before TV took hold, and even my mom and many of the war babies and early baby boomers weren't raised by TV's electronic baby sitter as much as our "Generation X" was.

Furthermore, my industrial hometown (now the poorest city per capita in the 50 states according to a 2010 census) had a vital downtown. You may think of the cliché or stereotype presented in the Christmas standards written around that time like "Silver Bells" (1950) or the glories of having "your own front door," which of course you didn't have to lock and a little roofed porch where you could sit and talk to next door neighbors on sweltering summer days. Some department stores even had piano players. It was a walking city: my grandma could walk to work, then walk (or perhaps bus) to the downtown, and walk (or perhaps bus) back home—all within a two-mile radius at most. They could go see regional celebrities, who didn't have to "go national" to make a living, perform. They did eventually get a car, but only used it rarely, for trips or family hikes to the woods. In retrospect, it's hard to resist the temptation to view this as a prelapsarian time, sheltered as they were from the horrors of racism.[16]

This walking city largely remained intact during my mom's post-highschool "courtship" years while she was in nursing school during the era of "Camelot." My mom wasn't old enough to vote for Kennedy, but had a button and volunteered for his campaign. She even went to Washington DC for his inauguration in the freezing snow—which was a long trip for our family who rarely left our own county—by train of course. Our town was a railroad town; you may have heard of it, because it's one of the railroads on the monopoly board that got swallowed up by Conrail and Amtrak in the 1970s, which paralleled the corporate music industry's takeover of the more independent music scene.

As a young woman, my mom was what you might call a "bleeding heart" liberal, and was excited about The Peace Corps, and hoped to join. She had converted from my grandparents' more secular Protestantism to Catholicism in part because of Missionaries like Tom Dooley (not the one in that old Kingston Trio hit), and because she found Protestantism too "wishy washy" and perhaps partially because she liked Italian boys from the poorer (less assimilated) side of town, though

---

[15] Notice, she wasn't worried radio would make her fat.
[16] On the other hand, the 1940s my other (Italian) grandmother was laboring in doesn't seem nearly as prelapsarian, trying to raise 8 kids on her own after her husband (who had sent for her as a mail-order bride from Italy) had died young, and not being successfully "assimilated" (though I hear she ran a numbers' racket, which takes some skills in assimilation).

she also had a crush on a Jewish med-school guy (perhaps I get my attraction to "Mediterranean types" (brunettes) from her. And perhaps she got it from her father, who though white with light brown hair, practiced his own little bit of "reverse assimilation" by marrying my dark-complexioned Polish grandmother.

Perhaps because it was the early 1960s—what some today would call The Mad Men era—rather than the late 1960s, she was too early for the hippie counter culture, or the women's liberation movement. She wasn't even really a 50s rock and roller, but more that Kennedy idealist and certainly didn't believe in the "pill" or in breast feeding (though her health conditions prevented her from breast feeding). It's kind of ironic that both "the pill" (with its promise of liberation through chemistry) and the return to breast feeding (a rejection of better living through chemistry) often go together in that development of second wave feminism in the late 60s/early 70s. I still have a floral suitcase of hers (one of the few possessions I was able to save when I became homeless) that has the name of the downtown store she bought it at on it. It reminds me of Petula Clark's "Downtown" from 1965, a song she liked, and through much of the 1960s, our town's downtown remained viable.

My mom was an excellent student, and a budding intellectual, and would have loved to go to college. Though college became more acceptable and encouraged for women, and for men from the working class, and even for more blacks during the 60s, have you ever looked at most college year books from the class of 1962? Mostly white men, and white upper (or upper-middle) class men at that. That started changing around 1965 when more affordable public colleges and universities were being opened, and you might even say, pushed by Government "Great Society" programs and a general aura of optimism about upward mobility through education and/or assimilation.

The blue-collar Flintstones were set in the past, while the white-collar Jetsons were set in the future. At the time, hardly anyone entertained the possibility that opening up more colleges could be part of a sinister long-term corporate plan to divide the working class more rigidly into "blue collar" and "white collar," to marginalize "blue collar" and undercut the economic base or infrastructure that created the "middle class" in the first place and help destroy the relatively self-sufficient, if not self-contained, county-seat city (whose produce often came from the farms in the same county, in contrast to today's needlessly inflated "carbon footprints") that my grandparents knew...

Nonetheless, college seemed like a shining grail to my "middlebrow" mother, as it did for me in the 80s, and even for many today---the promise of being a "first generation college student!" My mom was a thinker, a dreamer, a reader and writer, a social ironist, and a classic inwardly-directed introvert (but by introvert, I don't mean that she wasn't social; she loved to talk, to converse). Since my mother was of college-age pre-1965, however, it was still largely out of the question for her as it had been for her parents. Her parents had a decent "middle class" life, but it was still largely hand-to-mouth, or paycheck-to-paycheck, and, under the regime of 1950s mind-body dualism which cast the working class as "body" more than mind and the upper class as "mind" more than body, she had two strikes against her—class and gender, if not race.[17]

In the history of Euro-America, mind-body dualism has long been a tool of sexism, classism and racism, for it expresses, in more abstract terms, a social order in which the rich white male (say banker or real estate investor) is superior, and a poor black physical maid is inferior. Both of my parents, in different ways, were ushered more into the losing side of this dualism. My dad, raised in an orphan school as a second-generation Italian American cut off from his heritage and his mother's tongue, after a brief stint in the army, settled into a non-union factory job (they wouldn't let him unionize, which explains his envy and anger towards those in unions) and, that, coupled with his ailing wife (this was before the word disabled) and duties of raising a family, stunted his artistic and/or "hedonistic" pursuits.

And though my mom didn't nurse, she did become one, and a damn good one, overworked, but she loved her patients and the other nurses who loved theirs (often doing work that other slacker nurses didn't in addition to her own). She took her job home with her; she tried not to, but luckily a long phone conversation with my grandma could distract her, and as a kid, I was often transfixed by her stories of prima-donna doctors, even if many of her stories were "could've, would've, should've" stories.[18] She had a sensitive sarcastic sense of humor (what some would call gallows humor) that redeemed whatever regret she had about the way her life had turned out. She taught me more than most of my teachers, and was more entertaining than most TV (and that's saying something for a pre-teen TV addict).

These prima-donna doctors were all men, and more mind, while the nurses were the body below, and got paid (and respected) less, especially because my mom was only an LPN (Licensed Practical Nurse) rather than an RN (who had gone to college), but my mom was a mind, dammit, a heart, a soul, and not just a mere body. My mom, officially at least, was not allowed to be a cultural producer, though it was clearly her calling, and her hope was that I (and my sisters) would have the advantages she lacked.

---

[17] Like her mother, she married and had her first child at 20, yet in some ways my grandmother was more liberated than her, because of that late 1940s/1950s official ideology designed to get women to be submissive homeworkers (even if they had to work too) had played a larger role in my mom's upbringing; even if they were smarter than their husbands, the husbands were supposed to be the mind (see for instance the coffee commercials of the era, and my mom loved MGM endings).

[18] A characteristic this memoir no doubt shares.

If I, perhaps, had the male privilege, of being a cultural producer as a "mind" (or "mind/heart"), I would not do so in hopes of *rising above the body* the system reduced my parents to, but to *speak for* it, as well as the laborer they called they called "the consumer." I wanted to undo the hierarchy, the false association of women—especially working class women—with mere consumer, and in order to do so I'd have to labor on the level of language, even if they just called it "stand-up comedy" or, writing for a high school underground newspaper (in the so-called cultural superstructure my dad scorned), and I thought that, as an adult, becoming a commercial radio DJ might be a way to achieve this.

In the meantime, despite the much touted upward mobility promised my mom's generation (either through suburban "status symbol land," FM Rock Radio, or college), it's kind of hard to be forward looking when your dad's laid off at the factory and wondering whether they'll "make it through December" (as the Merle Haggard song would put it) and your mom's working double shifts at the Geriatric Center, and your town is dying (and even a 6 year old kid—who still believes in Santa—can see that), and though my mom didn't vote for Reagan, my dad did (and I was too young to be a tie breaker).

Muddled Thoughts On What a Gil Scott Heron Song Meant To A Teen In 1980 (& What It Could Mean Now)

"it's 1980, and there ain't no way back to 1975, much less 1969,"—Gil Scott Heron

While I was in high school, Reagan became President and my sense of cultural decay was confirmed by the first Gil Scott Heron song I ever heard (on one of the last commercial radio stations to still allow a sliver of self-determination for a DJ at 3AM): "B Movie." In the spoken-word "poem" part of the song, GSH diagnosed what happened to America during the period of 1970-1980, which some referred to as either "the me generation" or a "Backlash." They didn't teach this stuff in school, and certainly people like John and Yoko (who they pushed as political after I got hooked to songs like "Power To The People," before I knew the Chi-Lites one), weren't going to take risks to be political now that it was out of fashion (and their *Sometimes In New York City* bombed), and even the punk I was becoming aware of didn't quite get as deep into it yet, but Gil was one of the few who dared to stay political despite the "industry mandate" to depoliticize.

And revisiting those lyrics now, I find their brief but suggestive sociological analysis to be still as relevant almost 40 years later as they were then, in understanding the roots to Reaganism (or proto-Trumpism), and cut at least as deep in a few minutes as Adam Curtis did in 4 hours. In order to fully do these lyrics justice in a scholarly essay would take me at least 20 pages, but I'll just take a small section that had a big effect on me, to try to put myself back into how I thought at the time (I obviously didn't get the entire message):

"What has happened is that in the last 20 years, America has changed from a producer to a consumer. And all consumers know that when the producer names the tune...the consumer has got to dance. That's the way it is. We used to be a producer – very inflexible at that, and now we are consumers and, finding it difficult to understand. Natural resources and minerals will change your world. The Arabs used to be in the 3rd World. They have bought the 2nd World and put a firm down payment on the 1st one. Controlling your resources will control your world. This country has been surprised by the way the world looks now." ("B Movie")

According to GSH, The 1973 Oil Embargo from earlier in the decade had more to do, in the "cultural imaginary" at least, with changing America's position (he's bracketing, for instance, the loss of Vietnam and how Nixon's opening of relations with China began the trend toward outsourcing jobs to China, but so is Adam Curtis)[19] as an Imperial hegemonic player, leading to what some would call an identity crisis. We may trace the roots of 21st century Islamophobia to this economic fact (unless you want to trace to it the media's coverage of Elijah Mohammed, Malcolm X and Mohammed Ali, but generally the 60s was a time of the more "Ahab The Arab" kind of ethnocentrism, more arrogant than based on fear of 'immediate danger').

Although 9/11 is probably the most significant watershed mark in the history of American Islamophobia, in 1980, it began to be a national craze after the Iranian hostage crisis, with the rise of Ayatollah dart-boards (or novelty songs set to the tune of "My Sharona"); never mind the fact that Iran, a Shiite nation, was in a fierce conflict with the fundamental Wahhabi sect that ran Saudi Arabia, the principle beneficiary of the Arab Oil Embargo. This distinction was hardly in the American "cultural imaginary" of the time, just as it isn't today. Most Trump voters (and some Hillary voters) tend to lump most Arabs, or even most Muslims, together, and Bush could exploit that when bombing Saddam Hussein for Al Qaeda, as Trump exploits it with his Muslim Ban (that not excludes Saudi Arabia, but has Saudi Arabia's approval), yet the real source of the problem, then, as now, is domestic.

What America lost was *control*;[20] it had once had more self-sufficiency (or a temporary 'sustainability'), but consumption of oil began to outpace production of oil under US imperial control (even if we don't just mean the 50 states, including Oil Rich Alaska). Of course, the major corporations were doing everything during

---

[19] It must also be remembered that the Oil Embargo lead to a general acceleration of inflation beyond the "energy sector," or some could argue that the Inflationary Regime that began in the late 60s simply used the Oil Embargo as an excuse to effect its plan of destroying the American middle (and working) class.

[20] though I could claim coffee would be right up there with oil, and that clearly wars would be fought if an embargo occurred, and it would become less available to the mass of Americans

this time to increase U.S. dependence on oil, as if it was synonymous with the American lifestyle. Beach Boys were a walking talking singing advert for California and The Car, and Nasscar was still pushed during the Oil Embargo, and plastic use was on the rise. Oh, there was a little move toward "smaller cars" (thanks in part to that award winning "Think Small" VW Beetle campaign) in the 70s, but that didn't last long. It wasn't long before cars got bigger, more armed...or you could say fatter just like the country that drove them. They certainly became more expensive.

GSH connects the international player "America" to the domestic economic and cultural situation: "Jobs are down, money is scarce – and common sense is at an all-time low with heavy trading."[21] And this job-loss could've happened even had the Arab Oil Embargo never happened, but what caused it didn't make the headlines as much as say Watergate did, and why? Because "the free press went down."[22] In fact, it was all part of the same system; he also mentions the Tri-Lateral Commission, "David Rockefeller of Remote Control Company," but David Rockefeller dart-boards did not catch on....

According the GSH, the root problem was that America had gone from being a producer to a consumer, but it seemed that most every other adult voice was doing its best to deny it. There was a sign on a steel bridge crossing the Delaware River, not far from where George Washington made that legendary crossing 200 years earlier that said, *Trenton Makes, The World Takes*. That sign was once a source of civic pride, but by 1980 it was an absolute joke—hardly anything was made there anymore-- yet they dutifully lit that neon every night, while us kids felt about it the way a kid who sees his dad beat his mom while saying "I love you" would feel about the word "love."[23] And, things were so bad in my town, that when that Billy Joel song "Allentown" came out a few years later, we were *envious*. Our town was much worse off than Allentown, and at least they got a song.[24] All across America, factories left, downtowns had died, the radio had become a gated community, as the takers got the makers to think of themselves as takers, and think of the takers as makers.

++++

But what did GSH *mean* when he used the words producer and consumer in an era of supply-side trickle-down economics that marginalized labor? It's one thing to say that America as a country (as a government) became more of a consumer (and indeed the deficit grew under Reagan), but it may be less accurate to say that

---

[21] Reagan didn't bring jobs back, but sent more away while busting unions at home; and Trump follows suit
[22] And I could relate to that because I saw the more autonomous radio DJS go down.
[23] The sign, despite itself, became more honest, when the "M" burnt out, so it read "Trenton Akes"
[24] Before I heard the GSH song, I didn't realize the death of my home town wasn't just local (we were told the jobs were moving south and west; I didn't realize they were leaving the country!)

most *Americans* became consumers, at least in any absolute sense. As economists like Robert Reich and Joseph Stiglitz have pointed out, Americans became more productive since the late 1970s; production didn't decline, *wages did*.[25]

Thus, many Americans became more "consumers" than "producers" in name only. The "change' from producer to consumer signifies the loss of "working class" identity, as many of the smaller, local, papers, that had labor sections alongside of business sections, had folded, and all the major TV networks advertising (as well as the planted 'native advertising' in the official entertainment fare) was telling us we are primarily consumers, and are (only) valuable as consumers.

The elevation of the "American consumer" over the "American worker" was enshrined in the constitution in supreme court decisions to benefit the dictates of monopoly capitalism. For instance, "from [Judge Robert] Bork's point of view, if Walmart ended up as the only general retailer in this country, as long as prices continued to fall, this could benefit *consumer welfare*." (emphasis added). Never mind the lost jobs, and lower wages that would effect people's ability to pay these 'lower prices.'

What are they protecting the consumer from? The worker! The worker, not the boss, is the one who suffers most from downsizing and outsourcing.[26] And since you're likely to be worker as much as consumer, they're protecting you from yourself, or dividing you from yourself through this brilliant rhetorical sleight of hand. When they invoke the American consumer, you might think that they mean you (or at least your wife), but they may not even be talking about you; the pure consumer is the super-rich, the investor class, the leisure class.

So, the invocation of the "consumer" may be a very ingenuous way to make people sympathize with the 1%, those who produce no real wealth, but determine the value of things. For they certainly have the most consumer spending power. Of course, this consumer often goes by other names, including Job Creator (another oxymoron), and corporate *person*, all of which are expressed in anti-labor policies, and "B-Movie" is clearly saying it's time to think of ourselves as labor again.

In the context of B-Movie's complex, suggestive, breakdown of the American sociological landscape of 1980, this short excerpt about America's decreased production, and increased consumerism, is invoked to support his claim that

---

[25] "since the early 70s, median rates refused to rise even though productivity was rising dramatically." It doesn't matter that more people were actually producing more, but production was no longer defined by how much work you did, but how much you got paid (which is totally circular reasoning).

[26] And even though Bruce Springsteen was kinda presented as "the white Bill Withers," a working-class hero," is it really inaccurate that he was called the "boss" rather than say the employee.

"we're all actors in this I suppose." And, fittingly, Scott-Heron's Song culminates in the repeated chant:

This ain't really your life
Ain't really your life
Ain't really, ain't nothing but a movie

And a B-movie at that! Like a more analytical sequel to "The Revolution Will Not Be Televised," a decade later, the weary call to action that is "B Movie" places the election of Reagan in a broader cultural context that suggests that the rise of American consumerism (and the decrease of American working class identity) cannot adequately be considered without considering the role of the Hollywood film industry (of which television, and, increasingly, radio, was a part), in rendering us more passive. Amiri Baraka, too, had made a similar diagnosis in his 1974 poem, "A New Reality Is Better than a New Movie," though "B-Movie" (even on the page) cuts deeper.[27] In Criticizing Hollywood, you might even say he's criticizing the coastal elite (and, damn, I wish he were alive today; he'd have a field day with Google and Zuckerberg!).

So how can we fight it? How can we once again elevate labor over consumer (and include childbirth in labor too!)? Perhaps writing *our own* screenplay, or, better, a song, as if uttering your righteous democratic visionary thoughts could rescue us from the hell of a consumer society, and empower us to be producers (and, maybe, just maybe, yoked to a funky haunting bass line, it can!)[28] Rest-In-Power Gil Scott Heron!

In any event, despite these muddled thoughts, listening to GSH's song made me burn with the "fierce urgency of now." "B Movie" implies that too many were watching TV and movies instead of exercising the hard-won right to vote, unionize, etc, and, yes, this song made me despise myself for being a mere consumer, even as it inspired me to immediately go out and *consume* every Gil Scott Heron album I could find (some of which I could find cheap at used record stores). Sure, I wasn't 18 yet, and kids are allowed to be (or supposed to be) a consumer, but this song had a lot to do with getting me to stop watching TV. I remember a friend saying to me, as we watched some Late Night show, "just put those celebrities in our living room; we're way more interesting than they are!" In fact, I remember Saturday Night Live stole one of our jokes! (though of course we couldn't prove plagiarism since they never met us, and doubtfully were paying Google to surveil us since it didn't exist yet).

---

[27] I guess Dylan, too, was saying something similar in 1965: "advertising signs they con/ you into thinking you're the one/ that can do what's never been done/ that can win what's never been won/ meanwhile life outside goes on all around you."
[28] This was before I read page-based poetry.

I also gave up soda, and avoided the car as much as possible to minimalize consumption, in hopes of becoming a cultural producer as part of the Reagan Resistance, and the anti-Hollywood army. I vowed that someday I'd be able to pay GSH back (he taught me the word, and concept, of *reparations*), just as I vowed someday I'd pay back my mother!

Besides, I knew I'd be having to leave home, and make it on my own soon. And, even though I had a "working class identity," I, like many of my generation, was not nostalgic for the good old days of factory labor. I lasted about a month in one sweeping up the chocolate Santas that had fallen from the conveyor belt to the floor, and one night on another conveyor belt sealing and lifting 50 pound bags of Dietrich powdered milk. My dad wanted me to work in the factory with him (if I wasn't good enough to play football--I could blame my height--this is the least I could do). "But, dad," I said, "the factories are dying anyway!" And that "deserved some discipline." But I thought it would be possible to be a commercial DJ (disk jockey), a role that I thought could allow me to be exactly in between being a consumer and a producer. I could, for instance, *play* that Gil Scott Heron song, and *turn people onto* it. I could feed people's bodies, minds, and even hearts. The job didn't pay much, but I'd have free access to a wider range of music than most stations now allowed.

Yet, by 1984, it seemed there were many large forces conspiring to make our generation mere consumers (of politics, of movies, of music). Even a baby-boomer culture worker with a proven track record like Gil Scott Heron wasn't immune. Arista, the record label that got its start making GSH their first signing, had rode him and now abandoned him for safer, and more lucrative acts like Whitney Houston; if even *he* was finding it hard to be a producer, how could I become one in a country that's become a consumer?[29] Maybe I'd have to wait 30 years to write an essay that shows the role the Compact Disk played is changing America from more of a producer to consumer, and read it with musical backdrop on Delia Tramontina's *Poet As Radio* show on KUSF. I'll excerpt it here:

The Rise Of The CD

On March 2, 1983, only 7 years after Sony's first public experiments with the new CD technology, CBS launched the first major CD sales campaign (with the release of 16 titles that had already sold well in vinyl-format), in conjunction with Sony, maker of the players. This date is often celebrated as the Big Bang of the digital audio revolution. "Time To Upgrade" become the new mantra, like a patriotic duty.

---

[29] I saw GSH live around 1988 in Philadelphia with Linton Kwesi Johnson, and I remember him saying, "a lot of people ask me when I'm coming out with a new album. Well, once y'all buy my old albums….)

While a ticker tape parade of enthusiasm had greeted the new development of the 45 in the late 1940s, and eventually the LP in the late 1960s, it was harder to persuade a skeptical market that the CD was an improvement either aesthetically or economically. It was first marketed to audiophiles, as an elite object. Once it established some audiophile cred, its prices came down a little, as if to democratize the audiophile feeling: you too can feel classic when listening to Van Halen's "Panama."

As for content, the classic back catalogues were repackaged and pushed so the CD benefited from the 1980s economy of cultural scarcity. Advertisements for record stores that used to feature 5 new releases now featured 3 classic reissues with bonus tracks, and two new releases--at least one of which was usually a corporate-sponsored pop smash.

As "Time to Upgrade" became the new mantra, the record industry could make more money off the dead without having to spend as much money discovering and promoting new artists, and put more people out of work. Much less new music was being played on commercial radio, and a narrower range at that. The industry had lured the casual listener back into the market for a novelty spending binge, quick fix, which would show immediate profits, big bonuses and make them more attractive to potential corporate buyers (Bertelsmann, Sony, etc) in this merger-happy era.[30]

Vinyl was still hanging around though. Since the seductive approach was insufficient to hook people on CDs and get them off their addiction to vinyl, the major labels had to supplement it by force. Although CD sales lagged behind the sales of both vinyl and cassette for most of the 1980s, vinyl sales sharply declined between 1988 and 1991. I remember buying a Columbia vinyl record in 1991 that was warped and returning it; the second one was warped as well. The third time I bought it on cassette. The record store owner was as exasperated as I was. We both knew why:

[In 1988] the major label distributors restricted their return policies, which retailers had been relying on to maintain and swap out stocks of relatively unpopular titles. First the distributors began charging realtors more for new product if they returned unsold vinyl, and then they stopped providing any credit at all for returns. Retailers, fearing they would be stuck with anything they ordered, only ordered proven, popular titles that they

---

[30] This was an extension of the general cultural slow-down & reification that had begun in the 1970s; a conscious decision to sell history. CDs helped slow time in ways that soothed many who were still shaken up or burnt out from all the social and domestic disruptions of 1955-1975 with the promise of a "return to normalcy." Casey Kasem narrated documentaries: "A decade like the 60s can only happen once in a lifetime," because his bosses were telling him he better! While waiting for a new song to sweep you off your feet, there was plenty of time for thoughts of technological gadgets and upgrading where once you might have thought about what new music to check out.

knew would sell, and devoted more shelf space to CDs and cassettes. Record companies also deleted many vinyl titles from production & distribution, further undermining the availability of the format and **leading to the closure of pressing plants.** This rapid decline in the availability of records accelerated the format's decline in popularity, and is seen by some as a deliberate ploy to make consumers switch to CDs, which were more profitable for the record companies **(emphasis added)**

Thus, the rise of the CD also occurred at the expense of the last-bastion of decentralized local music retail: the record shop owner and salespeople. The death of vinyl during Bush's increased censorship policies & "Desert Storm" also froze out more 'marginal' and less popular cult-albums and had the effect of narrowing selection; this also hurt independent labels who were slower to make the transition to CDs or, in some cases, outright defiant toward the CD.

Furthermore, the change from vinyl to CD was a perfect excuse to close down domestic vinyl plants without having to directly "bust" a union. CD factories were built in other countries; outsourcing was sold as progress. At least Wallmart's outsourcing made things cheaper; CDs never were. The CD was used by the major record labels to consolidate their power, outsource jobs, limit consumer access to variety, and crush independent musicians and retailers. And, for what? I don't think you can ever persuade me with your scientific studies that prove that CD technology is more accurate to "the human ear," just as I probably can't persuade you that I *heard* the soul-less sound of exploitation, slavery, and censorship in the CD. It's just a coincidence...

The CD also helped the labels accelerate the phasing out of the single. Regardless of the fate of vinyl, the form of the album benefitted by the CD when the single didn't make the transition to CDs. Formats like "Album Oriented Rock" did not suffer in the industry transition to CDs. The 10/12 song album was now the new Reagan-deficit gold-standard. In the 80s, the Vinyl LP and the CD worked together against their common enemy: the single. Even though the double-sided single had long ceased to operate independently from the album, sales of 45s were still high into the mid 1980s (Five *Thriller* singles went platinum, for instance). Yet, since albums by major label artists came out on average two to three years apart, the single existed in name only, as a physical object, no longer a mode of cultural production. Although the "Cassingle" had some success during the transitional time of the late 1980s, the CD single never caught on. The record labels themselves were never all that enthusiastic about it from the get go.

CD-singles were not competitively priced compared to other singles formats (and the album-length CD), but the labels still feared they were cannibalizing the sales of the higher profit-margin CD albums. They pressured Billboard magazine to change its "single charts" into "song charts," which allowed album cuts to chart based only on airplay, without a physical single ever being released. The labels would still publicize an album track as the new "song," but just think of all the people who made things they put out of work.

Meanwhile, Back In "What Do You Want To Be When You Grow Up?"

Since my dreams of being a DJ were deemed unrealistic (one of the few things both of my parents could agree on)—and any hope of becoming a musician myself seemed as far away as it did for my mom (as far as I could tell, my town had no music scene unless you're into "The Beer Barrel Polka")[31] in that far away TV-land, I began to seriously consider college....and being that first-generation college student my mom had wished she could've been 20 years earlier in the 60s. *Don't Wanna Die At 18; Don't Wanna Die At 18....*

College may have been a luxury my mom and grandparents couldn't afford, but now it seemed like a necessity (even if we still couldn't afford it). And going to college was paradoxical, because even though I was a veritable "firehouse of activity" there, when it came to the banks, I was first and foremost, a consumer, hailed into the debt economy (going more into debt for it than I would have if I had gotten a car). Yet, I could not only please my mom, but also get a Federal student (start-up) loan to go to college, while I couldn't to rent a garage to form a garage band. Certainly, in college, I saw no point in majoring in music; it wasn't like there were classes in punk, or funk, or even a slow sad pop ballad...

In college, at least, there was college radio, and by the early 80s, I found myself in that paradoxical position of listening to pro-working class music that I could only find if I left my dying blue-collar town to become aware, through college radio, of the working class punk and hip hop that, by contrast, the blue collar kids who stayed in my hometown didn't have access to. If the metal being played on the corporate stations was generally considered to be the music of the "white working class," (an association Trump's campaign's soundtrack exploited), no wonder those who stayed in the small dying factory towns would call us "blue state snobs." And commercial radio was even worse in the 80s, and not so much because of MTV, but more because the corporations began to purge music from the AM dials, and replace it with right wing political talk like Rush Limbaugh. At least in the 70s, you still had the option of choosing between FM and AM for music, but now they had just about halved the number of radio stations playing music (of whatever genre), and 30 years of that can go a long way to creating the phenomenon known as the "Trump Voter" who kills Muslims on mass transit in Portland (for instance).

---

[31] I used to always think I got my love of, or passion for, music from my mom. My mom played piano from the book as it were, but since we were poor we couldn't afford a piano. My grandparents had rented one for a few years while my mother was a girl taking piano lessons (an acceptable lady-like pursuit), but they no longer had one by the time I was born. Since my grandmother was a singer myself, I wonder if they had family sing-alongs like the Davies family (with little Ray and Dave roughly my mom's age) had? Or had the rot of

But, as I left for college against my "red-state" working class dad's wishes, though with my "blue state" mom's approval, I was plagued by the question: was my dad right? Did the fact that so many of us in the 80s/90s drank the college kool-aid as it were, in a belief that college could mean upward mobility, or more "freedom," mean that we abandoned the fight to save factories whose death all around us was destroying our town from the ground up (and would eventually trickle up to white collar workers on the cultural superstructure). Was I, were we, class traitors? Is that a major source of any justified resentment many of the "white working class" have that some say lead people voting for Trump?

I became very aware in the 80s and especially the 90s that they were trying to sell a distinction, and widen the split between white collar and blue collar, to increasingly devalue blue collar, and, in effect, *force people into college* and its debt economy, and devalue the college degree, while I danced to The Godfather's singing, "things ain't what they used to be/ we're living under a false economy." Still, maybe my mom was right, and college could allow me to be a producer, and maybe, once she was divorced, she too could take college classes….

As I walked along the chartered streets (where the chartered Schuylkill flows) of my abandoned hometown's downtown (while the Replacements sang "Anyway, I got no place else to go!" or Dead Kennedys sang "Burn Down The Malls,"), past the burnt, destroyed train station that must've been something when my mom went to see JFK before he was an airport, and stood in front of the boarded up moldy ruins of the Art Deco theatre from the 1920s with the words "HELP _AVE

TV already set in, so that replaced family singalongs for far too many just like "instant cake" was replacing the rigors and/or joys of cooking?

I do remember my mom telling me that sometime in the 50s (maybe she was 12 or 13), she had proudly told my grandmother that she had written a song. "What's it called?" my grandmother asked. "I'll Be There," my mom answered. My grandmother replied, "you know there's already several songs called that." Though I'm sure my grandma didn't mean any malice in saying this, listening to my mom tell the story, I feel it thwarted, or repressed, her creative expression or artistic ambitions, and this made me terribly sad. I longed to hear the song, but we didn't have a piano and she didn't remember it.

Still, years later The Four Tops reached #1 with "Reach Out (I'll Be There)" and a few years after that, the Jackson Five topped the charts with another song called "I'll Be There" and a few years after that The Spinners hit #2 with "I'll Be Around (I'll Be There)" so, who knows, my mom could've been Ellie Greenwich? I wish I knew more about the story, but I was always afraid to ask my grandmother more about it because I feared I'd sound accusatory. Still, there were bigger external forces that prevented her from pursuing music, just as there were obstacles in pursuing college, chief among them class and gender.

I do remember she got a cheap chord organ when I was growing up (this was before Ca sios), but it wasn't until the 80s, as I approached 18, that she could finally afford a

ME" on its marquis, and cried, I remember vowing that, if for some reason this college degree ever does allow me to make more money, I'll come back and save it, just like Lou Rawls vowed in "Dead End Street" or was it "Tobacco Road." I envisioned all those abandoned railroad buildings becoming an art center! And, to paraphrase Shelley, if urban and industrial decay comes in the 70s (and Reagan in the 80s), can punk and hip hop be far behind?

2. CAN COLLEGE MAKE-UP FOR THE LOSS OF A WALKING CITY AND HELP MAKE AMERICA GREAT AGAIN? (or why meeting John Yau was better than winning the poetry prize)

I went to college as a political science major, and imagined that I'd become a politician, or at least one of those idealistic lawyers like Al Pacino in *And Justice For All*. I know I associated college with political protest, and found 60s footages of college protests kinda glamourous, even if I found CSNY's "4 Dead In Ohio" cloying, preferring D.R.I's "Reaganomics Killing Me. I joined the college "radical" organization, *Student Union For Peace And Justice* and on one field trip to an Anti-Nuke and U.S. Out of El Salvador rally, I saw Senator Alan Cranston speak. He was running for president and, at the time being touted as the most progressive candidate, as, say, "The McGovern of 1984" (this was before McGovern himself, and, later, Jesse Jackson decided to run). And, as a young idealist, who loved *Fear and Loathing On The Campaign Trail*, and held out hope that we could learn from the mistakes of the 60s, I decided to drop out of school for a semester and work on his campaign. They were willing to pay me $400 a month, as well as provide a free basement, and at the time that was a lot of money. If Cranston did well in the early primarieies, they'd make me the Nevada Coordinator.

To make a long story short, when McGovern decided to run, I defected from Cranston to work for him (even though he paid less, and I was homeless for two months before finding a leaky room in a Scientologist's apartment for $100 a month), and when I returned to college, I ran as a delegate to the democratic convention for my district, but by the time Pennsylvania's late primary came around, he had

piano. And when we finally got one, I remember my dad having to cover it up and hide it from his mom when she came to visit so she wouldn't think we had squandered money on a decadent expense. It's perhaps coincidental that both my mom's mom and my dad's mom were figures who devalued music in these stories. It reminds me of James Baldwin's "Sonny's Blues," in which the family doesn't appreciate and represses Sonny's musical talents and obsession, and how this may be to blamed for his subsequent drug addiction. In "Sonny's Blues," the familial fear of music has its roots in an incident where his father, as a teenager, witnessed white racists kill his brother (Sonny's uncle), crushing his guitar in the process, and as far as I can tell nothing so horrifyingly traumatic repressed music for my parents or grandparents, but there was nonetheless a stigma against creating it, if not against consuming it via radio and/or records....And, back when I was a Casio or piano busker, many other people have felt this need to tell me how their desires or needs to play music were often crushed when they were children. Mine weren't crushed, but just deferred.

dropped out (The (neoliberal) Gary Hart people wanted me to switch to being a delegate for him, I demurred and I got 24th out of 27th). Yet, even in Washington, something told me, "don't put all your eggs in the basket of electoral politics," as, during some down time from the campaign, I would prowl around the streets of DC shooting Super8MM films which I'd edit and create soundtracks for when I got back to college.

I thrived in college, especially a small college with around 1500 people; I developed a system so I could get good grades while still having a vital social life: one semester I'd take all the difficult courses, and be more a hermit; the next semester, I'd take the easy "blow-off" courses, and be very social. Thus, I could graduate with a 3.7 even as I flitted from social scene to social scene (even before I had read Frank O'Hara's "grace to live as variously as possible"). Dorm living (or even nearby off-campus housing) was more like the convenient walking city my grandmother knew![32] College allowed me to feel more like a producer (to test your art on a focus group of teachers and peers) even while you're going into debt (ah, the purposeful purposelessness of the sublime!). It also allowed me not having to settle on a specialization. Sure, my poem won the poetry prize, but I also won the philosophy prize....

Though I was originally a political science major, I gradually came to switch to the "less practical" majors (especially after coming back somewhat disillusioned with electoral politics), eventually landing on English after Jane Androne and Gary Adelstein began to make me seriously consider how the college professor could be a pretty cool adult role. Gary would regularly "blow my mind" with such statements as "So-called high culture and so-called low culture usually have more in common with each other than the mainstream culture of the 'official reality.'" I'm sure he said it better than that, for some reason its visionary pragmatism meshed with my sensibility.

Adelstein turned me on to both The English "High" Romantics, as well as The Michael Benedikt Surrealist anthology, and experimental "visionary" Super8 Movies (he scorned video!).

He had made an amazing film called *Reading 1974: Portrait of a City*, which I'd be happy to do a showing of, since it documents the death of my hometown— the poorest city in America according to the 2010 census-- a decade earlier (and

---

[32] Important Polemical Digression: Dear Bosses, you claim you care about students dropping out, and not being able to compete with those at the more expensive schools. You know what would help: dorm living! Pay the students in the construction department to build affordable dorms to help alleviate not just the college's crisis, but the city's crisis, and put the community into community college so the civically minded students who would love to be involved in extra-curricular activities but waste 3 to 4 hours a day commuting, would have a chance for community engagement!

since "the death of my hometown" is kinda fashionable these days thanks to Lynn Nottage's *Sweat* [2015]). And at this time, I was much more interested in Super 8MM films than poetry.

Extra-curricularly, I strove to engage in as many school activities as possible. You could say I was a kind of "renaissance man," or more pejoratively "jack of all trades" or dilettante: I not only made films and was in the SUPJ, but also wrote for the newspaper, had a radio show or three, worked at the summer dinner theatre, the literary magazine, and developed my sideshow piano act (and I'm sure I'm missing some things). I was trying out the "kitchen sink" strategy, spreading a tablecloth for the necessity to specialize I was hoping to put off for as long as possible, but even though college teacher seemed now a possibility as an adult profession, I remained very skeptical about devoting myself to poetry.

If you asked anybody who knew me in high-school whether I'd be a college professor, with 7 books of published poetry, they'd surely scoff. I know my younger self would've told you you're crazy. In high school, I had done stand up comedy, made videos (hmmm, I was on TV before I was ever on the radio), got people laughing at my human beat-box, and wrote tentative first satirical pieces for the mimeographed underground newspaper my friend Glenn Frantz (who was a brilliant introvert who turned me onto The Fall for instance) edited. There was no teen punk scene in my home town, and the only poems I wrote were parodies. I was definitely going for humor more than brooding or whatever the teachers' Force Fed Frost was telling us poetry was.

Yet, they'd bring in visiting writers, and I realized that "free verse" had become the new orthodoxy when creative writing teachers would "try to beat rhyme out of me." I didn't want to write Pope's kind of rhymes, but the kind of rhymes you could set to music (or at least with many parenthesis, lower case letters that would be scorned by Scrooge McDuck Ivy League Southey-esque Poe-Purist Professor for being too much like e.e.cummings). Pause For An Old R&B song on KPOO:

"I'm mad.....and you have the nerve to try to be glad."[33]

I know there's a lot of big deep theoretical works about the superiority of free verse over rhyming woks, but I felt "free verse" as poetry forming a little gated community to keep music out; even the somewhat lame offerings of Paul Simon or "Eleanor Rigby" lyrics in the X.J. Kennedy *Intro To Poetry* anthology still would taboo such poetry as:

I got no kick against modern jazz
Unless they try to play it too darn fast

---

[33] https://www.youtube.com/watch?v=IvBB8ObRfZQ

They lose the beauty of the melody
Until it sounds just like a symphony...."

Damn, I love the working-class pride in that song, especially when the *Oxford Anthology of Literature* was calling the "English Ballad," a mere "hybrid" art form (before academics started elevating the hybrid)—not quite music (meaning "high" music) or poetry (meaning "high" poetry). Yet, there were other ways to bring the two forms together (as in "B Movie," but also in the Velvet Underground's "The Gift").

When I first heard the Velvet Underground's "The Gift" at age 18, I was blown away (and not just because its lyrics were designed to appeal to the adolescent Piscean introvert). I loved that they took full advantage of stereo separation and made it part of the art: if you wanted the instrumental band without the words, you had the left side. If you wanted the words without the instrumental, you had the right side.[34] Despite the words (which I can say I've outgrown in a way I wouldn't say what Gil Scott Heron did in his 20s), I knew that art like this was what I wanted my life to be like: low-fi, but loud, powerful (and by some definitions cacophonous) dance music on one side, with no words to distract, with no words to distract me from my "interior monologues" or even a holy state of wordlessness. But on the other side, if I really wanted to hear the words and a musical Welsh accent, I could have that too (and don't forget "The Murder Mystery" which also uses stereo separation).[35] Furthermore, at the time they recorded the song, they, like the Syd Barrett Pink Floyd on the other side of the pond, had developed a division of labor between the Dionysian noise dance trance performances and the more artfully constructed songs on the album which they wouldn't perform live. This, too, had the power to bring two audiences together, like introvert and extrovert. And perhaps that was the standard, or soulmate, I always measured myself against—someone who likes both, but doesn't always need to mix them up, and there have been times I found it (if not, alas, recently)....

Some academics say song lyrics are working class poetry, but, from my perspective, poetry was upperclass (or older people's) song. That's how it came to me, and I know I'm not alone (just as novels are upper-middle-class *Hollywood*). So, even though I published some tentative firsts in the college literary magazine, I maintained some suspicion toward the poet role.

Then Harry Kosauros, the art teacher, brought a New York art critic to campus (who had recently written an art-catalogue about his new paintings) to give a slide

---

[34] All the while, in performance, Andy Warhol's got films going for a multi-media experience better than a Meme

[35] Perhaps this is true of No Trend's "Teen Love" too, though I only had it from cassette on the radio....

presentation on contemporary art. The art critic also wrote poetry. In fact, he'd just won a National Poetry Series prize for his recent collection, *Corpse and Mirror*, so Harry and Gary also wanted to set up a reading for him, to get him a little extra cash and make it worth his while. Others in the English Department (including Lillian Robinson, that otherwise very personable feminist theorist, who had told me not to rhyme) objected strongly to "that surrealist New York School kind of thing," but Harry and Gary prevailed, and John Yau was able to read his poetry. Even though I had seen his slide presentation, I and my friends in the poetry magazine (such as Andy, Kevin, maybe even Roberto, and of course that non-student Yuri, then still going by Riq, Hospodar) were somewhat skeptical that this reading would be any good, with the school's track record in the poets they brought. But we went anyway (perhaps for the cheese and strawberries) and were all pretty much floored from the first lines he read. Finally, here was a real live poet who was conversant with infinity, funny, and full of youthful angst (he was about 33 at the time)—yet not too blatant about it.

After the reading our gang went up to him, and he'd say things (in his Boston accent) like, "you know, the problem with Robert Frost in that poem is that he should've taken *both* roads." This quote confirmed to me that Yau *was not a purist, but a visionary pragmatist*, and something in my soul meshed with this attitude. He also confirmed my interest in O'Hara, Ashbery and Creeley (and, later, Laura (Riding) Jackson). It gave me the incentive I needed to put more energy into studying poetry during my remaining time at Albright. It wasn't until Yau came to my school that I began to see the advantages to, and the possibilities of, writing non-rhyming poetry, and finding enough infinity in the specialized genre, if forced to specialize (and I wasn't really; after all, Yau was also an art critic; and his two arts complemented each other).

Yau also made it clear that NYC was like walking city my grandma used to have than what's become of my home town, and, as I soon found out, even Philly was....

A CULTURE WORKER AMONG SPECIALISTS: THE PHILLY YEARS (1986-1992)

In the late 1980s, Temple University's advertising campaign was based on the slogan, "I chose Temple," often spoken by Bill Cosby. You could say I chose Temple, since I did receive my Master's in English/Creative Writing, and gained my first experience as a teacher, there. Besides, unlike undergraduate school, I didn't have to go into (further) debt; the school paid for itself. It helped me make a transition from adolescent college student to adult professional, and allowed me to live in a big city, and in close proximity to NYC at that, and actually suggest the possibility of being able to survive into my 20s in a way that could make my mom proud. Yet, it would be more accurate to say Temple chose me.

Temple wasn't my first choice of graduate programs. Once I had come to the realization, however reluctantly, that as an adult in this society, one must specialize, and narrowed my undergraduate degree to a dual Philosophy/English major so I could apply for graduate creative writing programs, my first choice was Naropa University in Boulder, Colorado, which I had discovered through the film *Poetry In Motion*, and my increasing interest in the "New York School" of poetry and visual art after John Yau visited my undergraduate college, and made poetry—or even the poet role—seem *cool*!

Naropa seemed to offer a more capacious notion of poetry for one, like me, who was skeptical of over-specialization, and who hoped to emphasize the similarities between poetry and music rather than the differences most colleges are institutionally mandated to stress. Against the backdrop of cultural signs like the "revised" 1988 Edition of *Norton Anthology Of Modern Poetry* (which had become much more conservative since the 1972 Anthology which included many writers from the Black Art Aesthetic for instance alongside of Yeats et al), the teachers and graduates of Naropa I knew valued a more populist, and didactic poetry, one less exclusively beholden to the written page, but, through multi-media and dance, could help bring some "fresh air" (or a much needed cultural revolution) into the literary world: a belief that we could help create a space for a wider definition of poetry that had become systematically narrowed especially during the reactionary Reagan years (just as my mind was widening....)

Naropa, at the time, gave some institutional sanction to many of these populist ethical and aesthetic goals for poetry in contrast to most M(F)A programs; writers like Amiri Baraka and Allen Ginsberg who had become increasingly "unfashionable" as the 70s became the 80s became the 90s, among whites at least, were staples there. It also actively encouraged its students to start their own magazines and presses and build a community (something which more M(F)A programs should require, for their own good!); my second book was published by a Naropa student.

Perhaps as a "poet" at Naropa, I could kind of have my cake and eat it too; if I was going to be forced to specialize to survive as an adult; such idea(l)s of poetry seemed to offer the closest to infinity in an institutional setting I could get a grant or loan to work in, and "buy time" (an important function of college). Sure, one couldn't take out a loan or a grant to study music with, say, Sly Stone, but Naropa had some connections with bonafied musicians I loved as a teen (Lou Reed, Patti Smith, Richard Hell, Jim Carroll, The Fugs, etc). I would have gone there myself had I been able to afford it. Instead, I chose Temple because, unlike Naropa or Bard (where Yau taught), it offered me money to pay for room and board (a rundown apartment with no heat on a largely burnt down block in North Philly), and yes it was a foot in the door to the big city with the cool college stations I couldn't get in my hometown.

One advantage of Temple—though I didn't realize it at the time—was that, in contrast to Naropa, and many other Creative Writing Master's programs, it offered an MA rather than an MFA. Theoretically, an MA may mean less than a MFA because it's not a "terminal" degree, but there wasn't a significant difference in curriculum. If anything, the MA model was better because it provided the practical on-the-job training that too many MFA programs lack, leading students into increasing debt.

While Temple was not the cultural hotbed that Naropa seemed to be from a 2,000-mile distance, and didn't harbor the revolutionary possibilities that seemed so glamorous to this restless first-generation working-class college student (even though Temple's advertisement claimed Black-Arts pioneer Sonia Sanchez was on the faculty of the Creative Writing program, she was not teaching classes when I was there, but rather doing cultural work through the provost's office), it did have the advantage of being in Philadelphia.

Philadelphia had many other literary and artistic scenes that I could find common ground with, such as the poetry scene that I became aware of through Lamont Steptoe's amazing work with the Painted Bride Art Center. This scene was more based on orality and fast-talking anger and humor than Temple's was. As a friend, Steptoe also became an important teacher; he not only immersed me in Philly's strong black culture (introducing me, for instance, to the great artist/poet Jerome Robinson---years later tragically gunned down while trying to keep the peace at the Wheels Of Soul clubhouse---and many others), but also arranged for performances for many writers and musicians who were prominent figures in the national Black Arts Movement (Baraka, Troupe, Baldwin, etc). He also supported my own fledgling work, and nourished my tentative firsts embracing the angry young man energy which academia was trying to channel ("Remember, Chris, Wallace Stevens didn't publish his first book until he was 44;" I did love, and learn from Stevens and others of that ilk, but not as a be-all-and-end-all).

Steptoe gave me my first featured (and rather high-paying for the time) reading and also introduced me to many other young writers, black, Latina, Asian, and white (some of whom have since become very well known—such as Linh Dinh, ex-Philly poet laureate Frank Sherlock, CA Conrad, Major Jackson, Dave Roskos, Ken Greenley, among others). This, coupled with the experiences and non-accredited education I was receiving in the West Philly Punk Scene (helping to co-found Killtime Warehouse in 1988), and through radio station WKDU, was at least as valuable as the degree, and the exposure to a range of academic poetry, I was receiving at Temple. Philadelphia at this time, even with its huge cultural chip on its shoulder viz-a-viz NYC for instance, was a veritable cauldron of activity that certainly rivaled Naropa. In this sense, I received a degree *from Philly*, and just like any academic institution, the various factions were segregated, and often territorial.

Double (Or Triple) Life?

On coming to Philly, and being confronted more with the seemingly "adult" mandate to specialize, I developed a division of labor between the two arts I was most passionate about it: music and poetry (I had abandoned film because it cost more to make now that the college wasn't providing free equipment to edit on). *"In music, I consume more than a produce; in writing, I produce more than I consume. In music, I practice (though sometimes in public); in writing I perform. Form is something you do for others; content yourself."* Though I fancied myself a bridge between music and poetry, I knew I had to respect specialization enough to keep them somewhat separate.[36]

---

[36] you can start (again)
with how music & words
could come together as a kid
as mind and body could
but growing "up"
meant a split between them
in you of course
in society
college meant choosing
words, but
with ample room
for music
but they split further apart
the more advanced you got
the more in debt you got
the more adult American
and the yang wanted
to fight to bring them together
and yin let them be separate
and develop a working
balance, a division
of labor between them

it wasn't that the body
was more social
than the mind
(classrooms
and extracurricular think tanks
were as social as any dance party
and you could get off
on solitary homework
at least as much as going
for a solitary walk
with the precursor
to today's ipod
or bike, singing on swings),

it was that you
were able to earn a living
off that which was called mind
more easily than that
which mind calls body
(insofar as mind,
by definition, is
that which divides itself
from body, and body
wouldn't be caught dead
dividing itself from mind)

and this specialization
or you could say
alienation (the difference
between work and
working out) of labor
was given to us
as an obstacle to navigate.

for yes the white collar
world rewarded the hermit
as self, but even if
what mind calls body
didn't pay as much
as what mind calls mind,
it was body at least
as much as mind
that allowed me (& others)
to find, through dancing,
a cheaper way to live
so we wouldn't need
as much money

which was important
coz of the college debt
we hoped to be able
to pay off, so as to be
able to pay back the real debt
to the elders, and each other,
but others said "screw
the middleman," & they
warmed me, even if
sometimes they scorned me
for working the straight job
until I reminded them
my teaching job
brought in more money
than they did to pay rent

Caesar salads &,
as for the academics,
well, they didn't have
to know about my 'secret'
'underground' affordable
life that fueled me for
their disembodiment (this
was before Facebook
mixed it all up

Just because I sacrificed making music (aside from busking with the Casio) doesn't mean I was going to sacrifice being fueled by it. I had two good legs and loved that Magnolias song, "I gotta gotta….reach-reach-reach out!"[37] even if I couldn't afford the musical equipment I'd need to be in a band and could be appeased by a Casio and university practice rooms which allowed access. This served as double duty, since I was not only recording possible ideas for songs for later use, but playing music every day (even if, or especially because, I didn't commodify it). It cleared my head so I could write better. And dancing while louder, often faster bands played, often broke down the fourth wall because the dancers were on stage too.

In my hometown, I felt that the loss of my city's downtown, the subsuming of its musical culture into Hollywood culture, as well as niche marketing were all part of the social engineering that helped create The Reagan Voter, and helped criminalize the Reagan resister as well as the corporate TV/Hollywood/Radio resister. Certainly, as young (aspiring) musicians and culture workers, it was clear that the powers that be were conspiring to cast us as consumers. But in Philly, by contrast, there was enough of a critical mass of Reagan Resisters and pro-local, anti-TV/Hollywood/ Mass Culture resisters that it felt like we could actually do something and if not exactly be a cultural producer, at least not be a mere cultural consumer.

And I definitely felt this fuel a kind of defensive generational fervor that wasn't merely a "lifestyle choice" or "personal self-expression." The punk band The Minutemen spoke of the necessity to "Jam Econo" and hip hop's reliance on two turntables and a microphone was a brilliant attempt to make a virtue of a necessity, and a make beauty when the powers that be impose an austerity measure like making it harder to afford "real" instruments, and legal places to play them.

Thank god, I found, or was found by, punk and hip hop music, and this music had the power to beat much of my retro-centric taste out of me, and lead me to a social scene which gave me a new lease on life, and gave hope for my generation (because, dammit, we were making great music too, and why weren't songs like

[37] https://www.youtube.com/watch?v=irudgfBqUTswith how music & words

The Descendents' "Cheer" smash hits)[38]. Although you could say, in finding punk and hip hop, I was part of a "consumer niche" too, and it is true that punk and hip hop could not really escape the commodity culture of specialization (as "youth culture," "more male than female," both generally tabooing ballads), they at least were rooted in the local. You could say they helped restore the local basis that had been lost in the 70s, even if on a smaller scale than in the 40s and 50s before TV culture took hold.[39]

On Philly subways and street corners, I remember hearing guys trade raps with each other, and thinking about how "Hip hop" rhymes with "doo wop" and all those legendary street-corner acts from back when my parents were teens. My ideal mixtape of that time would include this as much as local rappers who got more famous like SchooleyD. These rappers, often unnamed to me, seemed to be as much what hip hop culture was about as the list of the 10 who had crossover hits in the 80s. Sometimes they wouldn't even take money! From my distance, rap seemed far more democratic and multi-media. And, despite the fact that hip hop and punk came to be called niches, in Philly at least, there was a unity in diversity attitude that celebrated eclecticism both in live/work underground warehouses, as well as in the non-commercial (college, community) radio.

Seeing the Philly "hardcore" band Ruin, in the basement of a building at Temple (I think F.O.D, and Gang Green was also on the bill), in December of 1986, was my first real moshpit, and this experience changed my life in more ways than one. I didn't necessarily go to this show to meet people, but to "dance the devil out" (as Jerome Robinson would put it at a "free James Brown" dance party a few years later), or at least to dance out the stress from the rigors of being a "disembodied"

---

[38] https://www.youtube.com/watch?time_continue=12&v=nA7D6BxtVpg

[39] Philly '87

"the white man is at best corny"--Baraka

One radio station stepped on one foot,
and another got in my other face
And I realized they were working together
Against everything I love
And this pressure mounts
And the only way to find quiet
To drown the noise
Is to make my own
And I can't afford an instrument
But I can be a Human Beat Box
An image to build something from
While walking or even running
But I'll slow down (or, if I'm singing
On the swings, get off) for your boombox
And am glad I found a noise I like drowning out mine.

poet for the day job at Temple. I didn't go to listen to words either (if a few became audible, fine), but to feel the sounds. At $3 for the price of admission ($1 if you had a Temple ID), it was cheap entertainment at its best, but it was also a work out.

Afterwards, I walked back, covered in sweat which froze to me (but I felt warm inside!), a few blocks back to my apartment with no heat on a largely burnt out block in North Philly which is probably gentrified by now (though I was receiving a stipend for the T.A., I got the cheapest place possible; after all, I had an undergrad debt to pay back), and blasted Drexel's 80s underground station WKDU…..the neighbors (mostly black) didn't mind; they were blasting music too. And, as I rocked myself horizontally to sleep on the mattress on the floor (beneath the salutary burnt out lightbulb), I heard one of Ruin's song I recognized from the show just an hour or two before.

As I listened, I realized the words to this song sounded strangely familiar! And then it hit me: Oh my god (this was before OMG), it's Leonard Cohen's "Famous Blue Raincoat!" Ruin had so thoroughly transformed the song that I didn't recognize it in "the pit." Listening to how Ruin had re-rendered Cohen's slow plodding waltz into what I'd call anthemic power pop, or *melodic* hardcore, allowed me to appreciate the song much more than the original. While Cohen's speaker seemed somewhat cold and smug in his original (placing more sympathy on the male "you" of the song who had slept with the speaker's lady, Jane, than on the "I" of the song), in Ruin's version I could hear the pain, and *believe* the speaker of the song.

If all of this means nothing to you, oh historians of the rock music orthodoxy (including you Michael Azerrad with your narrow sense of the 80s 'canon'), you may think of how the Byrds transformed "Mr. Tambourine Man." Now multiply that pleasant surprise that song must have been to some like Greil Marcus in 1965 by 10X and you'll get a little of what I felt.[40] Sure, Nick Cave had also recently transformed a Cohen song to make it come alive more for the 80s kids, but on the continuum of aesthetic expression, Ruin went further in taking one of the most bodily forms of art I knew and combining it with some of the most mental, well-wrought poetry set to music (even if Cohen, as a poet, was not really embraced by either the Temple MFA crowd, or the more spoken word scene at the Painted Bride Art Center).

You could say they also straddled the line between the seemingly more sophisticated "high" art that Cohen increasingly symbolized (though this was before the craze when everyone would do precious covers of "Hallelujah"), and the more working class art of the punk underground scene; furthermore since Cohen was over 50 at the time, it pointed to a way beyond the mere "youth culture" parameters of punk into a way that I appreciated, since I craved art that had staying power (like the

---

[40] Here's a studio version, for some approximation, but it was even more powerful live: https://www.youtube.com/watch?v=UHM1VTeel4c

older, and even dead, poets I was into). I felt a power that could be strong enough to undo the dualisms within the confines of white culture at least, the dualisms on which white supremacy, classism and racism (restlessly) rest.

And, to top it off, they were a *local* band, Philly's own little secret. Some of Philly's best bands had a hard time making it outside of Philly. The Dead Milkmen were an exception, but though I enjoyed them, they weren't really "of," and had kinda bypassed, the scene. I could evangelize Ruin to the poet people who would listen. I even learned their version of this song for my little one-man band Casio punk busker act I would do in Rittenhouse Square, or even by Temple's bell tower (you can think Billy Bragg, and yeah sometimes I'd do faux Brit accents).

Furthermore, this experience was an example of the symbiosis that college radio (like WKDU) could have with the local, live, underground, scene. College radio provided me with more of a solitary introvert connection to the music (I'd listen to the words more on the radio), and WKDU was eclectic enough to play hardcore, both local and national, industrial noise rock, Britpop and art rock, hip hop, and slower brooding songs sung by women.[41] WKDU worked in tandem with the live-music, and political activist scene, to connect radio listening introverts with the more extroverted crowd that went to shows to help create a well-rounded, multi-dimensional, eclectic local (youth) scene…. Unlike corporate radio, it wasn't barren, but provided a portal to a social world, so the live local scene was no longer merely transient because it was connected to the radio station, even if, alas, Philly (in contrast to other national scenes) lacked a viable record label as a kind of clearing house.

The college radio station also played more national acts, but maintained a strong connection to the local live scene (in contrast to what I would hate in California 20 years later when college stations like KALX would often have ticket giveaways for local shows and *not even play a song* by the act they are giving away tickets to see): the live scene and the radio scene fed off each other, and mutually empowered each other (even if we really didn't have much of a record label), and saved each other from their excesses. The college radio stations for the most part drew a generational line in the sand and were much more focused on new (or at least 80s) stuff that wouldn't get played on commercial radio (in those days you wouldn't hear Abba or *Sgt. Pepper* on college radio)….this allowed it to make room for a wider range of music from the here and now.

WKDU made me feel safe and secure. I mean, if such an exciting free flowing source of new edgy sounds could issue forth from the boombox even in the darkest Reagan/Bush times of the 80s, certainly it would always be there with its

---

[41] I also really loved songs like Area's "With Louise" played on these stations at the time: https://www.youtube.com/watch?v=8u1mkjXyTwU

morning motivational, and help-me-fall-asleep-after-midnight, music. As one on a shoestring budget who had largely opted out of consumerism (the used record stores I used to frequent didn't carry this newer music as much as *Frampton Comes Alive* and other baby boomer music), I fit the stereotype of lying in bed with my radio/cassette recorder culling gems for mix tapes just in case I couldn't count on it being there someday.

In the Philly activist/artist scene (there were a lot of anarchists, but enough of us commies that I wouldn't call it "an anarchist scene"), I noticed a split between the people who first and foremost went to shows and who often had a "harder core than thou" attitude (as mentioned before, in both punk and hip hop in the 80s, ballads were, if not exactly forbidden, at least extremely rare), and, on the other hand, the college DJs and community radio stations whose ethos was much more eclectic and made more room for ballads and quirky introverted bands alongside of the loud fast dance music that was kind of the core that held the scenes together. Despite my earlier defense of the necessity of local grounding that had existed in my grandmother's day a little more, in the Philly "underground" scene I discovered, on the other hand, the potential tyranny of the extroverted local, which made me realize that in some ways the more placeless national culture can be the introvert's best friend. But at its best, there was a bridge between these scenes, just as graffiti helped bring punk and hip hop together:

Graffiti Bridge
I wasn't a graffiti artist
But sometimes I'd follow them
& watch, catching myself in the same posture
I would viewing the Guston retrospective
Or when being invited over to John Yau's loft…
Or when they're watching the statue of Hermione
Come alive in the last act of *The Winter's Tale*
And in Philly Graffiti
Seemed the main bridge between punk & hip hop
Between white and black youth
At least for those of us who didn't play ball
And I want to say that louder
Coz graffiti is not crack
Graffiti might even be a way to avoid crack
Like the music can be
Despite all those stories that love to link them
More than they link right wing corporate talk radio
To Rush's Oxycodone…
The Anti-Graffiti League murals
Were never as pretty as a great subway tagger
If only he had time….

I remember when he said
"My dad used to own
the building we just tagged.
I'm just doing what I
Would have anyway
Without getting paid for it—
They should be happy…"
Indeed, a beautification project
Where punk and funk could meet
Even if you reduce it to
Blacks listening to the Beastie Boys
And whites listening to Public Enemy
Or Cop Killer by Ice-T's Body Count…
Beyond rock against racism…
And yeah we saw it generationally
And that was the first box
We tried to mosh ourselves out of
Don't wanna die at 23, don't wanna die at 23

I became a regular at small, local, often underground, shows, and at one of these shows I met Hugh Wattles. He was a charismatic presence at local shows with his glamorous tall dyed hair girlfriend Lisa Curmine. They were two of the main forces behind that anarchist 'zine, "Talk Is Cheap," that I had read. I later found out he was the financial backer as well. They had published a poem of mine and invited me to one of their editorial meetings with the staff of 4 or 5, many of whom worked at the Wooden Shoe Bookstore on 21st St. They weren't just politically radical, but in varying degrees socially radical too, anti-racist, pro-gay and lesbian, free-love, and clearly interested in putting together an underground coalition.

Not long after this meeting, they decided to fold the magazine, which at first bummed me out, but Hugh, it turns out, had bigger fish to fry, and it'd be far better for me. He already owned a house at the edge of Powelton Village, on the 3800 block of Spring Garden. When he bought it, it was nothing more than a shell, but with the help of Joe Tiberino—who had run Bacchanal, and whose wife Ellen, now dying of cancer, was somewhat of a local celebrity for her "Move Confrontation" mural (which had rendered Mayor Wilson Goode centrally with Devil's horns)—and his own not inconsiderable carpentry skills, Hugh had converted the Spring Garden house into a funky living quarters, with weird haylofts, a pit in the first floor, and rickety spiral steps leading up to the 3rd floor bathroom. It had no heat but a wood-burning stove and pipes leading from it to various locations that were never quite warm enough. It even was set up with glass and plastic ceiling in the rear of the second floor where the kitchen was, for possible conversion to solar heat somewhere down the line. This place was grungy-homey, semi-illegal, and those who lived there had names like Bolo (after that book Bolo Bolo), Kat, Krow,

Paradox, jackrabbit, well, and Denise, Jeffrey Stovall, and Cheryl Dunye. Hugh himself had lived there, but now spent most of his time at Lisa's loft in Northern Liberties (which she shared with folks like Greg Giovanni, founder of the Big Mess theatre, whose play, *Napoleon Pull-Apart*, I had recently seen at the somewhat more "legit" Painted Bride Art Center).

But Hugh was ready to make another move, and the demise of "Talk is Cheap," just hurried his sense of urgency along. Around the corner from the Spring Garden house, on Lancaster Avenue, was one of many abandoned warehouse spaces. At the time, Philly may have been the international capital of abandoned factories and warehouse spaces!). It had recently been used as a rehearsal and performance space for the "industrial" noise band Sink Manhattan (the 80s kind of industrial band, which was much more cacophonous than later uses of that word; they had two bassists, and banged on metal, similar in a way to the Motor Morons in Baltimore, who I saw perform in 1983 or so at that Ad Hoc Fiasco which that guy "tentatively: a convenience" had told me about when he came to Albright dressed in pants entirely made of zippers and showing such underground film classics as "Pee On Bob's Head" for Harry and Gary's film class; but while the Motor Morons' main instrument was a car-engine connected to an amplifier, sparks flying from the battery as the audience dived into a giant clear plastic bag placed in the middle of what would have been the dance floor had anybody thought of dancing, Sink Manhattan used heavy industrial equipment, like toxic drums and the like, that had been found in Philly's abandoned factories).

The space had been vacated by Sink Manhattan due to a fire at one of their performances. When the firemen came to put it out, the water from the hoses caused the concrete floor (which had been built over wooden beams) to cave in, leaving the place even more ruined than before. It was dank with that post-fire water smell; icicles dripped from charred rafters, piles of snow covered holes in the floor. Junk, from old newspapers to metal, was strewn everywhere, and a good chunk of the roof was gone. No electricity—it would need a lot of work, but Hugh had a vision, had stars, or a glint, in his eyes, had some money, and a scene of people he was recruiting. The landlord, a shady character, but one who thus had no qualms with letting a bunch of punks break zoning laws if they were able to come up with the rent, was willing to let it go for cheap rather than hold out for more money for the space to remain empty as a tax-write off. So Hugh had been talking up this idea since I met him, and now he was recruiting me to get in on the ground level. This would be that communal living performance space I had dreamed of! (or had vague inklings of ever since I first set my sad child's eyes on the abandoned roundhouses of my home town, and no longer had "dorm living" to fall back on).

Hugh's offer in short: I'd move into a room in that Spring Garden house (on Xmas eve) for $100 a month. This was a total steal, cheaper than the slums of North

Philly, with no strings attached, or if there were, they were the kind I wanted to pull at me. I'd help clean up and build the warehouse space. I assured him I wasn't a carpenter. That didn't matter; there was enough else to do. So we set to work, first on removing the large chunks of concrete from the caved-in floor, hurling them into the window into the weeds and rusted junk behind the building, then we'd help paint the walls, wash the floors, that kind of stuff. It took about 4 or 5 months to clean the place up enough to open it for shows. In the meantime, Hugh and I moved in to a little "apartment like" area above the warehouse that had until recently been an ambulance dispatchery. I set up my mattress (who needs a bed?) on the cold concrete floor, and went around the block to shower and shit in the Spring Garden house (who needs a bathtub? Or hot water if you got a scene? And back in those days, there were more free public restrooms) It wasn't really secure, and once we got robbed, but that was water off my duck's back. At least it was a rudimentary shelter, and we'd eventually get a real door. It was a labor of love!

There was also a café that was built, just beneath the ambulance dispatchery and adjacent to the larger warehouse space. You could tell by the floor that to had probably been a café before, and so this didn't take as much work to get in running order. Many people started hanging out there while the carpentry work went on next door, black and white, straight and dyke, young and old, artists of all types, activists. Almost daily, Tim would bring big bags of day-old bread he got from community-minded restaurants to eat and help make a place a haven for many homeless and displaced folks who were being driven further west by the same process that allowed me to get this space.

We were in the gap between white gentrifiers and poor black families, and fancied ourselves were part of a bridge between neighborhoods (as well as generations), we were trash-pickers, industrial musicians; it was a place for displaced of all races, dropouts, and queer blacks ostracized from the black community as well as straight blacks who didn't ostracize gay blacks.

The open-minded permissiveness of the older interracial Tiberino couple shone over the venture, which was excitingly utopian but also becoming a reality. Sure, there were factions, but "unity in diversity" was still Hugh's motto, and as his roommate I saw him wrestle with many demons, internal and external, to hold himself and others to that standard.

Besides, the place was so big that it could accommodate most, maybe even all, of the various factions. Hugh was kind of a visionary (he was into Deleuze and Guattari's *A Thousand Plateaus),* and kept himself kind of in the background, not drawing too much attention to himself, as he solicited input from just about anyone. It didn't even feel like I was *pitching* an idea to Hugh. It wasn't about money, or even about fame. The place could "take a loss" on twenty events a month as long as it had one or two dance parties that could draw in the hipster hedonist kids from Penn or Center City, or maybe even a name band or two, like when the Laughing Hyenas played, and Thurston Moore sat in (I got to stamp his hand; even he paid to help out). All of these official and non-official happenings provided a constant and extremely convenient social life, available for the taking, yet at the same time "a room of one's own," a place to go to if I needed to get away from it all—this was the closest I had found to being able to straddle my introvert/extrovert sides I had ever, up to that point, found, and in retrospect, maybe even since).[42]

[42] Kill Time

In Philly, we lived in a place
in the burnt out border
between black and white
and we thought we could create
a more desegregated fortress…
that could grow up to be a bridge
(to repair the nation's ailing infrastructure!)
It ended up being called a punk warehouse
but we had funk DJS and
Jerome Robinson would bring
the Wheels of Soul…
and I found soulmates
between the activists and artists
(and activist mates among the souls)
to join the fight against time itself,
against specialization and its diminishing returns…

Could our warehouse space
radiate outward and push back
against the gentrification they wanted to use us for?
push back against the overhyped skinheads
and the underhyped
mayors who bombed The Move
& University of Pennsylvania developers
eyeing and buying the land
could we side more with the soul
of what was being driven out
more than the soullessness of what
was threatening to move in?
Could we make this warehouse last,
grow dignified and old in it?
What can the word community mean without it?

We were deluded enough to hope…
It was 1989 and James Brown was in Prison
and the "Free James Brown coz he freed me" dance parties
brought young and old together

Part of the ethos of the warehouse was to live as cheaply as possible, and to be sustainable, to reject the debt economy being pushed in the 80s, which Hugh believed, and many of us hoped, would have to crash (again, I thought of the Godfathers singing "we're living under a false economy.") Although the rising cost of housing, even in the 80s real-estate bubble, made me reject the mortgage debt economy (and, perhaps, now I could have my regrets though it may not have even been available to me), I did join this collective with one disadvantage compared to the others: I was already laboring beneath the debt imposed by my undergraduate education, which, alas, had been my entrance into Reaganomics. Thus, I had to have at least somewhat of a day job to survive to bring some money in. And, in the process you can say I was living a "double life" (like that silly old cars song, "it takes a fast car, baby, to live a double life," or my attempted answer song, "Nah, it just takes a fast bike!").

My teaching gig helped pay for the warehouse, but the warehouse was also helping me be a better teacher. On a few occasions, I would see some of my students at punk shows, and, after a brief, momentarily embarrassment, realized that being associated with the punk warehouse scene helped give me a kind of cred, at least with the white students like Brooke Sietinsons, later of the band Espers). And, I found that many of the black students encouraged my, as I encouraged their, straight talk, and knew how to call my bluff, and put me in my place (don't worry, they were very gentle about it). I remember a class at Peirce Jr. College (I was only 23, many of my students were also older than me), which was roughly 50/50 black/white, when a white woman said something like "I was talking to my, uh, uh, uh, colored-complected friend," and a black student interrupted and said, "just call me black. I'm black!" And that really helped open things up....and cut through the BS of "post-racial" America. Anyway, I was learning more by teaching than by being a student....

College at the time was a booming industry, despite its inflationary costs. I also had students older than my dad having lost their blue collar livelihood and trying to be "retrained" for white collar work, but that didn't mean that we could "bank"

as much as black and white
and I learned a lineage deeper than poetic—
the older blacks called it dancing out the devil
the younger punks losing bad religion…

No longer their consumer
and they couldn't quite call us producers,
our social involvement with music
(broadcast and live) grew
as our spending money on it declined
as if we stumbled on some cozy,
even cuddly, alternative economy.

on white collar work either and so I encouraged my students, as I encouraged myself, not to rest content with a specialization if they caught themselves feeling too comfortable in it, to diversify (and start wondering if the increased divorce rate has anything to do with this seeming increasing necessity not to put our eggs in all one basket).

Meanwhile, some of the purists at the warehouse scorned me for having this job (and for having been to college), which saddened me because I wasn't going to get all "moral high ground" and snitch on the shoplifters (they had a code of ethics, and would only steal from corporate chain stores). Luckily, Hugh was able to explain to them that I deserved a second chance after my youthful stupidity (or transgression) to go to college in the first place. Afterall, some of these folks were from more money than me, so "dropping out" from college, which was *expected* by their parents, was radical for them while, for me, it could pass as rebellion against my dad. Besides the money I brought in was keeping the warehouse afloat as much as the amazing finds that trashpickers brought in. "Unity in diversity," indeed!

I imagined that one day I'd be free of the college debt so I could pay back *"the real one"* (as I was fond of saying at the time), to my mom, to GSH, etc.... And though there's always going to be some who say "white collar" isn't as "honest" a buck as blue collar is (even if it's a white collar teacher who rejects the 'banking' model,' as well as bankers), I strove to dig myself out of involvement with "the debt economy" even as I watched others, in the more 'above ground' poetry world take bigger economic risks and be rewarded ("you have to spend to make/ I learned it from a snake"). Still, perhaps the punk scene was the closest our generation could get to a place where I could exercise the ethos I learned from my grandparents' working class (miserly?) thrift, or "self-imposed" austerity measures.

Indeed, I retained a healthy skepticism to whatever "boom" they were trying to sell in the 80s. In Philly, there had been a temporary downtown construction boom in the mid 80s, but once the construction was done and the buildings finished---the building had also been used to destroy older, cheaper, locally owned businesses--, they had a hard time finding clients to fill them, and the economic downturn was worse than what it had been before the boom. It was never a boom to most people I knew, but that could be a positive, right? If what comes up must go down, if we don't go "up," we'll have less place to fall!

I liked that credo, and the spirit of making a virtue out of necessity and Tikkun Olam, leaving the world in a better condition than you found it. It jived with my sense of poetry as cheap entertainment, and my love of New Orleans. After all (pre-Katrina) New Orleans may be one of the poorest cities in America, but the flipside is that it's also one of the cheapest cities in America, cheap enough that underpaid street musicians can actually afford the rent (as many will tell you, tips are not keeping up with inflation), and it was clear to me that poorer, or cheaper communities were generally more musical, or more musical communities were generally poorer and cheaper, and music brought people together enough for them to want to pool their resources for the collective good. Ah, if only the poets believed this as much as the musicians did. For all the (self-proclaimed working class) poets' valorization of minimal involvement in the acquisitive economy, when push came to shove, in terms of community crisis, I felt they weren't able to put their "money" where their "mouth" is, and pool their resources to create a collective.

Perhaps the reason for this is that poets tend to feel their highest creation occurs in solitude, but, even though I loved poetry (and the kind of "obscure" and "generative" poetry that some of the folks at the warehouse didn't take too kindly to me wasting my time reading), I felt the poetry community dangled more on the cultural superstructure or was more superficial, or alienated. Because of that, I had no qualms about commodifying my poetry as I did about commodifying my music, since poetry, in the very act of creation, involved a physical alienation that music didn't. Did I feel "in poetry but not of it?" No! I was in it when I was in it, and it takes a fast bike, baby, to live a double life.

"Grace To Live As Variously As Possible"

Even though the warehouse seemed to offer a wider range of culture, connected to a national underground movement that hadn't yet been coopted, it wasn't the be all and end all; I knew I could best "jam econo" by zooming in on poetry to see infinity open up between 5 different people who all called themselves poets, and this seemed part of the meaning of Blake's injunction to see the world in a grain of sand. And, just as there was a split, say, between, introverts and extroverts in the underground scene, the poetry scene had more than enough of its share of divisions.

In Philly, the poetry scene was very fragmented.[43] Most of the Temple students didn't go downtown to the Painted Bride Art Center, and most of the Painted Bride folks didn't go to Temple. It was racial, but not just; it was also a distinction between page and stage, or between "town" and "gown" as they say, but these are all short hand terms. It seemed that most of the academics didn't want to be known as stage poets until they first got published as page poets, but even though I had page ambitions, I felt the stage was a great place to work out ideas at least as much as the workshop was. My performances would often be a hit even if my poem wasn't.

You could say I was a straddler between these two literary worlds—not trying to take sides between "academic" poetry and what was only starting to be called "slam

---

[43] Perhaps it's less so since the University of Pennsylvania's Writers House's outreach programs, and the city instituted a poet laureate, but I'd have to ask others about that

poetry"—or, one could say, between "elitist" and "populist" poetry. In doing this, I met resistance: "too street for the academics," and, for some, "too academic for the streets" though most of the resistance came from the academics (I didn't meet Jeffrey McDaniel or Edwin Torres until years later, but there are some similarities in how we navigated aesthetic/scenes during this time)

This fragmenting Zeitgeist I was walking into in the more specialized poetry world I was already familiar with from my training in the pop-culture industry; as a pre-teen and teen I had witnessed the resegregation of the radio airwaves, and the *Norton Anthology of Modern Poetry* signified an analogous trend in poetry (which, 30 years later, still has not had its "Charleston movement" like the pop music industry had, on several occasions, in the last 100 years).

In the 80s, in music, in Philly at least, there seemed to be some collective push back. Was there an analogous collective push-back in poetry?[44] You could say that the word "poetry" itself, by definition, would be anti-Hollywood/TV, if not necessarily anti-Reagan. After all, the various poet factions, from "mainstream" to "avant-garde" to "spoken-word," could at least agree on the value of this cheap, and somewhat marginalized form of, activity over the inflated larger-than-life economy and culture of Hollywood, and most were horrified by Reagan even if blatant politics were often tabooed. Nonetheless, I didn't see it yet, though there was some talk in the wings of a generational identity to overthrow the tyranny of the old folks who, for some, had become as stale (or repressive) as the old folks they overthrew back in the 60s and 70s. I had too many older poet friends and even mentors to fully accept the poetic generational identity at that time, even though I knew, at 23, that I still had twenty years of being a "young poet" ahead of me if I could survive. I loved the intensity of those who valued "Live fast, die young, and leave a beautiful corpse," but I didn't want to die young.

I valued writers who seemed to get better with age and, at the time, I saw that in Ashbery and Baraka as opposed to say Ginsberg (who, to his credit, acknowledged that he was too busy with his activism to devote as much energy to crafting poetry as he did when younger). More importantly, at the time I held much of what Frank O'Hara achieved (both as a writer and socially) to be, if not exactly an ethical ideal, at least a template as he straddled and bridged what, in NYC centric terms, the difference between the "uptown" (more upper-class) and the more proletarian scenes, but I didn't think of this as abandoning politics for mere self-expression (as Adam Curtis criticizes the 60s generation and Patti Smith for doing).

---

[44] To pursue the analogy, one could say that L=A=N=G=U=A=G=E poetry was similar to the 70s/80s Corporate hard rock, while the American Poetry Review Crowd was more like 70s lite rock, but screw that analogy, for however liberal most poets are vis-à-vis the general American population, it must be said that the literary scene was less desegregated than music (or even football for that matter)

I didn't just think of my poetry-related social role as merely an ingénue (or "new kid in town") "trying to find my place" (as Honor Roll? sang[45]) and piecing together an identity through trial and error, but believed, as I'm told many 22 year olds are prone to, that I was serving some social cause greater than myself (whether God, country, revolution or art, even if some call this institution "nothing"). And, my noble cause, perhaps more than anything at the time, was a kind of "grace to live as variously as possible," but in order to do that, I felt I had work on de-specialization, and de-segregation....to form coalitions, a broader front to stick it to the man like when Ashbery lobbied to get Baraka out of jail....for instance. We could do more!

But the New York School aesthetic/ethos wasn't really part of the mix in the late 80s in Philly; I had to travel to NYC for that, which I did quite often, but I seized on any opportunity to help despecialize the various factions that existed in the Philly landscape, and no doubt failed as much as I succeeded. Even though I was still officially an apprentice (writing *juvenilia*), I knew that given the more individualist ethos of the literary scenes, I would have to operate as kind of a "lone wolf," or what Judy Juanita calls "an army of one" if I was going to get anything done, but isn't part of the point of networking to introduce two people to each other even if they're in different scenes. Still, compared to the rappers and punks, who had little or no time for the poetry scene, I was moving kinda slow.... Sure, I spoke about bringing music and poetry together, but they were *living* it.

When I auditioned for Lamont Steptoe, I was impressed that he didn't hold it against me that I was in grad school, but I could tell some of the folks at the grad school weren't too keen on my associations with Steptoe's scene. Steptoe's vision was much more capacious. He certainly was no separatist, and cultivated young white talent as much as black and other POC. He asked me if I was "raised catholic." I told him, "*razed* Catholic," and he liked that I was probably a fairly devout secularist at that time too, disillusioned by my upbringing, if not quite as much as he was with the military industrial complex after Vietnam.

The first feature reading Lamont offered me at the Painted Bride Art Center (and it paid three month's room and board) was with Gerald Stern, a then 60 something white male bourgeois apolitical quotidian poet I probably, unfairly, didn't really appreciate, especially as a 23 year old cocky punk/mod ingénue, who cared more that my teenager sister, and Alexey Berlind, an amazing young drummer, said I blew him off the stage than what the older poet establishment said. I guess I'm glad there's no video, nor even much audio of my early readings, even if some people dug them, but a lot of trial and error. You may picture the stereotype of the wild haired, wild eyed, cocky-awkward poet. Stern, by contrast, seemed to take himself too seriously. I remember him introducing a poem: "This is a story about a time I was sitting out on the back porch, and my parents were inside watching TV." Then

---

[45] Honor Role, My Place: https://www.youtube.com/watch?v=V_Qfg04gpIo

he started the poem, "I was sitting out on the back porch, and my parents were inside watching TV." No humorous awareness of the situation whatsoever. Yet the place was packed! He was huge! APRers mostly;[46] neither the academic avant-Temple crowd, nor the Painted Bride Art Center, Bacchanal, or North Star bar spoken word crowds really came, but even though I was a fish out of water as I tried not to be disrespectful, I both pissed some people off, and left others ambivalent enough to at least be on their radar. Surely it was a sign, the sign! Choose poetry! The poetry world needs me! The rock music world doesn't really need my songs; there's so much I already love there, hardly any in the contemporary poetry world (you cocky young turk!).

A few months later, I was approached by some folks who had come to the Gerald Stern reading who asked me to be a co-editor of the local glossy magazine Painted Bride Art Quarterly. Even though the magazine shared the name Painted Bride with the art-center, and was originally a kind of house organ, it had grown increasingly disconnected from the spoken-word scene at the PBAC. They were mostly 50 or 60ish white folks, who were not into the New York School, much less the L=A=N=G=U=A=G=E poets or those who taught at Temple (and, it must be remembered, there was during the 80s a contentious split between the L=A=N=G=U=A=G-E poets and the New York School at the time; see, for instance the poetry wars surrounding the "Stalin As Linguist" essay in *Poetry Flash* at this time), or even the Beats.

The way I saw it at the time, the PBQ was stuck in the mushy-middle (like Gil Scott Heron's "Oatmeal Man"), and if this was a kind of war, I would have to attack on both fronts, from the "beat/black arts" scenes that they felt above (still holding onto that Louis Simpson dictum that taboos poetry that is too recognizably black, unless it fits into that 70s feminism mode that attacks black males more than white males) as well as the New York/Language school that often felt it was *above* both the PBQ kind of writing, as well as the black arts aesthetic (though it may make an exception or two for diversity or quota reasons). These hierarchies made me laugh in a way, and I tried to cut through them as if they didn't exist.

DIGRESSION: A funny thing about the avant-garde at the time: it often positioned itself "left of center" in the politics of poetic form, thus implying that so-called "mainstream" poetry was more "conservative" or "white moderate." PBQ might be called "mainstream." It was kinda like a minor league American Poetry Review, though APR would get more of the big names and would publish Ashbery, Creeley, Forche and Yau, but the way these self-proclaimed avant-garde leftists spoke of the mainstream had much in common with the way the early 20th century "High Modernists" art scorned the more populist arts (Amygism, etc) as "low." In the late 20th century poetic climate, it was not as cool to seem to be a

---

[46] American Poetry Review was based in Philadelphia, and Stern was a staple.

proponent of "high," so they flipped the verticle spatial configuration on its side to create a dubious horizontal left-right continuum, or as that song "Substitute" puts it: *the north side of my town faced east and the east was facing south.* It was still a hierarchy, on both sides (again, this was before the L=A=N=G=U=A=G=E poets moved to Philly). END DIGRESSION

I soon found out the magazine had an interesting history, and that back in the 1970s it, along with *The Hot Water Review,* had actually been much more like the way I envisioned it could become now—more black, more Beat, more "performance oriented," yet also more New York School. Turns out the founding editor, Louise Simons, had actually been a visiting "poet in the schools" who brought Richard Brautigan's poetry to my high school and indirectly got me thinking of myself as a poet (though at the time I was so "reactive," that even her reading "shit, piss, and fuck" poems inspired only parodies). What a small world! But she was long gone now, [47] and the magazine had passed through many regime changes since.

Editor Lou Camp was (at whose house we held the editorial meetings) an interesting fella; he did a classical show on WXPN (before their big "mainstreaming" purge of 1989), and at his audition he made me watch a video of Wagner's *Parsifal*. He sure loved that high German opera, and I could bond on Rilke with him. When it came to contemporary poetry, however, he was suspicious of what I'd call the "high" art of the day (Ashbery, etc). In fact, he thought I was kind of a snob in my poetry tastes, while I, with my punk, Dylan, and funk, thought he was a bit of a snob in his musical tastes. Nonetheless, there was a mutual respect that formed, and he, and the others, did grant me a few concessions in terms of what I wanted to publish.

In any event, it wasn't that the PBQ people didn't know I was dissatisfied with the status quo, so it's kind of amazing that they kept me on for 4 years. It wasn't like I was saying they can't have their Robert Bly imitators, and those who would translate Rumi into some New Age icon (but who seem to forget how central the dance was to him, and, yes, I think if Rumi came to America in the 1980s he would've seen the similarities between the punk mosh pit and the sacred Sema), but I thought I'd be doing them a favor, making the magazine a more visceral presence both locally and nationally, at least as exciting as, say, Paul Hoover and Maxine Chernoff were doing with *New American Writing* in Chicago, but with more room for essays on poetics like *Sulfur* magazine was doing at the time, and some of the "irreverent humour" and culture criticism I enjoyed about Andrei Codrescui's *Exquisite Corpse*. Make some room for John Yau; make some room for Lamont Steptoe and Amiri Baraka (not that they needed us as much as we needed them, and I was not averse to begging).

---

[47] I'd eventually track her down, and, through her, her sons who ran the Khyber Pass rock club, where Theresa Leo and I eventually able to set up readings for the PBQ. 15 years later, they still have readings there.

I thought one way to achieve this more dynamic magazine would be to change the way we selected poems. When I joined, I was one of 5 editors. In order for a poem to get accepted, 3 of the editors had to agree. I'm told this is how many editorial boards work, as well as grant and prize committees, and I suppose in general it's fair enough, but since most (if not all) of the poems I championed were coming from what seemed a different world than the other 4 editors (well, two different worlds actually): spoken word/black arts, and NY School/L=A=N=G poetry, many were constantly outvoted (with the occasional charity fuck). It made me hesitant to solicit from the "big names" I knew. Soon I realized that the other editors weren't exactly a unified front either, and each of them felt that some of their favorite poems—the one's they were most passionate about—were also getting outvoted, and, instead, most agreement was found with second, third, and fourth choices.

It occurred to me (after a great talk, or you could say consultation, with Robert Creeley, who told me of his similar frustrations on an editorial board back in the 60s) that we could create a better magazine if a majority didn't have to agree about every poem. Yes, the editors proclaimed, it may create a cohesion or consistency, and give the magazine an identity (and, despite myself, I did learn things about poetry from them), but it also tends to appeal to a lowest common denominator, a magazine of fourth choices, poems we can all sort of like, but rarely a poem any particular individual feels passionate about for that may polarize. Was I warring with the civic notion of compromise so necessary to get anything done in America? Was I planting seeds of division into this collective action by acknowledging it?

Once again, it wasn't hard for me to see analogies with what had happened to genres of American "pop" music. The PBQ's editorial staff was based on an editorial model not too different from a Radio Conglomerate like Clearchannel's idea of a radio station format, say a "lite rock," "urban contemporary," "Modern country," "classic rock" (and off on the fringes punk, hip hop---this was pre-NWA crossover). But, as a poetry editor, I wanted to take my model more from an earlier and seemingly more human, or humane, model of eclecticism of locally owned Am-top 40 singles oriented radio, or perhaps from college radio like WKDU. To make a long story short, I valued (and still value now) eclecticism, rooted in a place, over the foolish (and placeless) consistency that's the frightening hobgoblin that's stalking Europe or however it goes.

Anyway, I wasn't going to propose that we go to the other extreme, and simply divide up the magazine, so that each of us got editorial control of our own little 20% fiefdoms! That would defeat the point of any collective in the first place. It's good to agree on something (and Hugo's letters were kinda cool). Besides, if you got a friend who's a bad poet even if he's also an editor, you have the anonymity of the collective process to hide behind. But let's say the magazine is 120 pages long and we give each of the 5 editors 12 pages per issue to publish poems they are passionate about: in total, half the magazine. The other half of the magazine can rely on the time-tested majority vote model.

I believe this can create a more eclectic magazine, in which more dialogue sparks would fly (especially if we make room for a poetics section). This could bring together a wider range of people (this was before the web, but could be applied to today), even if we're just talking within the confines of poetry (though watch out for that Stroffolino kid, you know, give him an inch and he wants a yard. Soon he's going to be asking for a wine-and-cheese reading party art the gallery with a chamber quartet and then he's gonna want a dance party and those punks he hangs out with are certainly not poets, and no CD!).

But, hey, nonetheless, I got 12 pages to work with, and I can make room for both the New York School and the Philly Spoken Word Crew. I even got a review of Bob Perelman in there, and wrote a piece on the editor of the American Poetry Review that put me on his map, and also got to branch out into visual art with an interview with and feature of the amazing Ellen Tiberino.[48] It was a start, and I'm grateful, and largely embarrassed by my own tentative firsts (juvenilia) published there….

And I have no idea, in retrospect, 3000 miles away, largely cut off from Philly and NYC (but for the ghost of Facebook) if this maybe did some good in breaking down some walls in the Philly poetry scene. I think PBQ did get hipper, especially when Theresa Leo took the helm, and we did those reading series in the same rock and roll bar where Pavement made their Philly Debut that was coincidentally owned by the two sons of the woman who was the original editor of the PBQ in the 70s. But, stop me, please before I get all nostalgic and warm and fuzzy and just want a group hug with all the folks I knew there, if they are still alive….

While many of the older folks, both in Academia and the New York scene, were warning me that being known more as a "stage" poet than a "page" poet could prevent me from getting a book published, luckily, in 1990 I was able to get two chapbooks in print. Both Dave Roskos (Vendetta Books) and Steve Roth (backyard press) were in their 20s as well. David was part of a proudly (but not snobbishly) non-academic blue-collar working class literary scene based around New Brunswick and The Court Tavern who I met through Lamont. Steve was a Naropa student 2000 miles away in a scene Chris Funkhouser was helping to put together that had one foot in and one foot out of academia. Even though David and Steve didn't know each other, and their aesthetics diverged (David had a magazine called *Big Hammer*; Steve had one called *Make Room For Dada*), we all shared that generational chip on our shoulders, comparing ourselves to heroic tales of how The Beats and the "New American Poets" burst through the gated community of New Criticism dominated poetry in the 50s & 60s, and convinced that Reagonomics was using the elders, even though we respected them, to keep us down (just like Stalin only made Mayakovsky official state poet after he had him killed, to prevent others from becoming like him)….But, screw that, *Carpe Diem!*

---

[48] Insert Move Confrontation picture if editor allows.

I am eternally grateful that both these editors indulged my need for immediate gratification, and these books taught me the valuable lesson that poems that could be crowd pleasers at readings rarely hold up on the page, in my case at least (if not Lorri Jackson). And, it probably would've taken much longer to realize that otherwise. Being embarrassed by making some work public may make your writing better. In "Hunting is Not Those Heads On The Wall," Baraka notes how the artist can be cursed by the artifact, and that the artifact's main point is to enable the process. Try telling that to an editor if he says you're not doing a good job promoting your book! And, yeah, I gotta get better at either not being embarrassed by a book the minute it comes out, or writing a better book, dammit! In the meantime, the great thing about a limited run chapbook is it's transient, it's more like "testing the waters" with a double-sided single, and if it bombs, three months later come out with another, and thus be more open to human feedback or what Kenneth Koch calls "Fresh Air."

I also began curating various reading series, mostly for the local writers, at Barnes and Noble and Borders downtown, as well as West Philly's Community Education Center. In addition, the kind folks at the swanky avant-garde Schmidt Dean Gallery on Rittenhouse Square also gave me a forum to start a poetry and experimental film series where I could bring my NYC Art Critic friends like John Yau and David Shapiro and Clark Coolidge (who had recently published a book of poem-drawings collaborating with Philip Guston), along with other NY School writers like Alice Notley or Eileen Myles. I didn't think of bringing these NYers to Philly as "colonizing," though I could see why one would think that---I thought of it as more mutual; creating more opportunities for local writers too. Besides, it wasn't like I could pay these writers more than what we got at the door (rarely more than 50 people). In addition, I brought Cheryl Dunye (before *Watermelon Woman*) and Gary Adelstein, the college teacher who had taught me that counter culture art can unite against the mediocrity of the mainstream culture of the "official reality." And, at the time, I believed I was beginning to do this.

I still wasn't really getting paid to run these readings (though I got some gift certificates from the Bookstores), but *The Philadelphia Inquirer* phoned me (in my role as poet/reading series curator) for a quote for one of their puff pieces about poetry based on the perennial question the mainstream press almost always asks when it decides to write about poetry: Is Poetry Dead? Is It Still Relevant? Oh, I could've said, "well, if you guys gave it more press, it could be more alive!" But instead I said, "Well, the novel kind of replaced poetry; then movies replaced the novel; then TV replaced the movies; poetry keeps getting pushed further behind. But it's popular enough." Well, at least that's what they quoted. They edited out what I said about music as a kind of poetry that can fight against Hollywood. Poetry doesn't need to do that as long as music can. Poetry doesn't need to be popular, if it can be *deep* (and cheap!). Poetry doesn't need the quantitative measures of success (popularity, wealth), and its lack of popularity has freed it to work on a level that can transcend class and race....

The "official reality" of Hollywood may keep poetry marginalized, but if it allies itself with the art gallery kind of economy, it's popular enough.[49] After all, poetry, even in deepest solitude, can have the power to "select its own society" and there's a kind of magic that has the practical power to bring introverts together, through the page, just like an artist who needs to spend most of his or her time in the studio loves the occasional social formality of the yearly group or solo show of their abstract still lives! High art at its best, but not at the expense of the more oral forms of communication. We need a symbiosis. That was my vision, but the *Inquirer* of course doesn't like to get that deep about poetry, but certainly there's a way to change that. I was conforming and yet had integrity? They were no longer so either/or?

Perhaps I was being absolutely selfish and needed to try all these attempts at social organization (or Praxis) stuff just to get the creative sparks flying, and synapses popping for the principle of linguistic juxtaposition that so often fueled my writing, that fluid imagination I craved, transcendence or letting go, as if to "reflect in tranquility" to translate the "spontaneous overflow" of the (structured) moshpit energy that fueled me and many others. It also inspired me to be able to talk to two different audiences at the same time, years before I understood what "code switching" was all about (except perhaps in Sly Stone's "them summer days, *those* summer days"). Like, some days, I'd wear a snazzy jacket, but (sometimes) ripped jeans back before the rich would pay $500 for simulated peasant look, like I was some kind of Ashberian punk centaur apprentice!

In addition to teaching, by 1990, I also had a night job working on the 10th floor of a skyscraper in downtown Philly for a company named *Video Monitoring Service* (VMS), thanks to Cheryl Dunye. This company was a video newsclipping agency which meant it taped the local 6PM and 11PM News (Fox was just starting with their 10 O 'Clock News), and my job was to play these tapes back, and look for corporate keywords. Corporate clients (from Big Oil, to Big Pharma and Hospitals, Fast Food, and even Donald Trump) would pay for videoclips of news stories that mentioned them negatively, so they could work on how to "spin" the news or censure the news station by pulling advertising, or ones that mentioned them positively (often planted stories, or what's called "native advertising" like when the weatherman shows off his new *Sunoco* Tie, or the kids are shown at the *Crayola* Easter egg hunt).

Though I had given up watching TV after hearing the Gil Scott Heron song a decade earlier, the novelty of getting paid to watch TV (and also to get a little inner glimpse into the corporate machinations behind the TV industry) in a downtown skyscraper in the middle of the night had its advantages. I now knew what was

---

[49] In fact, the owners of the gallery (renters of the space) were telling me I could get a grant and pay myself to keep the reading series going. Really, I can make money doing that?

"up" on what the "official reality" called the news, and I made use of what I saw as the news story's absurd juxtapositions in my poetry. And truth is often stranger than "fiction" or what poets call the imagination! For instance, I heard a news announcer say, "Scientists warn that nothing but a complete change in lifestyle and attitudes can forestall global catastrophe.....next up, The Phillies Go Extra Innings!" And I remember including a line in one of "questionnaire" catalogue poems that went over well in the spoken word scene, "Why did Gorbachev win the Nobel Peace Prize on the Same Day MTV debuted in the Soviet Union?" And I have Video Monitoring Service (another casualty of the Tech Revolution) to thank for this!

Ah, how exciting and glamorous it was to Xerox and use the Fed-Ex machine at VMS, and then around 3AM go to the all-night 30th St. Post office. I also had more things to write about, or at least *from* (since I didn't really write "about" things that much), having "really lived" in a way I wouldn't have had I taken up Susan Stewart's offer to enroll in Temple's Ph.D program. The "real world" ain't so unbearable, is it?

In 1990, *New American Writing* published my poem "To Keep Meaning From Emerging From The Mesh," (dig that clumsy alliteration and assonance!) that shared similar hopes for this middle (less specialized) ground I hoped to find in my poetic activity between "high" and "low" along with the introvert faith that "the more inner you go the more outer you go." The poem began:

We meet like shoelaces, knotted by a need
That likes to act nonchalant,
Staring its object straight in the threat—I mean—face.

And ended with:

So whether or not you get the job
Has much to do with seduction
And whether or not you get to seduce
Depends on whether the job's the excuse.

It was an attempted "meta" poem, punning on the meanness of mere meaning, while still meaning. Apparently, this charmed not only Paul Hoover and Maxine Chernoff, but many others. In terms of publishing my poetry, this seemed to signify a new era. The poems I had published before were mostly in underground zines, youth culture zines, *Cops Hate Poetry, Chemical Imbalance,* etc. *New York Quarterly* had a national reputation, but *New American Writing* was read by a lot of the New York writers I brought to my reading series, and not long after NAW took a chance on me, I noticed that many of the other magazines that had previously rejected my work (*Sulfur, O-Blek, Caliban, American Poetry Review*) were now publishing it, and NAW opened that door to the world of the page more than stage....

Attempts At Synthesis
"I tried to keep my two loves separate"
—Laurie and Lou[50]

Mostly, I kept my two loves (music and writing) separate like music without words, and words without music, straddling, or bypassing, the song, as if it was some ideal I didn't think I could afford, economically (but also spiritually?). Still, sometimes the two worlds, socially as well as aesthetically, started coming together, and I welcomed it (this was before Facebook would flatten out personality by algorithmically screening your "friends" and the ontology its notion of "radical transparency" imposes on us).

WKDU DJs like Nathalie were heroes to me because they were into the kinda more psychy-folkie (yet still edgy) underground stuff (Sonic Youth, Galaxie 500, Spacemen 3, early--pre "She Don't Use Jelly" era--Flaming Lips on one hand, and Beat Happening and Agit Pop on the other) that became more accepted as "indie" when the early 90s seemed to promise that it would liberate the underground from a more macho male dominance....

I was privileged enough to meet Nathalie thanks to a fortuitous turn of events, I was taking the subway to West Philly from North Phllly where I had been busking with my Casio by Temple's Bell-tower to see Allen Ginsberg read and lecture and University of Pennsylvania with my Casio held tightly under my left arm. Out of nowhere, a group of teens tried to steal my Casio, attempting to yank it out from my arms (a lot of people liked the silly beats it had). I pulled back, until one got the bright idea of pulling my scarf, which sent me tumbling face flat onto the subway platform, sending my glasses down into the netherworld of the subway tracks (I rarely wear glasses, but I had been reading so much for school that my eyes were hurting me; perhaps the glasses made me look more like an easy target).

---

[50] A radio station is to a live music scene
What a literary magazine is to a reading series.
On the radio station,
There's room for many more than on a record label
In a literary magazine,
There's room for many more than a press that does books.
And for the artist who is more of an introvert,
And is not interested in social dominance,
And is happier on the social periphery,
Both the magazine and the radio station
Give you a context, or forum,
In which to be heard, and not
Shouted down by the louder
And/or more aggressive.

Out of nowhere, a young woman's voice from behind me yelled, "leave him alone" and they scattered. Then she shouted, "now go down and get his glasses." To my surprise, one did, and handed them to me; they were shattered, but they didn't get the Casio. Nathalie then introduced herself (I was a little shaken, but adrenaline— or is it fight or flight—in an interesting thing)-- and then told me that she too was going to the Allen Ginsberg reading. She was supposed to interview him, and get a station ID from him, but didn't really know much about him. I told her I did, and she invited me along.

The pre-reading interview, however, was a disappointment. When the two of us arrived, one of Ginsberg's "keepers," a middle-aged woman with a clipboard, told us that she had also booked an interview with some students from The Daily Pennsylvanian, The U-Penn student paper, and that while Nathalie and I could sit in on it, they would get top priority in asking questions. These students were very conservative, tall, short haired Wharton School economics republicans, and seemed to know even less about Ginsberg than Nathalie. They had a vague sense of Ginsy as a leftist political agitator who opposed everything they stood for, and most of their questions were decidedly contentious, and hardly touched on poetry at all. I got a few questions in while Nathalie sad silent taking notes, trying to turn the conversation to poetry, but it became obvious to me, by the few times Ginsberg met my eyes, that he had already detected in me someone who was A) Politically simpatico with him (well, save *NAMBLA* which I didn't bring up) and B) that I was into poets, like Ashbery, he didn't care to talk about. Though I had some polite exchanges, and occasionally even defended him against the Penn students, he was much more interested in trying to change, open, their minds, use the occasion as a socio-political forum than to talk about poetry, or even The Clash. Not that I didn't want to talk about politics, but he didn't want to "preach to the choir."

When it ended, at least we got him to do a station ID for WKDU, which Nathalie later made a cart of (with Tibetan chanting in the background); "Hi, this is Allen Ginsberg, and you're listening to WKDU…and if you're even smarter, you'll go down to the Philadelphia Dharma Dhatu and sit yourself down and meditate Tibetan Buddhist style." I appreciated the humor and chutzpah of this, and laugh-clapped (the first clap, "the sound of one hand clapping" appeared on the ID).

Nathalie and I stayed in touch, and I'd often make it point to request songs she had previously played. She also invited me to read some of my own poetry on WKDU, while she played glorious noisy jams by Minute Flag which made me feel like I getting closer to my dream of doing spoken word with a band that sounded at least as good as The Velvet Underground's "The Gift," or at least No Trend's recent (college radio) smash, "Teen Love."[51] I also introduced Nathalie to the

---

[51] https://www.youtube.com/watch?time_continue=14&v=MY79DYD2Y4o

great poet Lorri Jackson who read on WKDU (and, dammit, I lost the cassette of this reading, as well as all my WKDU "80s Nuggets" when being forced to downsize thanks to the gentrifiers, and it doesn't seem anybody has archived what WKDU was then).

I remember the exact day I met Lorri Jackson: March 20th, 1989, the equinox, Persian New Year, first day of spring, last day of the astrological calendar, John and Yoko's anniversary, and birthday of Spike Lee, Mr. Rogers, Sister Rosetta Tharpe, Marianne ("Piano Jazz") McPartland, Jerry Reed, Hal Linden, Ovid, Hölderlin, Henrik Ibsen, William Hurt, Maggie Estep, one of the guys from Frankie Goes To Hollywood (who I was never into), and me. Lorri was friends with some of the folks at the warehouse, and, covered with tattoos, was more known as a punk poet than those who came around to any of the literary scenes I was navigating in Philly.

Hugh and Roea and others from the warehouse scene drove me to go see her read in NYC at a reading series curated by (fellow Louisville native) Richard Hell at St. Mark's Poetry Project. Since Roea and Hugh had given me some of Lorri's poetry before going to seeing her read at St Mark's Poetry Project and meeting her, I was her reader before we became friends. And, she was the only contemporary poet I met in the 80s I knew was better than me....and she was a charismatic performer. I remember at one point she started taking pictures of the audience, a gesture which certainly Richard Hell (who had posed on the cover of his *Blank Generation* album wearing a t-shirt that told his audience, *You Make Me!*) could appreciate (and one which I stole for my readings as well, which Steve Malkmus could appreciate). Her poetry blew me away, especially coming from someone only slightly older than me. She could write poetry that spoke a common language to non-literary (and certainly non-academic) punks, but also had long rhetorical flourishes that rivalled sophisticates like Ashbery. I know she was into Kathy Acker, and it turned out that she had studied with Paul Hoover at the working class art college, Columbia, in Chicago.[52]

[52] **Thoughts After Reading *So What If It's True* 27 Years After Your Death**
Forgive me if I start with some phrases ripped out of context....
"praying for a sigh" (149)
"I will dare to breathe" (118)
how eternal of me/ to swell with the incidental" (89)
"it's not quite despair/ it's sharper and meaner than that" (89)
"He accuses me of believing I'm special.
'Well, at least I believe.' I counter."
"A man waiting for a cab insists I have
a piece of jewelry for the rest of my life" (67)
"I bet you wanna know the details
but the unnamable remains
the most dangerous, like a mute

I first became aware of Paul Hoover when I discovered that many of the best poems being submitted to the Painted Bride Quarterly were by students (or ex-students) of his, mostly women (Connie Deanovich, Jacqui Disler, Joan Fisher, Lydia Tomkiw, Elaine Equi, to name but a few). Yet, Lorri was different from all these, and brought her own style and raw-edge (and Louisvillian background) into Hoover's post-New York School Chicago school mode. Once Lorri and I got talking, I realized how similar we were in our aspirations to merge so called "low" and "high" in ways, and befriending her certainly helped make me a little less alien to some people in the warehouse scene who scorned me as a bit of a literary snob because I liked reading work they couldn't understand (not that I necessarily could either, only I didn't *mind* that!).[53]

who refuses to behave like a freak...."
"but don't tell her the worst part
of living day to day
is not having a place to cry in privacy"
("Things To Do When You Have No Home" 82)

THE POET RECREATES HER SELF BY FALLING/ IN LOVE/ IT IS NOT THE OBJECT/ OF THE FALL/ BUT THE FALL ITSELF/ IS IT/ THE BIRTH?/DEATH? RESURRECTION/ IT IS THE PROCESS OF THE CIRCLE" ....(119).

[53] Getting close to Lorri made me confront both my uptightness about getting a tattoo, and my snobbery about those who had them. Perhaps I had always been too much of a wimp to get a tattoo much less cover my body like she did. Tattoos were much less common in the late 1980s, they hadn't become gentrified yet, and were more common among men and kinda had macho connotations. I'm not going to pretend to understand the decision-making process that culminates in getting a tattoo (there's infinite variety, I'm sure), but I liked the way Lorri used the "image" and/or "symbol" of the tattoo (as both noun and verb), and it got me wondering if I write poems for the same reason others get tattoos?

Is a tattoo a hope to make something permanent, to honor that a moment can become a monument, an aid to memory, a need to honor a quick decision even if you'll come to regret it later? Is it a need to wear a past on your sleeve? To invent a new future? To decorate? To become less invisible? To accept a brand? To understand all the world's a stage, and all of us actors, or work of arts? To weed out the snobs who judge and/or prejudge? What's worse? Being invisible? Or too visible? What's better? Taking control of your image, or accepting that you have no control over it?

The superb "Flesh Dreams" can be taken as a defense of the poetry of tattoo, or the tattoo of poetry, and forgive me Lorri for excerpting from this major poem:

"A promise is never a medal. A good-bye
can be. We mark ourselves
with prison tattoos
because it does not matter.
We purposely think of that job
We won't get in the future

Even though Lorri presented a cool veneer, and her star was clearly rising, as she was soon to embark on a national spoken word tour opening for Lydia Lunch, it wasn't too hard to see the pain and suffering informing her work, the struggle to merely survive in an unjust world she just couldn't quite blitz out for all the state-of-the art poetic pyrotechnics. [54] She confessed to me that she was frustrated and

& we always laugh cryptically
when thinking of the last laugh." (6-7)

The tattoo's not just some superficial whim of defiance.... No matter what you do, you will be judged negatively so you might as well live for the moment, and make your mistakes public. Read the whole damn poem, I don't want to reduce it to such romper room advice! I'm so sick of the whole debate, "was she outcast, or did she just chose the outsider's life? Did she jump or was she pushed" (and forgive me Lorri if I fall back into it.....)

Oh, Lorri, no matter what I say about your work, it will misrepresent you. I'm just projecting, and selfishly using your work to figure out things about my life and/or art. I must stop myself to honor your beautiful mystery, because I know you got sick of how most of the people that spoke or wrote about your work would tend to devote less energy to the aesthetic beauty or your sublime vision and more to psychoanalyzing your ethics (like when Jacqui called you a nihilist)......and trying to use that to reduce your poetic achievement, or at least pin you somewhere you didn't belong (misfit from the misfits, thus queen of queens). And even though you were a good sport about it, forgive me for being guilty of that in that crappy review I wrote!

No, Chris, even if you think you're doing somebody a favor by hopefully turning people onto her work, you'd be honoring her work better if you asked the same hard questions of yourself that Lorri so rigorously asks of herself.

54 Are tattoos self-branding? Or body branding? And what is poetry but a kind of tattoo? Self-branding, or perhaps, better, self-unbranding? If the body is a tattoo, the poetry may be a defense of the tattoo, but it could also be a kind of tattoo remover (of course another tattoo can also be tattoo remover), better than a crown of laurel or graffiti? To help make one thick skinned? To show the world one is not thick skinned? Lorri, I saw you do both in your poetry (and of course could see it in Ashberian terms like "the shield of a greeting," etc), and aspired to do both in mine (or I aspired to do both in mine, so projected that onto yours?)

I covered myself with poetry tattoos,
Or I constructed myself with poetry tattoos
and if I regretted "a quick decisions tattoo" (63-64),
I could always get another to cover it up,
or otherwise redeem it.
I embraced a discursive maximalism of mistakes,
And I fancied it a flinging away,
A shedding of skins, unable to accept
Or commit to the brand,
And damn I admired your courage!
And still feel this burning need to defend you

felt hemmed in by her early (for poets at least) fame, that so many had reduced

Against those who called you a nihilist

Did I detect a tension between "body" and "self" in your poetry, in my poetry, in the relationship between life and art, in our society, in our attempts to transform society through art? Is it a war between self a body? a war between the actual and possibility? A war between what others think of you (and you didn't have to imagine the worst when it's already being said), and judging the judgers to get beyond judgment…("Yeah, I wanna 'inform' the popular culture, play a role in shaping it not relinquishing it to the ad people and Hollywood executives" (59)….or not a war but a negotiation, like breathing is mutual….

And we cannot talk about the figure in isolation. We must talk about the figure against the backdrop of harsh reality of America in the Reagan Years, the classism, sexism and other forms of judgment from the "norm" that had even managed to break into the underground "alternative" scenes. I probably should've started with the backdrop, but if I start with the backdrop I tend to never get around to the figure….

Your heroic fights with the backdrop of judgment, of social stigma (and the official reality's mandate to be a consumer). "Unlike the typical stereotype of the depressed woman, it does not make me better to spend money." (113), resisting the "meat hook glare of uncaring men" (89), and the voices of male authority who say "you have neither the face nor the body nor the brains to make it in the world." Switch To Third Person, Render "Thou" into "It"—

As a woman, using writing, in part, to help her carve out space for herself in a male-dominated macho scene, in "Life Of Crime," (42), she writes about developing a "new callousness" as a survival strategy, yet contrasting herself with "those bad guys, those tough guys" with a sublime heightened theatrical ambivalence:

"Oh to be able to fall from tall barstools
And get up smirking
Or scramble beneath tables
Away from bouncers in time
To loud angry music
Escaping unscathed and barely embarrassed
Is a dumbness that does not bless me."(42)

And even though the newscast constantly reminds her "of yet another killer of women/ who has struck again and/ skimming the law of man/ will strike again and again," (95), she overcomes fear: "I am not a missive of submissive/ but a weapon of torrential possibilities" (149). I love the way you took a heroic stand against not only the writer dude who wants to unlock her inner "hippie earth mother," but also such macho self-proclaimed moralist meatheads as Henry Rollins, after he called you "a piece of shit".

"that's part of the point—TO GET THE SHIT OUT, coherently, incoherently, whatever it takes not to be a shit, to come to terms with having been shat on by the true pieces of shit in this world."

In a scathing letter of barbed wit, Jackson begs Rollins to "try a little compassion—not for me because once wounded I don't stick around for the kill—but for all those who have fallen and are looking for the strength to stand up on their own again. Those are the kind your literary heroes write about isn't it? (54) I love the way she/you turn the tables on him, use his language against him, point out the holier-than-thou hypocrisy (though I don't know if it pierced his thick, callous, overrated, skin), And I love the way your short story, "Life Of The Party" (21-25), and the poem "Dear John" (43) satirize the way that it wasn't just the men in the "underground" scene, but also some women, who were as guilty of the same hypocrisies they allegedly droppe up of mainstream society to avoid, couples, who despite their Marxist, existentialist and or anarchist jargon, are as arrogant and petty as the normative prom king and queen. Lorri might have socially circulated primarily in these scenes, but that doesn't mean she was "of" them. As she writes Chris Peditto, "I'm a person trying to have a life separate from all that ugly bullshit." Similarly, "A Prima Donna Poet Replies" is a hilarious riposte to many of the male poetry editors (often older, and not really in the punk scene) who were publishing and championing your work you suspected for superficial reasons, biting the hand that thinks it feeds you and making it love it (47, 8)

Nor do you spare the more academic poetry crowd, and I love that you also put yourself, and your work, in relationship to the kind of judgment you got from the more sophisticated, or academic crowd, like those you were familiar with in Paul Hoover's classes at that working class arts college in Chicago, those who need to hear that "The exquisite needn't always be/ lovely, diplomatic, knowledged." ("With Love And Speed," 103), or the way you begin "Rat Stories (Number 4)"

"It is a difficult thing to keep from
making fun of those sincere connoisseurs
of words who read with such lovely
afflictations and side of the eye impressions.
Of modern things and divine things
Love that is camp when it's not.
The last word always rings in the ear
But the eye is empty: no recipes, no receipts,
No gameplans, no after lunch conclusions,
Nothing darling…." (63)

Ah, afflictations! When I read this, I could see enough of my reflection in this portrait to feel that you had my number, and such challenges are always inspiring to me, and earned my respect. She knew I was more likely to identify with this poet-type than those post-Bukowski cowboy bro-poets she satirizes in the "Prima Donna" poem, yet as long as I didn't have a snobby attitude about it, it was cool between us. Unlike some who reject 'sophisticated' poetry because they don't 'get it," Lorri got it all right, but it was only of limited use for her (Paul Hoover said that when he tried to turn Lorri onto the L=A=N=G=U=A=G=E poets, she asked him how old they are, and based on that, decided they were not worth the bother, but when I told her I saw similarities between her work and Ashbery's, she just told me "no one had ever told that before"). She knew what she's looking for, and that no one was else was putting together the kind of things she was, on the page, operating largely outside the poetry scenes, and always keeping some an awareness of a reader who generally didn't read poetry, or knew nothing about poetry, or "thought poetry sucked until I read Lorri" close by.

Yet, this poem is no mere satire or screed of the more staid poem based on such 'artifice,' but a realization that in criticizing these poets she may also be criticizing her self. It's a balanced, and ambivalent, expression of crisis, and attempt to construct a new poetics:

Get past this sentence:
I am appalled at the pretense
Of poetry, of life in poetry,
Of myself...
Who wants to be laughed at
Who wants to get caught naked by a stranger.

Yet, these last two lines (which may seem like questions at first until you notice the absence of a question mark) turn into what I see as a defense of poetry, in what I, at the time, referred to as "The Westerbergian Sublime," of self-confidence by default ("I suppose your guess/ is more or less/ as bad as mine"), but this via negativa allows her to evoke the Jacksonian sublime (or, just as Nietzsche wrote that it was the thought of suicide that kept him alive, for Lorri, it's imagining a world without artifice that keeps her writing):

I have to urgently remind myself
of what ripping away the plastic violets could leave us:
the garbage collectors will quit, move to Florida
we'll choke in our own refuse,
our own blank fear will gape back up at us
a quick decisions tattoo, the name of
a lover we hated, or the mere chance to get caught
in our beginnings.
It is really too much
And classically becomes a choice
Between the lesser of two evils. Welcome.

She doesn't say whether she ultimately chooses the "plastic violet" reality over the bleak dystopic phantasmagoria of society choking in its own refuse (as if the contrast could symbolize the widening gap between rich and poor), but I pause over the beautiful mystery of the word "refuse" here. The word also appears, as does the word tattoo, in "Over and Over Again Like A Tattoo," and may also help make more sense of why this poem is called "Rat Stories."

Forgive me, Lorri, if again I excerpt and distort---

"So much for glamour and grammar
Where nothing resists
In the everglades of truth
Where the evangelist has you
On the examination table, has you
Turked in this world." The art
Of the rats
Was that
They ate too much, for the city
Was made of trash, refuse
Of all colors and sizes."

her to an image. She felt that people liked her work for the wrong reasons and

And against this backdrop of backdrops, of 1980s urban decay, or American decay, of, quite, literally, decadence, the ruins from which Hip Hop and Punk cultures sprung (and I don't know why that cartoon on the cover of Lou Reed's first album always sticks in my mind's eye, like a scene from the old Spiderman animated series, maybe coz Jacqui liked to point out how Lorri was like the Lorraine in Lou Reed's "Wild Child"), I see Lorri's heroic conservationist tattoo-poem-rats (as if you could eat someone else's cancer and spit it out before it becomes yours).

The evangelist may scorn or envy the rat's art, but the poet as rat may have similarities with Dickinson's fly-God. The rats as god's garbagemen, like necessary homeless trashpickers, working overtime to try to purging this society of its poison. Are the rats able to avoid eating the plastic violets? Can the poem's less-is-more aesthetic help restore balance in a world in which we're constantly being bombarded by things we don't need? As if to say, even when you run out of skin to tattoo, there will always be "the void of the voice" to tattoo? Or, in a conspicuous consumption society of glut and trash, it may be the highest calling to make of yourself an instrument to ingest (in earnest and in jest) the garbage of reality, to become a true recycling center, and refuse (that word again) to spit it out, or sh*t it out, until you've made it into beauty, or got people to accept what they refuse ("everybody wants to go to heaven/ but nobody wants to die") or helped slow things down. There is no once and for all tattoo, just as there is no once and for all poem…..no resting on laurels, a poem is perhaps the least destructive way to honor the urge to create and produce without contributing to global catastrophes, and if the rats can do their work, we don't need a plastic violet poem to prevent the garbagemen from going on strike!

"During the fall
You had to live
Like a slaughter
Or you would have been
Yourself
The rasping laugh, the one hand clap….."

The slaughter is the rat, as the one-hand clap is the plastic flower. I see (perhaps mistakenly) the last line as a severe criticism of the faux unity of "the sound of one hand clapping," as any poetic hubris that may arise from a moment of transcendence (or suspension) that can all too easily puff poets up with pride. Rats teach humility. Is a poetic epiphany really more blessed than a tattoo? Though she rejects (or refuses) easy figures of poetic transcendence, and embraces the swampy "everglades of truth" (which may or may not evoke Wallace Stevens), I don't think this can be mistaken for "nihilism" dammit! In fact, Lorri had more faith in, and passion for, poetry than about anybody I ever met! And she did more before the age of 28 than many more celebrated of our generation has done in their 50s (she'd be 55 now, and may have published amazing novels as well as poems, as well as released rockin' spoken word stuff…and….

And, finally, for my greatest shame. I'm reading "How Egyptian of Me," another poem that takes a heroic stand of how others brand and commodify you: "Does the singular self deserve such inspections?" But the line that makes me feel the most ashamed is when you write, "if a woman says/ she is no victim don't argue by pointing/ out the semantics this gnawed at her as she worked on her third book. Jacqui Disler called her "the lure of nihilism, Lorraine," like Lou Reed's (if not Jim Morrison's) "Wild Child," as we sat in the cafeteria of the working class art college with Sharon Mesmer who was breaking up with Carl Watson and who hadn't moved to NYC yet. Yet, more than anyone my age I knew at the time, her writing was able to transcend many of the aesthetic splits in the poetry world. Even the other editors at the Painted Bride Quarterly (hardly a home for "punk' or "underground" poets) would accept a poem by her I brought in.

Lorri was struggling with heroin addiction, but had been clean for a year, and moved back to Chicago. We wrote, but I never knew if she got my last letter because she had a relapse and Overdosed….She was 28…..I can't go on…..and Lorri forgive me if I render you into a martyr of the cause to reunite poetry and music, and find a way to get "underground" (youth) culture and "high" culture to unite against Hollywood's mass culture, and create a space for people as beautiful as yourself….

But this would not be the only death that shook my world in the early 90s. The underground scene was dying…..and so was my mother….

THE 90S: CROSSOVER OR SELLOUT?

From the perspective of 2017, or even from the perspective of 2004, the 1990s may seem like a prelapsarian time. In 1992, I noticed that many of the same people who were excited, and mouthing the line that "We Won" when Nirvana and some other music from the 80s underground scenes started crossing over were also among those who cheered "we won" when Bill Clinton won the Presidential Election. It was easy to make that analogy because in the 80s it was easy to think of corporate Radio as Reagan radio; not just the right-wing talk that had taken over the AM dial, but the "trickle down" corporatized culture of Michael Jackson, Madonna and "hair band" metal. And the syncretic religion that mass culture peddles made much of that (often subliminal) connection between the "entertainment biz" and the field of electoral politics.[55] We could even have a little fun with it, if Clinton is

of desire. A fist is no theory worthy of such distinctions." And I remember the one time I overstepped the mark….in my crappy review when I wrote something like this poem's about "the kind of man she seems to enjoy being screwed over by." Am I eternally grateful for you being good natured enough to get past that, and kept corresponding, but it makes me regret publishing that review like it was some kind of tattoo, and maybe I'm writing this as a kind of tattoo remover, or can I integrate it into a larger more beautiful tattoo that would honor you better…

[55] Those who insist on the separation of church and state should also consider insisting on the separation of church and Hollywood (which didn't exist when the constitution was framed) since Hollywood has subsumed many of the functions of religion.

like Kurt Cobain, Gore was more like Eddie Vedder, or Hilary like Courtney Love.

Both Cobain and Clinton can be seen as appeasement gestures designed to neutralize the 80s underground opposition. And Kurt Cobain, like whatever was progressive about Clinton's agenda, died in 1994 with the Contract on America (I won't debase Tupac by making him analogous to Clinton; if anything, he's more like a third party candidate, or one who lost in the primary, whose platform never made the two-party plank for the general election, and what's the electoral equivalent of PJ Harvey and Sister Souljah? Certainly Dwight Yokum was no Newt Gingrich).

Rock and other cultural critics would sometime tease out the analogy, like "if the Civil Rights movement (to say nothing of the Beat Poets, and Kenneth Koch's 'Fresh Air' a little 'higher up' in the cultural superstructure) rode on the wave of 50s R&B music that signified a cultural opening at least as much as did the church's interventions (MLK's SLCL Atlanta Headquarters was located beneath the R&B radio station Jack Gibson broadcast from, and sometimes Jack would dangle the microphone out the window so MLK could make announcements over the radio; that is, when the KKK was not cutting the cable at the tower), then this promise of undoing Reaganomics that Clinton signified for some rode in on the waves of hip hop and 'grunge' in the early 90s. Clinton walked through the door they opened…"

Certainly, many felt a cultural opening, as the early 90s is portrayed as somewhat sunnier than the 80s, more outdoor, more "peace dividend" and less "cold war." I know I was excited, in the music scene at least, that more loud rocking women were being heard, and accepted, more than ever. But some of us, even then, saw the loss of what we worked so hard in the 80s to achieve (if I helped? Did I help? Or was I too drugged on slow futurity?), back when the "yourself" in Do-It-Yourself (DIY) was often really a more collective "ourselves" than the "every band for itself" it became in subsequent decades.

Ah, 1992. Remember all that talk of Bill Clinton being "the first black President," coz he played saxophone, even as he was stepping up the Prison-Industrial Complex and dismantling federal welfare programs for the poor, and though the figure of Clinton seemed more "body" in a positive sense, his policies were in fact closer to the relatively more disembodied figure of The Gores (and their PMRC). Not only did he demonize Sister Souljah's attempt at anti-racism, but also pushed the burgeoning Silicon Valley technocracy even more than Reagan was, as Clinton asked us to envision the good of a future with less factories and the new white collar tech economy, as if that transformation itself could "grow the middle class" since the word "working class" became virtually synonymous with "blue collar" which became more associated with the past (Flintstones) rather than the

Jetsonian future.[56] Whatever was forward looking about Clinton's policies were, if not exactly more "mind," at least less body. In retrospect Ross Perot was right, as he pointed out the similarities between Bush and Clinton; neither were a friend of blue collar working class labor, and the fact that his theme song, "Don't Stop Thinking About Tomorrow," was 15 years itself showed how "forward looking" Clinton's policies were. Would it be better if he made "Here we are now, entertain us" or "Brenda's Got A Baby" his theme song?

Beneath all this hoopla, I saw the walls tightening around the alternative economies, the underground infrastructure, the rising local rents, and the brain drain (and body, heart and soul drain) to Hollywood (or at least Nashville) and, for artists and poets such as myself, NYC. The fact that college radio was mandated to be advertising-free proved to be a fatal flaw when the amazing DJ has to "retire" to pay the rent, and the corporations are starting up those higher powered but more automated "alternative" stations (like the one that plastered "Honk, If You Hate Freebird" billboards over Albany, NY) to the new generation of 90s arena rockers with a generational chip on their shoulders.

I saw an increased segregation between hip hop (mostly black) and indie rock (mostly white); compare even photo shoots between 1989 and 1994; by 1994 white indie rockers had to appear more clean and collegiate, often than they really were, while rappers and had to appear more "thuggy," often than they really were. In music, the white male 90s indie-rock ethos was generally more slicked up, or tamed down (watered down) versions of the 80s. Hip hop and punk started losing much of the visceral small club energy that got the ball rolling in the first place.

The radio stations were less eclectic, but more formatted and niche-market splits developed between "modern rock" (more corporate and macho) and "indie rock" (more like Pavement), as well as between alt-country to say nothing of Nashville's contemporary country which increasingly had more in common with "modern rock" or "Classic (70s) rock"—the working class coalition both Bush (in his ZZ Top Hat) and Trump would stress, against the "coastal elites" who were more into "indie rock" or the black working class more into hip hop.

I saw a repeat of many of the same paradigm shifts I had experienced as a kid in the 70s. Lollapalooza signified the 90s Arena mandate (as Woodstock opened the door for the 70s arena mandate), and its accompanying change in sound. Many bands who were excellent in small clubs couldn't quite make the transition (or had to sacrifice what was great about their sound) to the Arena Rock circuit. And, in hip hop, Dr. Dre slowed down the beats to signify a move from the more peripatetic boombox culture to a 'cooler' California cruise-in-your-car culture. Despite these

---

[56] See the first 10 minutes of Michael Moore's "Canadian Bacon," for a great satire of this economic and cultural philosophy).

trends, between 1992 and 1996 I still held out a little optimism, especially because more women's voices and loud distorted guitars were being heard....and, besides, I got to read poetry at Lollapalooza with Bob Holman's crew.

The 90s was, in short, more "me" and less "us" than the 80s, and even though I didn't really know it at the time, I was following the fashion. It's also possible that my particular deep skepticism toward 90s notions of "progress" were deeply informed by, or but projections of, my own emotional state of mourning for my mother who had, at the age of 49 in 1992, lost her lifelong struggle against a variety of ailments that had been misdiagnosed ever since she was 15 when she lost her kidney---smack dab in between what Thurston More called "the year punk broke" and Clinton's election (and remember Clinton didn't win a majority; he needed Perot). After my mom's death, I felt too weak to keep trying to fight the zeitgeist, and hid in poetry as a kind of "third place" that, as Ashbery would say, "refused (the system's) right to exist." Or you could say I was running way, but in many ways *escapism* was the zeitgeist of much of the 90s, so that even in running away from it I was confirming it.

After my mother died, I felt the life drain out of me, I wallowed and couldn't muster the energy to dance the devil out. I fell into that "trying to get people to feel sorry for me" mode. That phrase came to me in a dream. My mom spoke to me gently but straightforwardly and firm, "Why are you telling people I died? You're just trying to make people feel sorry for you." My mom was never one to guilt-trip when alive, so I didn't know what to make of that. Mike Watt of the Minutemen said that when d. Boon came to him and said he was still alive, that you're supposed to assure the spirit, as lovingly as possible, that he (or in my case she) is dead. I don't know. I like what Iris Dement says. Let the Mystery Be....it isn't it like the Corporations pull death's strings. No, wait, she was misdiagnosed by inept doctors, and *you can't get cancer treatment on the wages of a nurse!*

Yet I couldn't stop wallowing, and though I knew she was proud of me, I still felt that deep down I had failed her, that I wasn't realizing my full potential, that kind of stuff. And I knew I had to find a way to translate this sadness, this grief, this mysterious *inertia* into some pro-active, or productive activity, And, you know what helped a lot with this! Coffee! Yes sadness (or grief) plus (+) coffee equals (=) anger (often unhinged), but add the cigarette to tame it down, and focus what was now being called Attention Deficit Disorder (though they used to call it imagination!). It was like the coffee was the anti-depressant, while the cigarette treated ADHD. Yes, I know the 90s was the beginning of *Prozac Nation* and *Brain Candy* ("Happiness Pie"), but I was old school, like cassettes and 7 inches of Otis Redding singing "Cigarettes and Coffee."

I was almost 30, and only now entering into the American Religion of "wake up and smell the coffee." Perhaps I was trying to run away from the necessary sadness, and had I been more patient I could've worked it out, but I believed in the sublime mode after all, and sublime means sublimated, or transmogrified, and perhaps I had to transmogrify to survive. Indeed, the pressure to survive, and earn a living (Drive your cart and horse over the bones of the dead!) made me once again rush headlong even more into that "abstract social life" of writing and publishing poetry, and choose the more repressed, less, embodied, path. Perhaps I had been kind of a slacker when she was alive, and it was time to "grow up" and focus, narrow and put away those "childish" de-specialized unification dreams. After all, they say you can "lose your center" trying to fight "the world," even if I wasn't fully convinced I had a center. What they call the "center" feels more like the layers of an onion (and "just coz it has no center doesn't mean it can't make you cry"—another witty quip that could be charming currency in NYC to defend Ashbery against Armand Schwerner).

In short, I held my nose and voted for Clinton, and traded in my "They Lie" t-shirt for more of a Mod button-down shirt and jacket look (which could also pass as a teacher's uniform), and went back to grad school at age 29 to study with a baby-boomer poet who was definitely an introvert woodsman (rather than an urban "social butterfly" like Frank O'Hara) who had a well-paying low pressure teaching job since the age of 23 (something much harder to achieve in our 90s generation of protracted adolescence with a chip on its shoulder). In Amherst, Massachusetts, I had no art gallery, no punk warehouse, no literary magazine, and no mother. It felt like a vacuum, or a monastery.

Perhaps I became a sell-out then. At the time, I probably didn't even entertain the possibility that "white America" was calling and I heeded the call. After all Massachusetts was the only state that didn't vote for Nixon back in the day. If this was selling out, I was sure being stoic about it. Doesn't Dickinson have some line about taking her power and turning it against herself? Renouncing, self-flagellating, and if you self-flagellate well enough it can become collective action!

Though I longed for the convenience and more visceral social nexus of Philly (unlike Philly, not having a car in Amherst and Albany put a severe constraint on social life), at the time I knew that I had to engage in what Chuck Berry would call "too much monkey business" (at least write a book, if not exactly settle down) and embrace the solitary mind/heart writer existence as a necessary temporary phase (or what Bernadette Mayer calls a "political nothingness text")

Perhaps I needed to be in a small town that didn't have a vital social life in order to concentrate on school (had I gone to a doctorate program in NYC or even Philly, there may have been too many social distractions). If I was sell out, at least it didn't have to be a permanent tattoo!

In the cold winter, in the Puritan land of witch burners, I put music (if not quite the body) even more on the backburner to sublimate the pain of mourning and loss (both personal and cultural) by developing a poetic "signature style" that won accolades in the 90s. Yet even in James Tate's workshop, I was kinda pleasantly surprised to find other students (like David Berman, Joe Pernice, Brett Ralph and others---perhaps you'd call us broets now) who worked at least as much in the field of music, releasing albums on small labels (though I suppose Sub Pop is bigger than Drag City?), and reaching more non-poets than many poets do. My writing may have been reaching people older than me, but their songs were reaching younger people. Even though Tate was not a musician himself, and his work would be derided by some of the more avant-writers as "soft surrealism," it was fascinating to see how he brought many of these young musician/writers together much more than my other teachers had (and Tate devotees could do worse than to consider this part of his legacy).

But even though I loved Tate's poetry, I soon discovered that I could learn more from *reading it* on my own than wasting my time and credit rating on another Master's Creative Writing degree. So, I quit after one semester to go for a Ph.D. In the meantime, I was excited that somehow the mere act of writing in solitude, and sending poems to magazines through the U.S. Mail had somehow managed to conjure up a real social scene (perhaps this is what Marianne Moore meant when she said that poetry is an imaginary garden with real toads in it), even if more scattered across the country.

Yes, but Peter Gizzi and Juliana Spahr were planning to bring many of us together, and I remember being very excited about being invited to attend (and even be remunerated for) the New Coast conference in 1993 in Buffalo, NYC. Indeed, this NY-centric, but nonetheless national, poetry scene I was finding had a strong sense of generational identity (even if generations were defined differently in poetry than in music). There was a sense of a younger generation working toward realizing a collective "strength in numbers" ethos (perhaps borrowed from the 'punk' underground of the 80s; it always takes a few years to trickle up, just as "second wave" feminism was fashionable in pop culture in the early 70s, but didn't really make an impact in academia until the 80s).

Yes, this New Coast conference may be somewhat analogous to Lollapalooza, in that maybe the older generation (who dominated both the music and poetry industry) who had ignored us in the 80s would pay attention. The fact that most of these poets (including me) were either working in (or aspired to work in) academia certainly qualified any clean generational break, or safe space, or temporary autonomous zone sense of community. At least The New Coast Conference was open enough to make room for my work, which however "repressed" and "mental" was still a little too unhinged, effusive and wore its protracted adolescent sensibility on its sleeves a little too blatantly for some. I am eternally grateful for Peter Gizzi for this opportunity, and I believed, in poetry, our generation could learn from the mistakes of our elders and emerge from this conference with many seeds planted it could take lifetimes to tend. I also continued to make trips to NYC to see readings, and now even be invited to read.[57]

As I contemplated a move to NYC, John Yau suggested that I become an art critic, but even though I loved reading his criticism almost as much as his poetry, as well as others he turned me onto, and loved going to galleries and museums, choosing to become an art-critic would require being a self-employed freelancer—hustling—while a Ph.D would provide an institutional setting (if not quite a live/work artistic collective warehouse, which I couldn't seem to find anymore), and could allow me to buy time to also work on getting more poetry published, even if I had to go into debt once a new Republican Governor (Pataki) took away the scholarship I was supposed to get.

Another Academic Attempt At Straddling Specializations

Many young poet people were now getting Ph.Ds, given the academic inflation that was occurring at the time that devalued the MA and MFA degrees, so the poetic specialized purists didn't object as much as they would've 20 years earlier. Yet, even here, many of the poet/academics were trying to channel me into doing my dissertation on contemporary, or 20th century poetry (as I was known as a poet, and allegedly it would increase my chances of teaching jobs). Yet, I wanted to engage in poetry on its in terms, as reading it inspired me to write it more than write *about* it; a bird doesn't need ornithology (though I would write some reviews).

[57] **Commodifying Conversation**

In NYC, I understood the art of namedropping as the "merry war" of the sophisticated intelligentsia. I am reminded of David Lehman's introduction of John Ashbery at a SRO reading at the KGB Bar in Manhattan sometime in the late 1990s. Lehman recounts a party in which someone asked Ashbery if he read the works of the then fashionable French social theorist Foucault. JA said no, but then later on in the party Lehman overheard Ashbery talking eloquently about Foucault: "I thought you said you never read Foucault." Not skipping a beat, Ashbery replied, "Yes, but I go to a lot of parties!"

This story got laughs, but Ashbery's quip does suggest a deep truth: Yes, you too can pick up everything you need to know about Foucault by being an astute attentive listener to all the conversations about him. In a way, the point of this joke is rather radical; if applied to a classroom it can give permission to get away without having to read the primary text, and it embraces spontaneity, improvisation and the primacy of orality. You could go so far as to say this quip is one of Ashbery's best *poems*, and the title—in this case Foucault—is not a can opener, for when people are talking about Foucault, they might as well be talking about football, and there's the thrill of drinking with any tinker in his or her own slanguage, which seemed to be one of the ethical ideals of the New York School.

Instead I choose Shakespeare, in part because I enjoyed reading Shakespeare critics more than most critics of 20th century poetry. It allowed a wider range. It also would force the discipline of a sustained 300 page prose work on my rather lyric (albeit discursive lyric) sensibilities, and I welcomed that challenge, in part to sublimate mourning for my mom.

My emphasis was Feminist criticism of Shakespeare's Middle Comedies. Linda Bamber had written a book called *Comic Women, Tragic Men: A Study of Gender and Genre in Shakespeare* that helped usher in a revolution (along with Carole Thomas Neely, Janet Adelman and many others) in Shakespearean studies that challenged the male orthodoxies that called the comedies lighter (less serious) plays because women had more power in them, or at least seemed to; reading these women talk back to Shakespeare (or at least the male critical establishment) really helped my poetry become more dialogic.

Perhaps it could be seen as paradoxical (or at least ironic) that I ended up writing "better"—or at least more celebrated—poetry during this time because I was also working on a Shakespeare dissertation. From one perspective, you could say that my poetry was largely "outtakes" from my Shakespeare dissertation, but that often "outtakes" are better than the ostensible task-at-hand. Or poetry was a "safety valve." They two genres complemented each other: I tried to keep an Apollonian line, and division of labor between them: one notebook (say 6" X 9") for poetry, and another notebook (say 8" X 11") for the Shakespearean related prose (as well as occasional review/essays of contemporary poets), but of course they blurred (my first full length book was originally going to be called "Better Known As a Blur" before I discovered Nick Piombino had a book called *The Boundaries of Blur*): when I thought I was writing about Shakespeare, I was really writing about myself, or *the* self, the author function, or placing a kind of relationship I found my-"self" involved with in Shakespearean terms: self-as-relation.

"Wow, honey, last night was just like Act 3, scene 4 of *The Merchant of Venice!*" And when I thought I was writing about myself, or my life, I was really writing about Shakespeare. Perhaps during this time, I lost the "rawness" (and aspects of my youthful cockiness) that my first two books written before my mom's death had, but you could say for a while there Shakespeare (and when I say Shakespeare, I mean all those contemporary Shakespeareans—mostly Feminist and Cultural Materialist critics) became my main "sister art," as music had been more in the 80s and early 90s before my mom died, and though you could say Shakespearean studies was a relatively disembodied pursuit compared to music (and required becoming a coffee and cigarette addict back before the Attention Deficit pill craze), it certainly was less disembodied than most poetry, and still had at least as much as that linguistic complexity as the most sophisticated "avant" poetry of the 1990s I was aware of (in contrast to those who claim that "the more disembodied you are, by definition, the more intellectual you are").

It also got deeper into the trenches of the ideology or ontology of "self--as--relation" rather than essence. It allowed me to make a pact with narrative, if not quite the novel (which, for me, at the time, seemed to get too bogged down into scenic descriptions). Another advantage to working in the Shakespeare coalmine was that it provided a little more of a common language (just, like, in music, say, The Beatles or Motown, were, even in the 90s, a jumping off point for discussion). 6 or so years of heavy immersion (not only reading every play at least once, and some like 5 or 6 times) can stay with you, and be pulled out when needed to talk to many with a "middlebrow" sense of culture. Even my dad, who was more working class than even "middlebrow" in his sense of culture (football, reruns of westerns; a modern day "groundling") was surprised when I took him to a play, and realized he could basically get what was happening on a basic plot level at least. I came to Shakespeare from the opposite direction; I loved the wild language; when I first read "Richard II," and was asked what it was about, I said, "I don't know; some guy in a crown blowing a verbal Coltrane solo!" It took a few years before I could appreciate what I call Shakespeare's "soap opera side."

There's a book called *Meaning By* Shakespeare that shows how many voices in our culture have often used the phrase, "as Shakespeare said" to make a point, and how much sway such a fallacious appeal to authority can have (for, instance, I was surprised, when looking at a catalogue for Naropa University that they included a quote, "one touch of nature makes the whole world kin," with a picture of a leaf. I had to laugh, because in context of the play, *Troilus and Cressida*, the line is actually referring to STDs.) I'm not saying this is the way it *should* be, only that perhaps I could use it to my advantage when talking to people who've never heard of Creeley, Ashbery, Notley, Baraka, Laura Riding or Carla Harryman (much less Jennifer Moxley, Pam Rehm, David Shapiro, etc).

In NYC, there was always at least one free or cheap Shakespeare play being performed if one wanted that (even though the contemporary playwrights like my friend David Rosenthal were struggling, especially after Newt's "Contract on America" decimated the theatre) and sitting in the park often with a date witnessing these costumed actors (even if the costume was sometimes cobbled together from trash) shouting at each other about philosophy and ethics in bizarre language that could dance, and that I sometimes had to strain to get, seemed to exteriorize what some would call the "inner turmoil" of my "interior monologue"—to create a kind of inner peace (or balance) the maximalist way—as words cancel each other out until "it appears in other ways than words." It very much reminded me of the feeling I got in moshpits, or while mod-dancing (and I'd run back home to *read it*, as I would run back to hear the song I just danced to in Philly).

I was no actor, but I did get to set one of Feste's songs from *12th Night* (which some argue was written by the actor who played Shakespeare's Foole, *Robert Armin*), which, anachronistically, has a blues structure, to what was then a kind of fashionable indie rock tune (in hopes to save Shakespeare from some of the pretentious music that often accompanies the plays). Indeed, if Frank O'Hara was a poet among painters, perhaps in NYC I was becoming a poet among actors.

Furthermore, even though there was a split between those who took Shakespeare primarily as drama, and those who took it primarily as poetry (as fodder for academic arguments), even the debates that the academic Shakespeareans had were informed by a sense of theatrical "negative capability" that, too often, was lacking in the poetry world, in which the poet ideologues had a tendency to take themselves too seriously while others just tuned out, as if poetry at its highest (or purist) best feared being contaminated by argument (but if poetry is really superior to argumentative discourse, what do you have to fear by making room for it, as a character at least?)

At the Shakespeare Association of America conferences that I was privileged enough to go to, I often found a radical Marxist critic, a psychoanalytical feminist critic, an old-school metadramatic critic, and a post-colonial critic could exchange their views with an equanimity that rarely happened at a poetry conference (or listserv). Perhaps this was because, despite the specialization of approaches, Shakespearean studies was not as balkanized as the dominant contemporary poetry fields (for instance, "performance poetry" still remained largely segregated from page-based poetry). Ah, if only the more "page" oriented and more "stage" oriented poets could come together as much as the actors, directors, dramaturges, and scholar/critics did, the poetry world would be less segregated. But while it's virtually impossible to get 100 poets to agree on any sense of a necessary reading list (especially with contemporary writers), or a shared common language, in the Shakespeare field, the wider range of ideological approaches could at least agree on the *field* of Shakespearean studies as a value, a common text as a jumping off point (even if the New Historicists would rarely appeal to Shakespearean texts). Besides, the SAA held a better dance party (shout out to Fran Teague and Christy Desmet) than any poetry conference I attended (except maybe *Assembling Alternatives*).

This doesn't mean that I choose "Shakespeare" over "poetry," only why I found some of that "grace to live as variously as possible" putting these two scenes, or disciplines in dialogue with each other (and a shout out to Stephen Ratcliff for instance). Yes, Shakespeare *fed* my poetry as much as the punk/underground scenes had in Philly, especially when colleges started offering me Shakespeare classes to teach, and in some ways a Shakespeare teacher is more like a DJ, what in academia and lit-crit, they call a "secondary source." Perhaps I loved the role of the critic/scholar because it was more like a kind of "sampling." Perhaps I had developed such a relationship to words (let indirections, or misdirections, find directions out) that made me only able—in words at least—to speak the truth of my heart by framing it as always already social and theatrical....like a Shakespearean foole, or comic heroine.

Yet, even though Shakespeare's "double perspective" and "negative capability" (as Keats says) could delight in its villains as much as its heroines, and thus be a very useful tool if I catch myself taking myself too seriously, it can run the risk of preventing any direct statement about social injustices. And, thankfully, during this time when I lived/breathed/ate poetry and Shakespeare, and was far away from the righteously angry "Black Arts" scenes in Philly & NYC, I was able to take a class with Theresa Ebert, the "vulgar Marxist" teacher the poet/academics had warned me about. She was encouraging me to expose the Euro-Centric, and ludic aspects to all the fashionable post-structuralists and tech-utopians, and how these much hyped politically-engaged academic theories (Foucault, Derrida, Spivak, Deleuze and Guattari, etc) are insufficient tools for trying to fight against, say, the racist administrators at CUNY who fired a professor (Jeffers) for Afro-centric views. The poets told me she was anti-poetry, but I knew she was into Brecht, and why can't I engage in some Marxist critique in the morning and engage in a little desire based lyric performativity in the evening? Is not this part of the grace to live as various as possible?

Ebert helped provide intellectual grounding in a wider social cause that I had to edit out of my poetry (at least that which got published) at the time, but I also found some grounding in my body in making up *a capella* melodies as I swung on swings sets. I couldn't have finished my dissertation fueled by coffee and cigarettes alone.

Albany—oh by the way that's where the grad school was-- in many ways reminded me of what had become of my hometown. Even though it was the state capital, the downtown was otherwise dead, especially after 6PM. The University, which had once been downtown, had been replaced by a new, improved "riot proof" campus sequestered in a northern suburb. While I did go to a few live punk shows (to see my publisher Dave Baratier's friend's band, 1000 Young, at the QE2), most of my dancing in those days was at the first Friday disco night at the Center For The Disabled (formerly the CP center). No, I wasn't disabled at the time, but I took a part time job as a leisure service provider there.

Yes, mom, you'd be happy to know that not only was I earning my PhD, but I too cleaned old people's asses for a year or two. But I also got to work in the pool with the clients who had cerebral palsy and autism (while the radio blared "Everybody Hurts" by R.E.M) and go bowling with them. We also had movie night and, yes, disco night, where I'd spin clients' wheelchairs around in a circle beneath an old disco ball while they played "Stayin Alive." They also had coffee house night where I played piano and sang with them (I guess this was my first professional gig). I wasn't really doing it for money though as much as to remember I was a body as I pulled all those coffee-drenched all-nighters.

Pavement Saw had released my second book *Oops!* In 1994, and Aerial/Edge put out *Cusps* in 1995, and my work was getting published in dozens of magazines, but it's 2017 and I'm sad because so many folks have told me they like the work I published in the 90s so much better than what I've done since 2005. One says I've "lost that Stroffolino sparkle." I feel times have changed, and that what may have worked in the 90s is not needed now, but I understand what Baraka means when he wrote, in "Hunting Is Not Those Heads On The Wall," "the artist is cursed with his artifact." What did people like about my poetry? Here's two blurbs from my 1999 book *Stealer's Wheel* by writers I deeply admire:

"The circular shape of mind in many of Chris Stroffolino's poems lends itself nicely to the relationships he makes between philosophy and traditional themes of poetry--especially that of love--using the language tatters of the heterodox culture he so clearly chooses to inhabit. His wholehearted inhabiting of such culture allows him considerable pleasure in treating the "hetero" male Eros with a marvelous teasing. This rare ability to tease the heterosexual species from within its own realm has allowed this reader some serious laughs she didn't realize she'd been waiting for."--Carla Harryman

"I think Chris Stroffolino's poems are the opposite of an 'in joke,' they are an 'out-joke,' meaning they are about the miserable hysterics brought on by suffocating grief and loneliness. How could that be good? I don't know, probably because he dresses it all up in a stunning syntactic Mobius strip, and in the midst of reading him I realize I feel less alone in my perceptions of the world. His poems may not DO anything or change anyone, but they are great. And, as with all great poetry, just because you know it's telling you the truth doesn't mean you can get anyone else to believe you."--Jennifer Moxley

These two readings complement each other; one stresses the intellectual, social, and humourous (or at least witty) qualities, while the other stresses the "miserable hysterics brought on by suffocating grief and loneliness." Still, even with such kind words from two amazing poets, since around 2005, I don't feel I can stand behind these poems, except perhaps as juvenilia that reeks of white male protracted adolescent broet "excellent scribbling in a period style" that is not at all adequate to the challenges of life in the 21st century (West Coast), in which many of the crises that were on simmer in the 90s---and not just to me—are at full boil.

I'm frankly *terrified* to look at my old poetry, but maybe I could borrow a page from David Bromige's *My Poetry* or Leonard Cohen's *Death Of A Lady's Man* (the book, not the album), for in both those books, the writers theatricalize the voice of their own harshest critic of their art to the point where you wonder: is the so-called criticism the more profound art than the so-called poetry that's being criticized? Or does the poem, after all, get the last word over the critic?

Underground Classic
        "I wish he'd explain his explanation"---Lord Byron

Reading *Light As A Fetter* (1997), a book that Ashbery and Creeley blurbed (and ex-roommate Joanna Furhman's favorite book of mine), 20 years after it was published (and 25 years after most of the poems were written) could make me feel like Rip Van Winkle or at least Wordsworth and Whitman making *The Prelude* and *Song Of Myself* worse with each old man revision-"corrective," but I'll look at the first poem, "Underground Classic.[58]"

It starts with the word "imagine!" (to set an imperative tone for those who say they hate being preached to, but kinda secretly like it). Then, a pun on "just desserts" (that suggests a world of glut). When you hear the word "dessert" do you think whipped cream cake, or 7 cherries? Dessert is to, say, veggies as an advanced class is to an introductory class (I often did better in advanced classes--in the humanities, if not math and science—but they say "Einstein couldn't tie his shoes" and thus rocket scientists may bow down before plumbers and their textile worker wives who can't even read and write…); or dessert is a luxury as veggies is a necessity. Imagine if someone gave you nothing but the food you called your favorite for all those years, would you still call it your favorite?

Anyway, this strikes me as a metaphor for the upward mobility promised by, say, Clinton's white collar post-industrial vision of the new America (in the post-punk 90s) or at least the disembodied obesity epidemic.

Then, another command: "Chisel something/ neurotic from that pre-narcissistic stone," as if the speaker is talking to himself (and trying to avoid the temptation to be too good to be true?) even if it has (or I have) to use Freudian terms. The "figure" enters, feeling deprived in a sea of riches (or glut). Then it mouths the diction of the high-sublime: "This is your task (not to have tasks)" climbing the heights of Parnassan Paradox! And mounts a defense of moods! (Matthew Zapruder wrote that my poetry negotiates moods, more than themes, and I think he meant it as a compliment). Is poetry a protracted mood? Is reason?). Is the mood of this poem smug as the reason is begging (I mean seducing)?

It seems to be trying to get the feeling of infinity in words by turning words and their denotative function against themselves as if to find a clear spot, a place of possibility… but there's so many commands! And, indeed, I'm too demanding and need to get my little jabs in against the "show, don't tell" taboo, even if Jennifer Moxley's right, and it doesn't do anything, or can't change anyone. Yeah, but Carla Harryman likes being teased, and that's kinda doing something, no?

So "the actor playing the phantom" is clumsy, and I kind of smile "Okay, maybe my younger self wasn't so stupid afterall, and can teach—or remind—me a few necessary things I have forgotten at my peril! "Embrace the clumsy!" So who am I to judge? Who do I think I am? The father in Cat Stevens' "Father and Son?"

You might even say this "actor" is a "bull in a chinashop" (or a pig with lipstick), but it's only the "Outtake"—the necessary outtake (or Ur-Text) perhaps, and yes I often

[58] I'll include the poem as an appendix

like outtakes (and "director's cuts") better than the official version (unacknowledged legislature) for the same reason I'd rather watch a painting change in an artist's studio than the finished product, and, besides, it's the early 90s and I'm really into "underground" movies like Hal Hartley (featuring PJ Harvey and Pavement in the soundtrack, and the amazing actress/director Adrienne Shelley who I met when she acted in one of Dave Rosenthal's plays years before her tragic murder) in my little academic-meets-post-punk-indie-rock name-droppy bubble.

Is this poem just asking, "can I, as person or poem, be an underground classic, who can 'sing both high and low?'" So perhaps the title of the poem in this case is a kind of can opener and the image, or at least the theme (or is it a mood) of New York Romance parenthetically enters ("A kissing storm by a subway stop") and, ah, allegedly romance was one of my big themes (but probably more like Amy Rigby's "Cynically Yours" or a love song called "(I Feel Like I'm Less Misogynist) When I'm With You" which, yes, some women liked!).

Or, if not Romance, at least "Id" as Gary Sullivan put it. I don't really believe in Freud's "id," but did I feel I had to play that role in my poetry. Exaggerate the id, and do it theatrically (is that why I called my first book "Oops?) Certainly, Gary saw that, and I suppose Steve Evans was right that I loved those "mordantly recursive sentence" like:
"...the middlemen I wish
To see myself as now that the autopsy
Proves what the author has died of
("refinery smoke") without proving it dead."

I can kinda stand behind this line 20 years later, no? Isn't that what I still fancy myself trying to do? I mean, even then, despite the seeming abstract and detached (scientific) tone---in a world that distrusts the "jargon of authenticity," you can still hear a collective working class cry that goes beyond post-structuralist differAnce, or structuralist "nothing." Yes, I can detect that seemingly perennial Stroffolinian need to be respected as one of the "middlemen" rather than the (more barren?) "Author" (say, Chris Stroffolino), while also de-hierarchizing a philosophy that claims (whether overtly or covertly) that an author (say the one who wrote "death of the author") is more important than a mere middleman (this was before I discovered the sideman role).

Perhaps what could seem third-rate grad school banter from one perspective could be spoken earnestly by the same frustrated soul who would rather be a DJ than a commodified musician (even if the DJ, too, is inevitably commodified; "I am what I play"), or who only publishes poems as an excuse to be allowed to continue teaching creative writing (where, yes, you may be able to change someone, just as Gary Adelstein changed me....)

At the time I sure thought the parenthetical "refinery smoke" phrase was "wickedly clever" (I could see how "wit" opened up to the sublime and/or revolutionary). In America, the rise of refinery smoke paralleled the rise of the middle class who could later send their kids to the college that was once their factory, and I think of "the lumberyard that's been closed down due to the environmentalists who will lose their job at the local college once enrollment drops like a tree...." (as I put it in Cusps in 1995). "You can't have one without the other...."

and, to paraphrase Ashbery's notorious opening lines of "Definition Of Blue"--
The (rise) of ("Clean, green, post-industrial) America
Parallels "the advance of" (post-structuralism)
And the (middle-class) is dominant until (the birth of the me-decade)

Or perhaps:
The (rise) of (Big Pharma)
Parallels "the advance of" (the obesity epidemic)
And (Big Tobacco) is dominant until (the birth of the cell)

This "refinery smoke" could be "cigarette smoke" though the "smokeless" refineries of Prozac and Zoloft nation (smokeless for consumers at least if not the producers in those Puerto Rican slave labor Big Pharma factories who have plenty of smoke) were beginning to replace cigarettes around this time. But "refinery" also referred to the status of "refined" diction, syntax, "high art;" for indeed such refinement can alienate one from the "raw" expressions of pain or joy like if the poem were set to a loud fast 80s "underground" groove that didn't mince words, but was getting all tamed down in the 90s era of Green Day and Dr. Dre.

We're kissing by the subway in the rain!
I love you like cheap entertainment!
Together, we can straddle the wealth gap!
Abandon refinement, and save oil!
I'll trade my crown of laurel
To be a clumsy middleman, or sideman,
Sampling the great mid-century middle-class classics.
Our naked cries will not be heard
So let's become our own worst enemies
And praise the absurd!
Prove me wrong! Prove me wrong!
Fuck Pop Tarts, Give me spinach empanadas!
Fuck Hollywood, Give me Cheryl Dunye!

I got a way to go to become a song lyricist, or even an elite bumpersticker tweeter
But that's okay if I can be a sideman, an art critic, a music critic, a popularizer, a community activist, Part time Shakespearean, Part-time Marxist, Anything but a purist, Anything but a purist![59]

---

[59] I wonder if the 90s self who wrote "Underground Classic" would hate what I just wrote, and cry, THAT'S NOT ME! THAT'S NOT ME. Nah, he was into the sport of being misinterpreted!

*"In order to rest in peace when dead
you probably have to be a firehouse of activity when alive."*

Eleni Sikelianos liked that line, but what did I mean? For Emily Dickinson, was death a place in language-life that can rescue us from the tyranny of prose-meaning? Is she, too, one of the middlewomen? "Firehouse" is a tricky word. It sounds like a house on fire, or could imply that I like "to set the world on fire," but firemen put out fires! Perhaps a less extreme way of saying this, is "I sleep better if I work out my body and mind more!"

"I'll come down from my cross for supper, but only if I can call it breakfast."

And perhaps one doesn't have to be medicated to be able to laugh at the martyrdom complex it was always so tempting to identify with (being "razed Catholic" and by TV), taking my "lofty ideas" too seriously. However cleverly expressed (the line got laughs and/or chortles) in the flow of words that can happen at reading where many poets are adept at making their readers feel they're on the torture rack and the only way out is to read the book, this line may get at what I thought was an important debate in any honest discussion of the American lifestyle, the health orthodoxy courtesy of corporate marketing campaigns from your friends in Battle Creek: Breakfast Is The Most Important Meal Of The Day (and a big breakfast at that).

Yes, Big Cereal (founded by Puritan Kellogg) didn't start adding sugar to cereal until the 1950s, and, yes, other cultures do not necessarily believe this; even in "advanced," first world Europe, they have very small "continental breakfast," and save their larger meal for later at night than the standard US "supper" (apparently, they also reject the idea that sleeping too close to sleep time is bad for you). And, even back in the 1990s, Europe had less health problems than the US.

So you could say this line gets at the issue of my eating habits (which have become more of an "eating disorder" in the post-2004 years in the west coast since the accident). In Philly and NYC, I preferred that European mode, not eating until later than day. Often supper, or evening dinner, would be my breakfast, in part because if you hooked me on food (especially on sugary freebies at the office) too early in the day, I had a difficult time stopping eating, but I always felt I got better work done when keeping food intake to a minimum (low-metabolism), in defiance of my upbringing. Ah, a song called "Stay Hungry!" could be an anthem, and living with such habits was encouraged—and even allowed me to be healthier—in NYC, the city that never sleeps, than ever in Oakland and San Francisco with the healthy food places tend to close by 6 or maybe 7.

Nonetheless, that's just a quick line in a poem, and I certainly wouldn't expect any reader of the poem to "get" this anti-Breakfast message as part of its meaning essence as much as I do here, making mountains out of molehills. To the more "casual" reader what may emerge is a very demanding speaker, expressing his "deal breakers," perhaps in an attempt to screen out potential lovers (after all at this time, I was fond of saying "a poem is a personal ad" though I always found it easier to meet women through music), an autocratic persona expressed and mocked simultaneously (as if poetry allows you to have your cake and eat it too), as Harryman's blurb implies.

Can there be confidence without the ability to confide? And who, but a cold-hearted abstractionist, would call "blood wine" like some smug insurance salesman speaking of the bloodshed after the aerial bombing of Black Wall Street in terms of Hollywood Stage Blood, a necessary sacrifice, the wrath of god, or in terms of dividend payments. "Pain brings out the best in you," chortles your manager as he electroshocks you further.... (Miserable hysterics? Loneliness "suffocating like succotash"?)

"Show me how you watch the tube
Without identifying with the walking
Advertisements"

And, of course, neither "the tube" nor academia (with the exception of Theresa Ebert) were making much room or space to talk about the continued bloodshed that was driving the American empire (in those years between the end of "Desert Storm" and the start of U.S. "Kinetic military action" in Bosnia). Bush had banned TV coverage of body bags, and the horrors of war, and this was before all the cellphone footage of police brutality, but perhaps I drop the clever masks here for a second to ask a substantive sincere question to the people likely to be the poem's readers: How have you (oh poetic elders like Creeley, Baraka, Ashbery and Gil Scott Heron, et al) created an alternative to the official reality of TV culture?[60]

Oh poetic elders, you may not be able to help our generation, after all Creeley and Ashbery were old enough not to have been raised by TV (were 30 in 1956, 57), but more than ever, we were raised by TV—not that it's necessarily harder for us. And even if the old defenses of poetry (as Parnassan, for instance) sounded more like O'Hara's school marm scolding a kid with "It's good for you" and didn't really work for our skeptical "post-punk" generation in the 90s, at the very least poetry can offer an alternative to TV, can it? Can you? Show me! Can I, as commodified self, be a walking advertisement for life without TV! (and, remember, this was before Facebook, which was an ingenuous way to rope many back in TV).

And perhaps this indicates a crisis of poetic faith (Harold Bloom believes that every "strong" poem expresses a crisis in poetic faith blah blah), and could remind me of a line Elizabeth Robinson read at the New Coast conference, in 1993, which expresses something similar, albeit in Christian terms (I'm a big fan of syncretic religions!): I believe, help me to believe.

---

[60] (think of all the great anti-TV songs by Public Enemy, The Disposable Heroes of Hiphopracy SP from around this time, or even go back to the Clash's "I'm So Bored With The USA.")

In my terms, I believed in the power of poetry to dig us out of our TV upbringing, and its narrow sense of the zeitgeist, but help me to believe....we can create our own reality from the ground up. I don't think I can do it on my own. And for a decade or so in the 90s, I found many who helped me believe, for which I'm thankful, or were they enablers? Well, in "moods certain of uncertainty" they can be both. You could reduce it to "it's just a game," harrumph says the old curmudgeon, frivolous, frivolous....but perhaps more importantly, did you feel refreshed then? And how can I help you better now....seduce each other off of facebook?[61]

Well, maybe I knew then that the somewhat densely packed ambivalences of the "suggestive intelligence" could serve as a time-capsule designed to be "unpacked" and read, by me, 20 years later, and if the poem knew more than its author did then, it may still know more than me now----but it still doesn't make me want to write that way anymore, but I know I have not yet—and may never—perfect that merger of "mass" (or "low") and "high" (or marginalized, or self-marginalized) culture that the title "Underground Classic" implies.

Meanwhile, "Outside The Poem"

In the 90s' poetry world, there was also a lot of talk about the democratizing and popularizing potential of the new medium of the internet. At SUNY-Albany, where I was working on my PhD, as well as SUNY-Buffalo, where Creeley and Bernstein had largely taken the initiative to start a Poetics Listserv (this was before the "social media" craze of the 21st century) many were embracing the new technology, which certainly promised a kind of "levelling the playing field" between extroverts and introverts (as college radio had done in the music scene). Quite a few were embracing the CYBORG ontology, and tech poets were being hailed as a new avant-garde.

I, however, was skeptical. It felt like I was being forced *by my elders* to get a computer (see my Op-Ed piece from 1995, republished in my book *Spin Cycle*). Like Carolyn Forche, I feared it could undermine the importance, or at least currency of, the contemplative mode, and also feared it would mean further marginalization (and/or destruction) of local culture. In one book, Tech Visionary Guru Mark Taylor said, "we don't all need to live in the same place anymore," but some of us wanted a sense of place...that walking city and downtown my grandma had, or that I found, on a smaller scale, in college, and in Philly (but couldn't find in Amherst or Albany). And if *Make America Great Again* can mean bringing that stuff back (without the White Supremacy), I'm all for it. Could Tech help with that? I didn't think so, but I tried (and I did find an amazing long distance romantic relationship through that internet in the first year I used it).

The University of Pennsylvania had just opened the Kelly Writers House, and

---

[61] Oh, by the way, did you get the final line's allusion to Rosalind from As You Like It?

their visionary manifestoes made it clear that they had the funds to use the new technology to aid the cause of poetry, and a wider more interdisciplinary sense of writing which, in the context of academia, could be seen as quite radical. What made it exciting to me was that it was attached to an actual place (rather than many culture oriented websites); they weren't using the internet to replace the local, but to enhance it. No doubt they were receiving funding by the same Ivy League patrons (whether public or private) who were funding R&D for Silicon Valley firms. Maybe they could fund projects like this for *every* college....

Meanwhile, the Telecommunications Act of 1996 was passed by congress (and signed by Clinton) and would soon play a large part in destroying whatever "victory" indie-rockers, or modern rockers could claim in the early 90s, as it strengthened the stranglehold the corporate players had on the U.S. music industry (of just about any genre) and helped effect a paradigm shift in which many who were fighting, in part, to open up the radio airwaves in the 80s and early 90s were now pushed off.[62] Of course the tech utopians (or tech determinists) who the Telecom Act benefited, told us to tell ourselves "that's no big loss, coz radio was dying anyway, and as long as you had a vital internet presence you may be able to distribute your music even better!" (though that took a few years to come to fruition), but I wondered, if radio airwaves were increasingly *passe*, why were the large corporations willing to spend more money than ever to control them?

Yes, even those in the Anti-Hollywood army could not quite bring themselves to start an Anti-Silicon Valley army... Still, I love Jesse Michaels' (of legendary Berkeley punk band Operation Ivy) take on this: for those of us who witnessed life before the Telecom Act and the "introduction" of the iPod and iPhone, it wasn't like most of us in the 90s were sitting around begging for social media, and the other 'perks' of tech culture. There was no vote: would you prefer to have an internet even if it means the death of your local bookstores, and record stores? No, we didn't have a vote....

But even though I didn't have a vote on that, I could leave "Smallbany's" placeless culture (which tech culture would only accelerate), and move to what I called *the last holdout*, perhaps the only walking city left in America with a vital downtown: NYC.

New York City
Chronologically, I'm supposed to talk about NYC now, but it's 2017 and I need a

---

[62] As Scott Timberg puts it in Culture Crash. When "Uncle Sam paid the Reagan debt by selling off the broadcast spectrum to the highest contract" with The Telecommunications Act of 1996, it "allowed a bevy of elite media corporations to ravage the airwaves with impunity, sweeping aside the remnants of local radio culture and replacing it with an endless stream of scientifically manufactured drivel to befuddle and distract the American people from their duties as citizens."

shot of futurity, or at least presence. "One of the biggest regrets in my life is that I ever left NYC."

Ah, New York City. In retrospect, you seem like "one manic explosion after another!" Duchamp said "Dada can't happen in NYC because NYC is dada." Still, writers like Bruce Andrews seemed to do a very good job of mimicking the zeitgeist of New York intellectual culture with their "non-referential" poetry. For some, this was like honey as a sauce to sugar. Others say, "if you can make it there, you can make it anywhere," but I made it there. I must admit I loved NYC's "culture hell that tests my manhood" (to paraphrase Claude McKaye), its constant stimulations and destabilizings—I called it a tight-fitting enemy, the bottleneck; it encouraged my workaholic charm even if sometimes I felt I was "Living for the City" more than "Working for the Weekend." It was the closest I came to being able to specialize (*Light As A Fetter* in 1997 was followed by *Stealer's Wheel* in 1999, and *Spin Cycle*, my essays on contemporary poetry, came out in 2001), and yet delight in dilettantism.

NYC gave me a new leash on life, or sprung me loose from a 4 year period of stoic renunciation! Another advantage it had that I couldn't find in Philly (and certainly "Smallbany") was that it was less ageist. You could be a young 40 year-old there, and I was in my early 30s. The so-called high arts so dominated this city, and many elder painters and poets "held court" in a way that promised more staying power than the "youth culture" scene that the Philly underground kind of was despite itself. NYC allowed (or even forced) me to become a man about town again as in Philly, and I became a regular at Bar 13's Sunday night Mod dancing parties with undergrad "kids" 10 years younger than me, who discovered soul oldies and brit invasion obscurities through movies like *Rushmore* (the problem was that it was primarily retro, like what had happened to much of college radio in the 90s, but, dancing, none of that mattered; James Brown or The Staple Singers 1965 is more alive than much being pushed in 1997).

In retrospect, it's still amazing how active I was in those years---working 3 and sometimes 4 jobs at a time: teaching at LIU, NYU, and commuting to Rutgers-New Brunswick, working as an artist's secretary for Pat Steir (thanks John Yau!), writing reviews for *Publishers Weekly*, and proofreading or factchecking for *The Reader's Catalogue*, *Teen People* (with its great view of the city from the *Time Life Building*) and *Women's Health* from *The Reader's Digest* Family all the while doing reconnaissance on the corporate world for my poetry which, amazingly, I had enough solitary time for (even if making music was largely consigned to a back burner since it seemed out of my price range).

I was even an extra on an episode of **Sex And The City**, a scene on a yacht for a party for the fictitious *Gab* magazine, with Sarah Jessica Parker and Mr. Big having a heated confrontation while a reggae band plays "Send Me The Pillow That You

Dream On," and if you look really closely in the back for a 5 second shot, you can see my girlfriend's hat, and my nose. I think we got $75 for that, and all the food we could doggybag. As an ex-girlfriend put it, "I'm not a social butterfly, I'm a social Firefly." Even though I rarely wrote "lunch poems," I kinda was living that Frank O'Hara dream, even though it was much harder to survive as an artist in the 90s than it was in the days of O'Hara (NYC's rising rent problems go back at least to the 80s when Yau told me his rent had gone up from $400 a month to $1200 a month, and, of course, Donald Trump had a lot to do with it).

And yes, many of us in our 20s and 30s in the 90s had that generational chip on our shoulder, given the backdrop of cultural devo, or "diminishing returns:" *Hell, if O'Hara was in NYC in the 90s rather than the 50s and early 60s, I bet he would have found that "grace to live as variously as possible" more difficult to achieve. And certainly no doctor poets like William Carlos Williams would have been able to pull off what he did in the era of corporate for-profit HMOS*....Still, I was humbled, when even an older artist, Richard Hell (*Blank Generation*) asked me if I had any leads on factchecking jobs. I felt like I was a link on a chain, I felt a kind of "we're all in this together" cross-generational solidarity despite the sometimes fractious nature of the poetry scene, though it saddened me deeply that even Hell couldn't make a living off his art. I think of Anselm Berrigan often, and befriending him helped to undo my skepticism to the concept of a poetry community since it was quite literary his extended family (quite a few poets babysat him), and he could inject that energy into the scene.....Too many memories. If I mention 30 of them, I will neglect 100 more.....[63]
--I can't go on....

[63] Back in the glorious pre-internet 90s when poetry was more conversant with letter writing and journals than a reaction to tweets, Grace Hartigan loved my interest in her collaborations with Frank O'Hara (a relationship at least as mythic as the award-winning trans-genre romance of Robert Mapplethorpe and Patti Smith), while doing a watercolor that became the cover to Stealer's Wheel. She told me "every painter needs a poet" and we could share a lament that my generation didn't have this dynamic as much as hers could (in NYC at least) & I tell her about how the painters came to Sam Truitt's Ichor Gallery poetry series in 1996, but eventually stopped once it became clear that the poets weren't reciprocating.

Many poets had painter envy to be sure, or some could express earnest solidarity (with painters who smeared dung on the Virgin Mary) by holding anti-censorship rallies while the art world laughed itself silly watching the artist's prices go up, with admiration, scorn or envy for this brilliant publicity stunt. Stunted alliances, but I can't blame the jealous gods of coterie poetry; the underlying economics kept more people divided; when you can't afford to live in the same neighborhood anymore, and are too busy *living for the city* to be *working for the weekend*, having to commute to 4 different jobs, and such, there's much less "free time" to cross-pollinate, to network, create and put together rent-control show of strength rallies.

--What?
--I can't really write about NYC at this (decade-long) juncture because it's too traumatic.
--Yes, but you've written about other traumas. Much of your recent writing is dripping with trauma, whether personal or cultural....
--Ah, but what makes New York more traumatic to write about is that there, more than anywhere else perhaps, I found a sense of home, I was accepted warmly as a fellow-artist by a wide range of people working as playwrights, filmmakers, musicians, dancers, actors, poets and the funky academic Shakespeare scene. To name but a few......I thrived in the walking city, even though I was poor....Oh, NYC, am I just overidealizing you, or the bubble you represent?

Could I go back there now, for at least a summer sublet, and join the many friends still there, no doubt scattered, trying to help their kids (who weren't even born yet when I left in 2001) to pay for college? Could I recreate some of the magic of my time there?

I know some musicians there who said they'd work with me if I visited, and we could spend the summer planning and rehearsing for an art-gallery performance including poets, painters, and other visual artists, actors, stand-up comics, dancers, fashionistas, and political activists (as well as probably a techie or two, since that's probably necessary these days)....for an event at summer's end, just in time for the fall start of the gallery season. It would be like kind of a reunion, or maybe at least a funeral party (ideally held *before* we die). At my age, it's never too early to start planning, especially given the cost of an affordable retirement home (a punk/hip hop retirement home for generation exers). My final request....

Volksboutique[64]

Ah, yes, dream big to act small. And I guess this was another aspect of my early 90s poetry, "like a car that has to dream of the grand-Prix to putt putt around the block" (with a nod to Samuel Beckett), in a world in which "it gets harder and harder to milk the taxi that hails the cow," and I think of the amazing conceptual artist Christine Hill who spearheaded Volksboutique (and is now based in Berlin). Though born in upstate New York, and a graduate of the same art program in Baltimore where Grace Hartigan taught, she first developed a reputation as an artist in Berlin (not long after the wall came down, when rents were cheap there). She set up a used clothes store in an abandoned warehouse beneath an elevated train. But it wasn't just a used clothes store, it was an art gallery.

Unsuspecting patrons would walk in looking for cheap clothes, but soon found themselves in the middle of an art project. Part of the gimmick was that the clothes

[64] http://www.volksboutique.org

would have no price tag so this forced the customers to speak to her and, as they haggled, Christine would get theoretical and metadramatic and call attention to the idea of conversation and transaction as art. This brief summary doesn't do justice to her vision, but hopefully it's enough to give a sense. I found it a brilliant and fascinating concept, with the potential of transforming society, or at least the art (including poetry) world.

Although some purists may object, it wasn't that Hill wasn't into creating beautiful well-crafted objects, but that they would be *part* of the show, the whole experience (and the show, in turn, could be part of the object). I saw what Hill was doing as fighting a war with our over-specialized society (from *within* its confines) more successfully than I had achieved. She was in New York as PS1 fellow when we randomly met on a subway, and we spoke about music (she was also a frontwoman for a German Hip Hop Metal Band on a major label), and invited me over to her studio when she worked on her *Tourguide* project, and eventually we collaborated on her *Pilot* project at the Ronald Feldman gallery.

The gallery had offered her a month-long exhibit. While the standard art-world protocol has an "opening party" while the work remains on display for a month, open to the public during gallery hours, Christine added a few things to this convention. First, *Pilot* wasn't just an art exhibit. The month-long gallery exhibit would also be a work space, which people were invited to visit as she, and a team of other artists (from all genres) were working. Christine, or the gallery assistants, would dutifully show them the art works for sale, but continued to work on creating the exhibit's culminating event, its closing show.

The theme for the show was to create a pilot for a Late Night (or Nite) Network Television Show like Conan O'Brien's (with an opening monologue, and its similarities to the variety shows like Ed Sullivan or Flip Wilson of a previous era). She was a big fan, or student, of Conan's, and lamented the absence of women late night talk show hosts (as she would have every reason to lament the gender bias in the art gallery world). But, since she was operating in an art-world context, allowing her audience to witness every "behind the scenes" pre-production aspect of creating this *Pilot* (whether constructing the stage, setting up bleachers for the studio audience, or taking pictures of her as she talked on the phone trying to book talent, etc.) not only seemed to live up to Baraka's great essay, in defense of *process* ("hunting") at least as much as *product* (those heads on the wall), it also broke down, or at least exposed, the walls between the "high" culture sense of art and the mass-or-popular art (The Late Nite Talk Show).

Sure, it would have been great if Executives from NBC or ABC or HBO would have showed up and recognized Hill's brilliance, and *broke the glass ceiling*, by offering her a late night talk show, but I'm not sure Hill would have taken the offer, since she had so many future *Volksboutique* concepts burning for realization, but I found it to offer all the finer, aesthetic and intellectual pleasures more typically found in a gallery context, as well as providing a template for my ideal of a literary event. For among the other achievements of Hill's project, it brought more collaboration into the picture, and broke down the wall between "the solitary creator" and "the social promoter," two roles most artists (at least in NYC) have to play.

If Christine could use an art-gallery context to explore the official boundary between gallery exhibit and Late Night Talk Show, why couldn't the poetry scene (the main scene I operated in as a cultural producer) benefit by being involved in an event at an art gallery called, say, *Dance Craze?* In this potential project, there could be a closing party in which one of the rooms is transformed into a "swanky" nightclub in which ten bands and DJS are invited to debut a dance song written on a shared theme for a compilation anthology. Of course, there'd be choreographers, clothing designers, visual artists and writers (surely, college students could do it as part of a work study community service project)… and, yes, even poets. They can perform in the front room, or with the musicians, and surely the show's catalogue would include poetry.

And, even if it fails to really create a dance craze that can sweep the city (just as Hill's didn't land her a late night talk show), in the smaller economy of the poetry and local music scene, it could certainly help create more of a context. Could I find an art gallery like the Ronald Feldman to host it? How do you get grants for something like that?[65] Why don't they teach grant-proposals in MFA Programs? In the meantime, I put most of my big dreams into my writing. In NYC, I really liked being a small fish in a big pond, even more than being a big fish in a smaller pond in Philly……

Poetry Wars and Poetry Detente

I, too, like Christine Hill was, trying to fight against overspecialization (from within its confines), but the poetry world has a different scale than the art world and music scene (to say nothing of late night TV). And a lot of the struggles that seemed so big at that time seem small now. For instance, I remember getting very excited that poet Sam Truitt had organized a reading series at the Ichor Gallery in Chelsea in 1996. As roughly my age, he decided it was time to start a reading series that had a generational identity (just like The New Coast Conference did, with many of the same people, who often were associated with the 3 Bs: Brown, Bard, and Buffalo), for even venues like St. Mark's Poetry Project (which we loved!) were so dominated, and mediated, by the old so we didn't have our own space like the St. Mark's people had when they were our age (actually, many were younger; it was easier to get books published in your 20s in the 60s).

---

[65] For an analogous proposal, but starting from an academic context, see my Notes To An M(F)A In Non-Poetry, and see apprendix 4.

Sam's act of generational separatism (perhaps borrowed from 80s underground music scenes) did get the older folks to pay attention. Eventually they wanted readings too, and when Sam started to give them readings, they opened up to our letting us read more in their spaces, and as a result loosened some of their dogmas. Sam's readings also brought in many amazing young artists in an attempt to bridge the social scenes between these genres like O'Hara and others were able to achieve 40 years before.

In the poetry world, it felt like some of the overly divisive factionalism of the 80s was waning, especially between the L=A=N=G=U=A=G=E poets and the New York School and others associated with the coalition lineage Donald Allen put together in his landmark 1960 anthology, but also between "avant-garde" (or innovative or experimental) and so-called "mainstream" (often associated with American Poetry Review and MFA programs like Iowa's Writing Workshop). My 1996 essay "Against Lineage" was written in response to a need to bridge these factions (or as Steve Tomasula put it in *The American Book Review*, "*Stroffolino holds out an olive branch to warring poetic factions, but sometimes the branch is on fire*"). It says some things that needed to be said at the time, but seems incredibly dated, and narrow, itself now.

I critiqued the narrowness of poetic "canons" from within the narrow Euro-American canon context, but didn't really ground it in music or a more collective sense of poetic creation in my attempt to reign myself in. But, however fractious many L=A=N=G=U=A=G=E and many New York School poets were—and it must be remembered at this time how loudly Ron Silliman pontificated on Poetics Lists and elsewhere about our younger generation's political failure---(which of course we could easily turn back on him), they generally could agree on the "common enemy" of the kind of mainstream stuff associated with the University of Iowa, for instance, as they even looked at me skeptically for having studied with Tate (yeah, I like Tate, but I also wrote a long essay trying to dialogue with Barrett Watten *on his own terms*, so there!).

Walls had already been breaking down between this factionalism with Iowa, largely thanks to women (like C.D. Wright, Jorie Graham, Brenda Hillman). So when a new generation of poets (and more women than men; I'm thinking of Fence Editors Rebecca Wolff, Caroline Crumpacker, Matthew Rohrer as well as Katy Lederer, Max Winter, Lisa Lubasch, Joshua Beckman) who had more associations with the MFA "mainstream" scenes began to move to NYC, and begin frequenting St. Mark's Poetry Project, the KGB Bar, and even the Segue Series shortly after I published "Against Lineage," more of the walls between what had been called "mainstream" (Iowa) and "experimental" (including both New York School and LANG Po), started coming down as well (like the Berlin wall?), and I welcomed that.

Fence magazine claimed to be formed as a frustrated reaction to one of the first major national magazines that had published me back in 1990, Clayton Eshelman's *Sulfur*. While I admired and respected *Sulfur*, and found Clayton very supportive of my work, I could appreciate that the editors (mostly women) challenged what they saw as his more macho "tough-love" editorial policies. In this light, the word "Fence" itself had a double meaning—not just fighting with swords, but also recalling Ashbery's "a kind of aesthetic fence sitting elevated to an ethical ideal," and Fence valued eclecticism (though some would say wishy-washy relativism), and also published fiction, to put these genres in dialogue with each other as well. Their presence helped liberate the debate away from the more reified, specialized lines that grew out of old 1960 battles of the anthologies (raw vs. cooked, for instance). They weren't as hung up on the "Pound-Williams" (gerrymandered) lineage.

Yet even though it seemed a good thing that some aesthetic walls were breaking down, it still needs to be said that none of these various factions really made room for declamatory music poetry a la Baraka or Ginsberg (they could be respected as elder statesmen, but newer writers were not encouraged to write "like that"). Perhaps the biggest mistake I made in NYC was when I tried to extend the spirit of the New Coast conference, in approaching Ed Foster about the need for a good anthology of people under 40 (which was kind of the new 30s, or at least the poet-timeline 30s, as opposed to the musician timeline) in which we could 'spread our wings' and maybe make a 'break' from feeling like we had to ape the fashions imposed by our elders.

To my surprise, he consented, and I'm proud of the fact that we achieved gender parity (just as the music industry allegedly had in 1996), but the end result only had 36 writers, a roughly equal number of pages for each. I thought (and still think) it would have been better to include less poems by more writers. Furthermore, it represented a really narrow aesthetic range. Most of the poets had affiliations with the 3 Bs (Brown, Bard, and Buffalo), with maybe a little Naropa or St. Mark's Poetry Project spice, but it tabooed writing that was "too raw." For instance, when I tried to get Yuri Hospodar's excellent performative catalogue poem, "To You In Your Closets," included, it was deemed "too beat." The narrow range of the anthology became even more of a problem, when the editors chose to put the word "American" in the title, which I felt was arrogant (at least, as a concession, I got them to put a parenthesis around it), and, despite the gender parity, racial segregation was still a problem.

Perhaps I still had enough of that working-class Philly guy in me to feel this "erasure of the raw" was a mistake. It was like with each successive generation, poetry was getting further away from what most claimed helped "open it up" in the 1950s (and I don't mean CIA backing), and just as tech culture was pushing America as a whole in this direction, the poetry scene felt more disembodied as the older generation was dying off. It needed some kind of a change, perhaps more of an influx of hip-hop energy, but that wasn't called poetry in these largely segregated circles...and, from this perspective, even a closet studio rock band (that didn't play live, and didn't really "rock") was a step toward more embodiment...

The Late Great Silver Jews (Or "I bathed in *American Water*")

"A lot of times I wish there were rock critics like there are book critics or art critics. Because I feel like I do a lot of work in the writing and there's no one on the other side that's willing - or maybe they're not looking because it's not there in other people's music - but they're not willing to do the work back,"—David Berman

In the spring of 1998, within a month of finally receiving my Ph.D, I got a phone call from David Berman, who I hadn't seen, or even talked to, since our time studying with James Tate 5 years earlier. He (who was "of no fixed location," during that time, having left Austin) was coming to NYC to record the next Silver Jews album, and remembered my piano busking from Amherst so auditioned me on the phone. Little did I know at the time that the album we recorded in those two weeks would take on a life of its own, and help transform some people's thoughts about the relationship of poetry to music.....even if we didn't play live.

I know that many of you have never heard of the Silver Jews, or even Pavement, but it's hard for me to talk about my life without talking about them and it's hard to talk about them without trying to clear my head of all the things everybody, in their small (by music industry standards), but passionately loyal, fan base has told me over the years.

Ah, the stories they told me of what David and Steve's songs meant to them. Some showed me their tattoo of the *American Water* tear, or offered me money if I played a Silver Jews song solo on the piano, or got me to play trumpet while they sang "Random Rules" to their estranged girlfriend on karaoke night. Or they'd name their bands after "The Wild Kindness" or "Trains Across The Sea" or other songs. Then there were the debates over who was better, David (Silver Jews), or Steve (Pavement)? "Would Silver Jews lyrics be as good on the page as the poems in Berman's *Actual Air*?" Quite a few were contemplating making that comparison a chapter in their dissertation (shout out, for instance, to Jeff Johnson), while others set poems from *Actual Air* to their own melodies (or even sampled my little 3 note riff from "The Wild Kindness" in a dance song)...

And you wouldn't believe how many times people have asked me questions about them (or us). "What's your favorite Berman couplet?" (Maybe *folks who've watched their mother kill an animal know/ that their home is surrounded by places to go*). "Do you agree that Berman, more than anybody has the power to plant melodies into our memories even as our 'rational' side is wondering whether we like them or not?" "Why didn't David release a solo album? Why did he have to hide behind the conceptual avatar?" "Do the words come first or the music?" "You were there, why did David (Berman) and Steve (Malkmus) break up?" "Was it because of personality differences or musical differences?" "Can you help get them back together?" "Is David a man who needs to closely guard his solitude, or a tortured genius?" "Why didn't he take that teaching job?" "It's not right for him to disown his millionaire lobbyist dad on moral grounds; blood is thicker than water!"…and I'm only scratching the surface.

It feels like a kind of community has formed around Silver Jews' songs and recordings—perhaps it's primarily generational, most of the fans I met first got into them in their teens or early 20s, but I also feel it's a community of introverts! As a connoisseur of vocalists who can get sadness in their voice (of any genre), an expert on song structure, and creating a "living room (or even bedroom) vibe" intimate connection with those who listen to his recordings, Berman, in the songs on *American Water*, certainly makes more space for those with a (at times apocalyptic) love-hate relationship with Solitude (and the municipal institution of solitude) than others at the time (like say Elliott Smith). Do songs like "The Wild Kindness" feel like introvert anthems appealing to the broken thus swollen selves who have faith in a power that "the deeper inward you go, the more likely your external world will be improved than if you tried to meet it head on," or those who understand that internal and external is a false distinction promulgated by the self-proclaimed glorious extroverts who pronounce us introverts or shy (not that those terms are synonymous) as cuss words in the first place, those Joneses we're supposed to keep up with, and of course our swelling interiority demands that we are misunderstood….?

I don't know. I obviously couldn't see the album as a *product* as these fans did, but I tried to follow where they lead me, for a possible 33 1/3 Book, so I wrote pretentious copy like this:

"*American Water* is a portrait of the seedy underbelly of life at the end of the "American Century." It appeals, especially, to wounded youth in an era of protracted adolescence, as they rummage through the glut of cultural artifacts for a voice they can identify with, a voice that can slow down for them and give the advice of an older brother (or ex-lover who's still willing to be friends) who's willing to submit to your angst if you let him crash on your couch for a few weeks, a rabbi with the kind of punk cred you crave, a kind of Tupac figure for the white gen-X crowd.

Yet, the personae the album's sonic "living room vibe" constructs also have wit and wisdom for the older folks; it's deepest prescient cultural insights gain more resonance after the crash of 2008. Though many have interpreted its lyrics as embodying a hope for personal salvation through art, this album is also an investigation of the cultural and economic decay of the US 80s/90s. For songwriter Berman, the political is the *inter*personal, and this is why the album still has (judging by its continued sales) the power to bring people together and speak across the ages more than the barren, if better selling in the short-term, artifacts of its time. Built around Steve Malkmus' sonic textures, *American Water* uses the lexicon of indie-rock against itself in hopes of luring listeners out of complacency, but it does so gently and unabrasively—so gently that many have not heard the cultural argument in some of Berman's most cryptic and seemingly personal lyrics."

But people also like to talk about it at parties, at least in NYC, dropping allusions to lyrics that come out great pain in the formal feeling of NY School "deep gossip." It's January 1999, only 3 months after the release of *American Water,* I'm at a poets party in Stacy Doris's loft in Brooklyn, and overhear some of the *literati* talking about the Silver Jews. They are playing the analogy game, comparing Silver Jews albums to Velvet Underground albums: "So, *Starlite Walker* is like The Banana album; *Natural Bridge* is like the "grey" album, and *American Water* is like *Loaded,"* someone adds. "What about *White Light, White Heat?"* I chime in. He quickly responds, "Oh, that would be *The Arizona Record."* "Oh, yes," I reply, "I had forgotten about that one."

Such parlor games were common in that scene at the time, and this analogy stuck with me. First, it shows the esteem in which these writers held Silver Jews. After all, the Velvet Underground was the quintessential "art/noise-rock" band, and Lou Reed was not only the rock and roll heart, or "godfather," of punk, especially New York punk, but, as Alissa Quart argued shortly after his death in 2013, a major template for the white "Generation X" sensibility (both male and female) of which both Silver Jews and Pavement were avatars. And Reed's *Coney Island Baby* was clearly an important affinity for both David Berman and Steven Malkmus; perhaps their most significant musical common ground while recording *American Water.*

Ah, Chris, but this is just superficial clutter. David Berman is not our generation's Lou Reed, or Leonard Cohen, or whatever. This analogy shows how many of our generation were compared, and even compared ourselves, to icons of the "baby boomer" generation, as the shared present 'independent' culture that was beginning to coalesce in the late 1980s when Silver Jews got their start had fragmented and was becoming increasingly colonized by the corporations and the past. As David Berman puts it in a song off *American Water,* "we've been raised on replicas of fake and winding roads/and day after day upon this beautiful stage/ we've been playing tambourines for minimum wage."

While some older gatekeepers would call this our "anxiety of influence" (as if DCB had an "oedipal" relationship to Leonard Cohen), Berman's lines suggest a deeper, more economically grounded, sociological interpretation to this dilemma our fragmented generation experienced. Lou Reed and his generation rarely, if ever, viewed their art in terms of musicians from 25 years previous to their arrival on the "beautiful stage;" neither was, say, Frank Sinatra or Charlie Parker being pushed on that generation the way, say, The Beatles, Hendrix or Neil Young were pushed on ours.[66]

Besides, Berman doesn't love New York like Reed did. Even though *American Water* was recorded in Brooklyn, neither Berman nor Malkmus lived in "Jolly Old New York" (as the title of an early Silver Jews single puts it) since 1992 when they were security guards at the Whitney Museum. As that song makes clear, they were much more diffident toward New York's culture than Lou Reed. As David put it in a 1998 interview with Amy Sohn of *The New York Press*: "I don't think I can really stay here because I get really self- destructive in New York, just party too much. I'm always worn down. I don't work enough ...I'm meant to be a good person and New York somehow seduces me into the dark side. I think I was born to be a rabbi or a reverend or something, but I'm turning into a fucking pimp."[67]

Berman's diffidence toward NYC was at least as aesthetic as it was ethical; his "country and western" influences were evident on all three of his albums from the 90s, but Music Critics usually registered these influences in terms of the burgeoning post-punk Alt-Country movement. Berman's musical affinities and aspirations, however, were much closer to traditional or "outlaw" country, while "alt-country" (from Wilco to The Scud Mountain Boys) fit snugly within 'indie' rock parameters (which Berman calls "the roped off theme park") and had much more in common with the northern tradition of the "singer songwriter," "folk rock" or an idealized notion of "Americana" than Silver Jews ever did. Even in corporate contemporary country, he heard a music with more working-class identification and staying power than much of the indie or "alt" youth culture was capable of. And David was not just trying to bridge two musical genres, but even the rift between the Northern white assimilationist "coastal elite" and the more fly-over rust belt "white working class," in defiance of the Hollywood dominated culture industry.

Within the context of indie rock, *American Water* was hailed for its synthesis of disparate styles; its "creative symbiosis" between David and Steve, who had come to represent mythic opposites in their approaches to music. Malkmus' music (especially in Pavement) was much more Dionysian; its power was in its physicality, its non-verbal (or trans-verbal) aspects. Steve was much closer to "free jazz," at least for a white boy. If David Berman was a singer/songwriter (or as

[66] And this is even more true in the 21st century—at least in the white scene-- hell, I know many indie musicians who are downright nostalgic for the days when you could make 'minimum wage.'
[67] "Not Mad About You: Interview with David Berman," Amy!Sohn; New York Press Oct. 14-20,(1998). And, in 2002, David called me from Nashville in a manic-mood, telling me he was working on a post-9/11 song called "Is It Okay To Hate New York Again?" He never did release-or finish-that, but that line appears in one of his prose poems in the Believer.

he liked to put it, "a significance provider"), Steve Malkmus was a *musician*. If David was the classic introvert, Steve was the classic extrovert. Not long after they began collaborating a decade earlier, it became clear that no single band could contain these distinct sensibilities, but it was magic when they could work together harmoniously.

American Water became an instant classic, establishing Silver Jews as a "full-fledged contender for the indie throne" (Pitchfork) as Pavement, who had been hailed as the best band of the 1990s by the likes of Robert Christgau, was falling off it. Yet David was not interested in occupying this "throne," especially if that meant touring and pimping. He didn't tour. For him, touring seemed a barren, self-indulgent activity, unless you could "really bring the music alive in a way you weren't on the record." Pavement, through their improvisations, could do that, yet Silver Jews' music came much more alive on college radio. It was through this medium that many fellow introverts first became aware of Berman's lyric depth. There is a communal intimacy to this one-on-one connection that transcends the spectacle of the live 'singer' songwriter' show (I personally would rather just stay home to listen to music that makes me cry; if I'm going out I want to, er, rock). In this sense, David's refusal to tour actually did more to increase the appreciation for the kind of songs he wrote; and, in the process, he turned many musicians onto poetry.

I came to *American Water* from a different angle, through the *back door* of poetry. So, while Pitchfork raves that *American Water* reclaims the word "poetry" as part of the "musical vocabulary," for me it reclaimed the word *music* as part of the poetic vocabulary (the kind of music that can only be real if performed collaboratively, even if only for the sake of recording, not mere *phanopiea*). The irony is that since I couldn't afford to form a band to create "low art," I devoted myself to the "high art" of poetry, for which I could get grants and loans. From this perspective, *American Water* was a porthole back into the world of "low" art that inspired and fueled me much more than the "high" Euro-centric art world in which I had been consigned. For even though I was more known as a poet at the time than David, he had more faith in the power of words *to* communicate feelings and ideas than I did.

And while Silver Jews fans may love the product, I loved, and learned much, from the *process*. Maybe I can't quite see the product because of the process....and Silver Jews was the first time I realized that being in a band was *possible*.

"You're too smart; you're too good," David tried to tease me out of my Ivory Tower (or was it NYC snobbism), and indeed Silver Jews was a step for me towards a more embodied art, which was just what the doctor ordered at this time since I felt I had become too "mind." As I realized all my friends were literati (and within that mostly poetry people) or academics, I felt I had lost a common language. David and Steve were much more conversant with pop culture, and though some may scorn this band as upper-middle-class Ivy League Broets,[68] the fact that they were into the NFL and the NBA (often with the Nicks game on the big screen while we rehearsed and recorded) helped give me another shared language so I could talk to the non-college-educated proles who ran the Yemeni store on the corner.

I realized later that the Silver Jews and their interest in major league sports also gave me a shared language to talk to my dad now that my mom had died (I sided with my mom when they got divorced). My dad was impressed when I started speaking about football with him on one of our rare conversations; sports, too, can be a useful tool in helping to undo that cultural segregation that J.D. Vance laments. Beyond this, football is generally far less racially segregated than say the poetry scene or academia, or even the music scene (and this is as true in 2017 as it was in 98), even if it comes at the price of gender segregation (white men and black men may often bond on locker rooms concerning women), but furthermore a rock band (even if the Silver Jews at the time was a "men's only" club) is more like what's good about a *team* than the literary world is. There's a cooperative formality I craved as much as the beautiful formality of David's songs.

In the studio, we each had a clearer role: Malkmus was the best lead guitarist in the room, Mike Fellows (ex-Rites of Spring) the best bassist, etc. The question is how to work together. At one point David compared himself (as singer-songwriter) to a quarterback and Steve Malkmus (as a wide-receiver) and I thought, at the group huddle at the wrap party, wondering whether I was a tight end or a place kicker, if only I can help bring some of this collaborative energy into the poetry world (Emily Dickinson bunts to first, while Laura (Riding) Jackson steals home?). In the meantime, have you ever felt like a player on a team that just won the superbowl, but still feel mad at yourself for not sacking the other team's quarterback just before he threw that game tying touchdown that could've cost you the game had their kicker not missed the extra point? Well, I just did.

I know I shouldn't be too harsh on myself, but....

I'm proud to be part of *American Water*,[69] but when I hear the tinkling meandering shapeless keyboard playing on "We Are Real,"(which at the time was called "Up The Hill"), I can't but look at it without a feeling of regret that I could've made it better, and have no one to blame for not doing so but myself...

Many were calling Steve Malkmus the best indie rock guitarist of the 90s. He certainly created music that helped get me through the all-nighters when I was working on my dissertation, as I'd take a stretch break and dance around my

---

[68] http://chrisstroffolino.blogspot.com/2013/10/how-we-devalue-poetry-long-essay.html
[69] 20 years after it's been released, it still appears on many "Top Ten Indie Rock Albums of The 90s" lists, and Scott Timberg and others have written that they wouldn't change a note.

bedroom when I had reached writer's block from sitting so damn long that it was like "there's a permanent crease in my right and wrong," (Sly Stone). And now, as he shook my hand and introduced himself, I felt in awe, and humbled. I mean, here I fancied myself a culture worker, a cultural producer, laboring for 4 years in the academic coalmine on a dissertation to be read by 3 older people while Steve was touring the globe, and David had put out one of the best song-cycle albums of the 90s, 1996's *The Natural Bridge*.

And though I was moving too fast, and too embodied, for some poets and academics (Charles Bernstein called me "exasperating"), compared to these two tall, Ivy-League professional musicians, I felt kinda like a hibernating animal emerging from her cave covering her eyes adjusting to the sun of music. It wasn't that I didn't dream of someday doing more music, but (in poet time) I was still young, and figured it would happen gradually (even if I was older in music time). Compared to Steve especially, I felt somewhat stiff, and with bassist Mike Fellows in the band (who had played with pre-Fugazi band Rites Of Spring), it was clear that it would take some time to get my mojo back and get back in the same shape I was when I moshed to his band a decade earlier.

In his art, Steve had kept the music part alive that I'd coated with the "refinery smoke" of words, and his guitar was like an extension of his body! He could tell I was a little starstruck, but did a damn good job of just being a regular guy, to equalize things, and was impressed by my book *Light As A Fetter*, which Ashbery had blurbed, and wanted me to introduce him to Ashbery (it would be great to watch them talk). He even flattered me, "you're the best indie rock keyboardist I ever played with," only to add quickly when he saw it going to my head, "now don't get cocky!"

Unlike the other musicians on *American Water*, I had never really been in a band before, much less in the process of recording an album (Tim Barnes, the drummer, was a no-nonsense session pro). It felt like I was missing a few necessary steps, like a baptism by fire, and I became acutely aware of my own bulky slowness, that I was one of those guys who can't just jump into what extroverts call action. I need time to scope out a situation, and the slower poetry world makes ample room for it, but in music, especially in recording, time is money.

We only had one week of rehearsal before we recorded a definitive object (which at the time was going to be called *The Late Great Silver Jews*) and I had to miss some rehearsals because of my job teaching creative writing at Rutgers. Dave and Steve were cool with that, but, in retrospect, I should've found a substitute teacher. For not only did my job prevent me from spending time in the rehearsal studio helping to develop a sound (which takes a little longer than just learning the chords), but it also took time away from the clubbing, or bar-hopping with those guys (who at the time were certainly living the rock and roll lifestyle, staying up to 6 or 7AM). For yes, I believe that bands can develop a better sound when they feel comfortable with each other, as the line between play and work blurs, but, no, I chose the fuckin' day job.

Despite all the hype about David and Steve's volatile relationship (many have told me they thought David was referring to himself and Steve when he asked, "why can't monsters get along with other monsters?"), they seemed to be getting along swimmingly when rehearsals began, like co-conspirators, and a general spirit of *productive fun* characterized the rehearsals. During rehearsals, sometimes a song like "Send in The Clowns" would get much louder and much faster than the way it appeared on the album, and the 3 chord "coda" to Blue Arrangement (which Steve wrote) would turn into a 10-minute jam in which Steve would unleash his Pavement side that he mostly kept in check with David during these sessions. Perhaps the high point, for me, was getting to trade rhythm (chords) and leads, back and forth with Steve during these jams, and even start to lock in with Mike (who was also playing restrained).

Obviously, we weren't really a jam or groove band, but even though time was money and we had a product to do, it was in those rare moments when the band indulged itself that we slowly honed a sound. We had more than enough tunes for the album, but time had been budgeted[70] to work on this half-finished groove song. Its working title was "The Lou Reed Song." "We got 20 minutes left, remember to leave some time for 'The Lou Reed Song.'" Steve lead the band in alternating two chord grooves--major to minor, major to major—a rudimentary verse chorus structure as he strummed a lazy, half-distracted Pavement riff, and started free-styling lyrics with that half-mellow crooner, half NYC street smart snarl of his. The words are largely inaudible, though Steve had "dummy lyrics" for the chorus: "(No One Loves Me) Half As Much As I Love You" (perhaps he was thinking of the Hank Williams song).

Apparently, Steve and David had pre-arranged that Steve's role was to create a comfortable sonic bed with the snarly NYC white funky groove so David would be free to sit back, feel the sound and song, and make up "Coney Island Baby"-esque lyrics on the spot, to see if any sparks fly while the cassette is running. Although Steve didn't bother to tell us the chords until Fellows asked him after a 6 minute jam, we had ample room to work on a sound and get a little tighter given the rushed circumstances. My fingers were enjoying their liberation from the tighter structures of the more finished songs... as Steve sang lyrics like "trigger trigger trigger come round again" or "ever ever never" or "I'm from Georgia tech" and "tryin' to get you again."

The second Steve stopped singing and left the melodic space open for his guitar to assert itself, my fingers, like the horse finally freed from the carriage of the marriage of true minds and David's tight song structures, took the perceived space and ran with it, usurping Phoebe's cart of the rhythm section, from Icharus Steve--and inched the groove toward the kind of funk that approaches what I don't like about Led Zeppelin's attempt to do Billy Preston or Stevie Wonder to a Doobie Brothers melody on my least favorite song on *Physical Graffiti*, eventually the playing got louder and faster and I caught myself what could be called wanking (maybe dangerously approaching everything I hate about Wakeman and Emerson, even on a little Casio), and while Steve indulged it as we traded off leads, I could tell David was getting more and more agitated. And I wondered if he was agitated at me for indulging Steve's more Dionysian style, and not fully appreciating what my role was. A rookie mistake.[71]

Steve was focusing more of his attention on David. On the tape, barely audible beneath my wanking, I could hear Smith (SM) tell Jones (DCB), "Alright, you got a song written?" Jones: "What do you mean?" Smith: "I wanna hear your voice..." Jones: "Don't worry---I got it." The song never did get finished. It does seem more like a "Steve" way of writing lyrics than a "David" way, but it was clear tensions between them were rising. Maybe I wasn't hired, like Billy Preston, to help smooth over tensions between David and Steve, but I certainly wasn't making it any better.

One night we were crammed in the back of a station wagon on the way to a bar after leaving another bar after finishing mixing sessions for the day. Out of nowhere, Steve and David were doing the drunken dozens wrestling each other and arguing over who's a better songwriter; I remember David saying, "Steve, your solos on my records are better than on yours. Pavement songs are antisongs and your solos are antisolos." (at the time I wrote, "He means it and doesn't mean it). I forget what Steve said. It seemed so obvious to me, I couldn't believe Steve would be offended by that. Besides, I loved many of Steve's "anti-songs" even if his lyrics were never as weighed down with empathy for human suffering as David's were. I thought, surely, they're just kidding around, but, nah.... *American Water* may have been an end for them, but it felt like a beginning to me.

Still, I felt I let David down. Oh, how stupid I was! Impatient! Non-professional! Bulky slow, thick, or, in terms of a (Freudian) psychomachia, I was appealing to Steve's "Id" (or his kid) when I was supposed to be the quiet poet shy superego to David's ego. So, forgive me, David, if I was more excited to work with Steven. In the long term, our long distance correspondence these last 20 years has meant much more to me, but, yes, at the time, I was learning more from Steve, as the two of us worked on coming up with just the right amount of reverb for my riff on "The Wild Kindness" or as he goaded me to dig up my trumpet for the first time in a decade to play that wounded, out of tune, melodic riff on "Random Rules" (Out of tune trumpet was in fashion that year in indie-rock, thanks to *Neutral Milk Hotel*).

---

[71] https://www.youtube.com/watch?v=xFjFk-ieCYA

And Steve taught me some valuable lessons
of how to step back as a keyboardist.
"When I play keys on my stuff, I try to think like a drummer."
To make the shift away from the one-man band
To let the rhythm guitar take care of the chords,
Double the bass, play octaves
And simple fifths---help create space
And weave in and out with the lead
As a kind of call and response.
By the time I understood these lessons
My 2 weeks with Steve were up
But they stayed with me
Awaiting another 2 chord jam
Or even better 1 chord with Sonic Boom
And Barrett and I got closer
Though unrecorded so far…..

I also found myself siding with Steve over David in wanting to play at least one live show in NYC before they left, but David refused. Nonetheless, with the experience and (undeserved, inmho) clout I got from playing with them, many other opportunities opened. It certainly created a wider aesthetic/ethical space to navigate, and opened up my aesthetic repertoire. At the wrap party, Dean Wareham (Galaxie 500, Luna) and I exchanged numbers and said he could use some keyboards. Brett Ralph (Malignant Growth, and Rising Shotgun) flew me to Chicago to record at Steve Albini's amazing Electrical Audio studio. By the time I had begun working with Greg Ashley in 2006, I had even come to prefer to work in the "confines" of the studio over the live experience (though being a cripple may have also played a part).

By the time *American Water* was released, they were long gone from NYC; Steve back to Portland, and David to Louisville where he'd meet Cassie Berman, and the rest (they say) is history. They, it must be remembered, hated NYC. I didn't, and there was certainly enough going on in NYC to keep me busy.

So did working with the Silver Jews make me reconsider the relationship between music and words? Not right away. As I listened to American Water, and what people were saying about it, I wondered if I should finally start trying to go through those old cassettes of my melodies with "dummy lyrics" from the 80s and early 90s, and try to put words to them, but I knew my poetic training, and positive external reinforcement, had not only not prepared me for the more three-dimensional art of songwriting in which words have more (or at least different) weight, but even put me at a disadvantage compared to a lyricist who had never studied poetry (at the risk of sounding like Jack Spicer crying, "my vocabulary did this to me." I don't blame my vocabulary, and if I find the right musicians, I bet we could have a dance smash called "Phallogocentrism" or such).

I fought with my oversophisticated training. *Don't think of it as dumbing down your poetry.* Trying to put "poetic" words to melodies made me realize how great David's are by comparison. It confirmed my youthful suspicion that I'm not really a songwriter; I could perhaps be great as part of a songwriting *tandem*, in which I'd be more involved in melodies (which many were saying was my strong suit), and someone else is the primary lyricist, though. Or perhaps I could be one of the guys in the band who gets one or two songs per album, but I just can't see myself as the "self-contained" singer/songwriter. Perhaps because I don't want to have to play that role live, but also because I may not believe in the power of the song, certainly as much David did. I felt that the band had to come first, and *then* the song.

I thought back to being 17, before I had learned the "specialized differences" between what's called "poetry" and what's called "lyrics," but that seemed as distant as the Ur-Continent of Pangea. It would take years to get that 'innocence' back, if I even wanted or needed it. But if I couldn't or wouldn't create songs as a bridge between music and words like David, perhaps at least I could shuttle (or swim) back and forth between the (social) shores, and I remembered there are other ways to bring music and words together. The way Amiri Baraka did this seemed a little closer to my abilities and/or needs.

"Some Of My Friends Love Le Roi Jones, But...."

Baraka, more than anyone else alive in America, it seemed, was able to restore and recreate what Clayton Eshelman of *Sulfur* Magazine called "The Whole Art," re-established bridges with the genres that had once been part of poetry but had been orphaned; narrative and plays were once poetry; same with religion and science and cultural criticism, to say nothing of music and dance.[72] And, whether or not you want to call Baraka a "conceptual artist," I have to acknowledge that he was as good as a talker (and in my experience listener) as he was a writer. Many times, I've seen him turn his "poetry readings" into conversations with hecklers (such as Sparrow), and be willing to risk spontaneity of trial and error in engaging his audience by thinking out loud. If he caught himself overspeaking or not making his point clear, he'd write an essay or poem or play, or all three, inspired by the experience.

Baraka was enough of a "student of Pound" to begin his first book with the line, "nobody sings anymore" and to know that poetry atrophies if it gets too far away from music, but he also knew there's a thin line between Pound's preference for

---

[72] In this sense, as I think folks like Pierre Joris understood, the most cutting edge installation performance art is, in fact, the most traditional poetry; this was the hope of many a modernist or post-modernist in his Poems For The Millennium Anthology, which I helped out on.

"the musical phrase" over "the metronome" and Goebbels' notorious Nazi Music Regulations that would not only ban Silver Jews for being "too Jewish and gloomy," but also staccato and "negroid excess in tempo."

Baraka was known as a poet and author before he began incorporating music into his performances, and you can read much of his early poetry as a lament for the literary world's alienation from music, specifically black music. He knew Robert Duncan may not have realized the double-meaning of the "process" he spoke about (just as I don't get the double and triple meanings in some of today's hip hop, without an aid like Jay-Z's *Decoded*), and he could also use his writing to catch the ear of many of his favorite musicians so they'd want to collaborate with him.[73]

And since I first saw him perform with David Murray back at in Philly until the last time I saw him at the Eastside Art Alliance in Oakland, Baraka's combination of spoken word with jazz, and sometimes funk, brought words and music together without necessarily having to *rely* on the Euro-centric notion of the song. And while David Berman, and Silver Jews were able to recreate that "living room vibe" through their recordings, Baraka (in his late 60s at the time), and his wife Amina, would open up the basement of his Newark home for monthly events, events which often spilled upward into the first floor of his house, especially if Amina had cooked, say, a thanksgiving meal.

Though they went unheralded by the mainstream white press,[74] these events are some of Baraka's greatest achievements. I witnessed Baraka come closest to unleashing his full repertoire of what could be called "performance art," as he and his wife combined the role of gracious host, nightclub MC, "Spoken-word" poet, often in conjunction with—as opposed to "accompanied by"—a musical ensemble, teacher (history, philosophy, etc), even preacher, and political activist presiding over organizational meetings with as much social acumen as he exhibited at the 1972 Gary Conference, and I'm sure I'm missing some roles. Perhaps most importantly, he listened and he dialogued.

---

[73] Have you ever read Baraka's early book Blues People? Even though it's a people's history through music, would you call me crazy if I told you that it's probably my favorite book of poetics? That what he says about music tells you more about what his aspirations for poetry than what he says when he's talking about poetry? I mean, if you're going to call the silent sound of words on the page music, wouldn't it be fair and balanced to call Blues People an epic poem? And, no, despite what some white historians say, The Black Arts Movement did not "branch off" from the "(white) Beats. Baraka's art is not just the "raw" side? What can be more "cooked" than the merger of high jazz and language (I was privileged enough to hear him perform from his lyric epic Whys/Wise).

[74] Most of the mainstream press's obituaries when he died were racist: http://chrisstroffolino.blogspot.com/2014/06/amiri-baraka-legacy-beyond-racist.html

Notes To A Sideman Manifesto

I didn't have a basement, so had to put in a file called "maybe someday" such dreams of hosting events like these in lieu of a traditional poetry reading, but I envisioned myself in a musical situation that could include both the Baraka way and the Silver Jews way of combining music and words, and perhaps I got it backwards if I felt I had to find the *musicians* first, and once I found them, *then* write songs. We could write them from the bottom up, from jams, collaboratively, even if we end up being the kind of band that DCB scorns who doesn't care about the words, or to paraphrase a poem from around that time, "if I have to err on one side, I usually prefer a song with great sounds over a song with great words and lousy sounds."

So, just because I'm known as a poet doesn't mean I have to be a songwriter to make music. The poets don't have to care about my music, and the musicians don't have to care about my words. I can be a sideman, just like David's band was called a "side project." I can back the songwriter (as with David), but also be a part of large instrumental ensemble like Wharton Tiers put together. I can stand as a kind of backup vocalist who sings *phonemes!* And sure, I'd be a *sideshow* and liked being a sideman in poetry too; and, yes, a creative writing workshop can be more like the band-like collaboration than the standard poetry reading.

In the meantime, I could use the money made from working on *American Water* to buy an Alesis Keyboard to join another "indie rock" band (who were friends of Greg Fuchs) that, in many ways, were the polar opposite of the Silver Jews. While SJ were primarily a studio recording project, Volumen wasn't so concerned or interested in recording (though we recorded a demo with Wharton Tiers), but the more visceral and transient pleasures of the live event (and even though no 90s indie rock legends were in this band, the New York name droppers might appreciate that the bassist, Fritz Chesnut, also a great painter, married Molly Shannon). We, or at least I, move by contrasts….

The imperative is more to get catharsis through dancing than thinking (so as not to cry) or crying (so as not to think), and Rocky Yazzie, the singer of Sweatlodge, reminds some people of The Minutemen's d. Boon, as he sings "Let's Get Dirty," repeatedly, each one getting louder, and he asks the band and the audience to join in, and many do, and the band walks into the audience like a 21st century retro grunge second line….Rocky grew up on a Navajo reservation closer to earth (or what some would deride as "dirt") than most contemporary Americans after the 20th century decline in the rural population of America from 40% in 1900 to 2% in 2000, which hardly any pundit brings up a source of today's economic and cultural crisis…and if he could settle down, then he would settle down….

In retrospect, my dabbles with music in NYC (despite the hype of being associated with *American Water*) seem "small potatoes," tentative firsts, baby steps in a shallow pool, even though I was in my 30s, which, given the ageism that infects the music industry scene more than the poetry world, was a little too late for some. As Bryan Ferry said, "the poet may slow it," like I was still waiting for someone, or something, to give me permission. But at the time, I'm sure I felt something like "for poets, the musical bar is set rather low." I mean, look at (listen to) Ginsberg's music. Even people who think Dylan can sing, know Ginsberg can't, etc. And the poet who did music could be kind of like a novelty, like the "talking snake" (if a snake can talk, it doesn't matter what he says).

Quite a few found the 'novelty' charming, or even cute, and I was more than willing to play that role when the Fence women (Caroline and Rebecca), who had managed to land gigs at the Poetry Society of America, and promised to liberate it from its stuffier previous regimes, put together an Anne Sexton tribute, and asked me to put together a recreation of her rock band at an event at Cooper Union, and even had a budget that would allow me to pay musicians for this one-time ad-hoc gig.

Wow! I didn't even know that Anne Sexton had a rock band! And, damn, at the time (before the internet), it took a lot of muckraking to find tapes of the recording. Caroline and I had to take a train to the Yale library in New Haven where they had, under lock a key, a reel-to-reel tape of some of their recordings, which they wouldn't let me make copies of, but eventually we tracked down a cassette from the member of the original band (sure, today, Youtube would make it easy, but I had great conversations with Caroline on those long train rides, and wouldn't trade it for all the Tech in Oakland!).

This band had some "hippie" qualities (Anne Sexton called it "chamber rock"), with Farfisa keyboard and flute, especially on the kinda funky "Woman With Girdle," and I was psyched about being able to popularize it to those who, say, loved Patti Smith (Sexton did it years before Patti Smith and I wouldn't be surprised if she knew of it) but didn't care for Sexton. Sexton also seemed to do this before Ginsberg really made his musical forays a matter of the public record. And all this made me re-evaluate her as a poet.[75]

It was my first experience as a "band organizer" (if not necessarily leader) This too allowed me to "hide" behind someone else's words, and because a woman played the role of Anne Sexton, I didn't even have to sing the words. The band also included Sasha Bell from Essex Green and Ladybug Transistor on flute, Angus Forbes on drums, and Shawn Vandor on guitar. I guess you could call it a small chapter in my (stunted) life-long journey to bring these two specialized genres together in a way a place like Naropa respected (I also dug Anne Waldman's new-wave inflected "Uh Oh Plutonian")? Another step toward embodiment, or "the whole art."

[75] https://www.youtube.com/watch?v=8O33wdQnN7Y

We got to share the stage with Eileen Myles! Eileen always seemed way hipper than Sexton, but also was way hipper than most "avant-garde" poets who would snub or disclaim any interest in or influence by, Sexton, and many of the old Sexton fans in the audience (who maybe could go for Sharon Olds as the "next generation") sure acted like *we* were being disrespectful to Sexton. They didn't want to admit that Sexton herself had put this rock band together. Their scorn and embarrassment at our rather faithful renditions of Sexton's band felt very much akin to my dad's family's embarrassment at the fact that his mother had been a mail-order bride and was basically living off of the money she had made running a number's racket in the Italian ghetto of Reading in the 1930s—things I took great pride in.

Alice Quinn was noticeably uncomfortable that the rock band was going to play, and probably never would have invited us to play at this event had it not already been set up by the previous PSA regime (The Fence women), and she felt she had to honor it. Because of this she told us that we were going to play at the end of the event *while people were filing out*. We thought this was unfair, and K and I went to talk to her about it. Yet, sure enough, Quinn got up in the middle of our second number (we were going to perform 5), and in the middle of the song interrupted K and told people they could leave. It was kind of comical, and at least I had the satisfaction that rock and roll (which many critics were calling dead even as The Hives and White Stripes were winning over teens and twenty somethings) can still *shock*. So, yeah, in the final analysis, the Anne Sexton night was a success.

All this was happening while my "stock" was rising in the poetry world (and, by poetry world standards, rather rapidly) so by 2001, I earned a NYFA grant, thanks in part to David Henderson, who wrote my favorite Jimi Hendrix biography, which reads like a 20th Century epic. I could hire an accountant and write almost everything off as a "freelance writer, teacher, musician" (shout out to Howie Seligman). I got to read my poetry on New York's Pacifica radio station, as well as a Lower East Side Pirate station. I was at the "top of my game" as it were (sure, I was poor, but there wasn't as much of social stigma against it in the art scenes, and "a life of genteel poverty was still possible!"). Riding high, perhaps too high, as if my balloon (or New York Bubble) would have to burst (like I wish the tech economy would).

Oh, and I finally begrudgingly came around to getting a CD player in 2001 just as they were launching the iPod.

I was offered a gig as a "Visiting Distinguished Poet In Residence" at a college 3000 miles away. Of course, I'm doing it. While this meant I would have to leave NYC, I had perhaps drunk enough of the "NYC-centric" kool aid to believe "if I can make it there, I can make it anywhere." It was a only a one-year gig. I certainly wasn't running away from, or turning my back on, New York City. There was a good chance I'd be back.

I remember saying goodbye to Anselm Berrigan as we sat on a bench in McCarren Park, and he told me that one thing he learned from seeing his parents (Ted Berrigan, Alice Notley and, later Douglas Oliver) struggle economically when he was growing up was that when you get a gig like the one I had just got to live cheaply, and try to save as much money as you can, because it may not last. I appreciated the straight talk, but it's a bitter sweet sendoff because I realized that thrift dictated that I wouldn't be flying back to visit. Still, I held out some hope that I could find something in California at least as vital as the professional social life I found in NYC in the 90s, or even Philly in the 80s, even if I needed a car. Hell, maybe I'd get to fly Anselm out for a reading…[76] If nothing else, at least I had a job that could start making a dent in the student loans, and finally get to see a real dentist after years of neglect.

MINING THE FAULTLINE: Oakland in the 21st Century Technocracy

Moving from NYC to California coincided with the 9/11 attacks and the collapse of the World Trade Center. This intersection of public history and personal history complicates any comparison I could offer between NYC and the Bay Area, because I'm also comparing pre- 9/11 America and post 9/11 America, and even though I had left NYC a month before the attacks, I felt the mass hysteria. My closest friends were in NYC. Had I not left, it's also possible I could've died (I often transferred from the Subway to the Path Train for my Creative Writing classes at Rutgers—New Brunswick on Tuesday mornings). My girlfriend was still there! I couldn't get through to her. She lived 20 blocks away, choking on the smoke of smouldering metal, and, yes, she was severely traumatized. And though we had decided to try out a long-distance relationship until either I'd move back, or be rehired for a second a year, the trauma of 9/11 put helped make the distance between us grow.

I was severely torn about what to do. My job was to start again in this strange new place if I had any hope of my contract being extended so she could move here too, but now I just wanted to be back in NYC with all my other friends. Yet I knew that this job, which almost seemed to be too good to be true, would require total devotion and would in effect subsume my artistic career as a poet (and burgeoning musician), if not exactly put it on hold, since publishing poetry is part of the job.

It seemed the country was going through a collective protracted mourning the entire fall, and Bush was promoting Islamophobia (as a Muslim friend—well, student-- put it, before 2001 we were considered a religion; after 9/11 we were considered a race) as well as consumerism, and a climate of increased distrust

---

[76] It's been 16 years, and I've only been back once….when Anselm flew me back, even though I never did get to fly him here……Still, maybe next summer I can do the 3 month sublet residency…

of strangers, of *any* stranger. I felt people became more closed in, but, again, my perceptions about what was changing about American culture may be biased, may be colored by the fact that I was also dealing with my own little personal culture shock, a culture shock that may have happened even had 9/11 never had happened—the move from NYC to the Bay Area.

When I first started teaching, one of my students, Nate Mohatt, who had moved to California from Alaska also expressed his culture shock: Oakland was *too loud* and *too fast* for him; but, for me, it was *too quiet* and *too slow*. And, indeed, from the perspective of a fast-talking New Yorker, who thrived in the more immediate walking city that "never slept," it was easy to feel that the Californians (or at least the white Bay Aryans, as one of the black elders at the Y would comically put it a few years later) were colder than the NYC (and Philly) people. Berkeley, for instance, may be known as the left coast, but it's socially much more conservative; ask any young musician who has had to struggle with its "no fun laws"

The New York Snobs say people are slower, and less edgy in their art because the California sun makes them kinda lazy, but I could see both sides. "It was easier to *sell* my art in NYC, but it's easier to *make* my art in Oakland." In NYC, hardly anyone minded if you had mastered the art of being able to talk and listen at the same time, coz they were doing it themselves; in the bay, however, it was rude and called "talking over someone." You don't know how many times I heard people say, "you're from New York?" in that kind of smug way that I suppose passes for politeness……

For awhile, I couldn't figure out just why rents were so expensive in the Bay Area (even in 2001, before the current record inflation). After all, the Bay Area does not provide nearly as many cultural opportunities as NYC did. Then someone told me, "in NYC you pay for culture, in the Bay Area you pay for the weather," and I certainly felt like a slave to the weather.

It's not just a temperamental and cultural difference between these coasts, and I must admit I loved, and quickly adjusted to, the climactic difference (and I didn't really miss the filth and humidity), rejecting the extremes of the NYC kind of moderation where "mood swings" are more permissible (and even rewarded, even as an adult, as long as it's theatrical) for this more moderate Mediterranean climate which, I'm told, is more like the Italian climate of Napoli (Naples) which my Italian grandmother had left to come to America as a mail order bride.

And though it runs the risk of a kind of essentialism, like the various historical transformations Aristotle's "climate theory" had to go through when the enslaving class moved northward and westward from Greece, first toward France and England, and then to Philadelphia (city of brotherly love)[77], 16 years of living in the Bay Area have still not refuted the theory that the cultural differences

---

[77] Or the way it was brilliantly turned on its head by CUNY Professor Jeffers….

between NYC and the Bay Area may be rooted in the climate (or you could call it the landscape, however artificial it is in both cities).

To sum it up: Bay Area (white) people may be less effusive, publicly moody, or seem nicer and more polite, more moderate and temperate just like the climate (of course the increasing role of prescriptions of legal mood stabilizers in both the Bay Area and NYC during this time may also contribute to this 'social norm'), but bubbling underneath this moderate climactic surface is the inexorable fact of landscape—it rests on a faultline! Civilization itself, as we know it, could be a house of cards. The violent forces of nature (to say nothing of "Radical Islamic Terrorism"), like the Freudian Bernaysian uncontrollable ID could be unleashed, destroying our way of life!

The Ohlone people certainly knew that building such a civilization as we ('the white man") has on this faultline land would come back and bite us. Their culture was much more in harmony with nature, and could bounce back from the necessary earthquakes (and even thank the faultline for its gift of uprooted fertile soil for next year's harvest). Am I just projecting my own post 9/11 hysteria on this situation? Still, the faultline kinda put Bin Laden in perspective, and I started working on a "lyric epic" called "My Friend The Faultline."

Like the faultline, the moderate Bay Aryans could explode and, in my experience, more violently than was more common among New Yorkers and Philadelphians, where people were generally more candid about their "negative emotions" often from jump, the get go. But here, I felt some of that NIMBY ("Not-in-my-backyard") kind of racism, like the kind Martin Luther King criticized in "Letter From Birmingham Jail," or the assimilationist "political foxes" Malcolm compared and contrasted to the southern segregationist "political wolf." And, after the bombing began in Afghanistan, Berkeley passed a symbolic resolution against the war, but if they really wanted to do something about it, they'd have more effect if they passed a resolution against *the car!*).

I was definitely alienated by CAR-ifornia. For the first time in my life, I needed a car, and for a bicyclist and runner, this was alienating, not just physically (I had to adjust to my confused body wondering why it's moving when it's not exerting itself), but also socially and culturally. Ever wonder why cars got fatter and more armed like SUVS at exactly the same time of the obesity epidemic. The car, perhaps, once symbolized a kind of freedom, and even a kind of shelter, but it could also symbolize a disembodiment and lack of immediacy (psychic traffic jams on the "Expressway to your Heart" with a nod to Gamble and Huff). I thought back to the much hyped east coast/ west coast battle beef in hip hop, but I sided with the east coast largely because it had faster—walking with a boombox-- beats than slower Dr. Dre cruising in a car beat, and I felt this culture shock even more among the white Bay Ayrians.

California's car based culture certainly affected social life. Since the subways (such as they are) stopped at midnight, many night life venues went out of business, or you'd see a lot of cars zigzagging on the Bay bridge at 2AM, and buzzed driving is drunk driving. Unlike NYC, or even Philly, one couldn't get buzzed and drunkenly sing songs to walk (or subway) home. Indeed, there was a kind of de facto curfew as well as de jure one. And perhaps NYC is the only city in America (aside from New Orleans) that doesn't sleep, but Oakland, years before I came here, according to ex-Black Panther Judy Juanita (*Virgin Soul, De-Facto Feminism*), and many others I've spoken to had a vibrant nightlife 50 years ago (when Laney, Merritt, and even SF State were basically free).

I could never figure out why Bay Area culture is so anti-night life. Someone said, "they're punishing Oakland for the Panthers," and I wondered if the fact that the Bay Area (as historically a colony of New York City disguised as Washington) just developed a culture of having to get up earlier because it had to do business with NYC. 9Am here is 12 there. This arrangement was great when I lived in NYC. I could call someone at midnight and it'd only be 9PM for them, but once in Oakland, I'd have to call east coast people at 6 to reach them before 9. Bay Aryans are also surprised when I tell them I ate better in NYC than in Oakland. For better or worse, I prefer what I'm told is a more European style of eating. Little or no breakfast, but a big meal later in the night, and since I was often a Noon to 3Am schedule in NYC (and, no, that doesn't mean that I didn't have like 3 or 4 jobs), I tended to eat after midnight, and in NYC one could always find many tasty vegetarian healthy food after midnight than ever in the Bay Area, where most of the healthy options are closed by 9, or more likely 6 or 7….

Another difference was the way people dressed. In NYC, more people dressed up; here more people dressed down or "casual" (some professors wore shorts and sandals when they taught). In short, even though I loved the Bay Area weather, I could never quite beat out my longing for NYC or Philly culturally… These differences were not just individual or temperamental, but structural and institutional (as a result of "urban planning").

Despite these culture shocks, I knew I'd feel more at home in Oakland than in the more expensive Berkeley and Frisco (and not just because it's cheaper; after all, water used to be cheaper than soda, but it also quenched my thirst more), but in part because it was still predominantly a "chocolate city" (if a little less than in the days of the Black Panthers), and had a warmer culture than the other two. What saves Oakland from my contempt for Frisco and Berkeley is the black community, or, if it's patronizing to say black community as if it's a monolith, a bunch of scattered (or even united) black people I know, who I felt more temperamentally aligned with, and who have more in common with much of what I missed in NYC and Philly….

As a New York Snob in exile, I had to laugh-cry at San Francisco's arrogance, "No, Frisco, you are not Manhattan. Screw your analogy. Brooklyn is bigger, and has more vibrant culture than you." I could invoke the God of dialectics and seeming opposites so that NYC and Oakland can unite against Frisco! But surely there's a better common enemy to rouse the fire of the harried Oakland proletariat into a sense of civic pride that would make Occupy Oakland look, in comparison, like the picnic it pretended not to be. Oakland can try to push back against Friscofication (or Silicon Valleyification), but Frisco's too busy comparing itself to LA, or NYC. It's not a fair comparison. LA is bigger than Frisco and Oakland combined (and Berkeley and Richmond. You could probably even throw in San Jose for good measure), so you can say LA has got its Oakland part. Its Richmond part, etc).[78] And as a New York snob in exile (though it was easy to root for the Oakland A's over the Yankees, it took a little longer to start rooting for The Raiders more than the Jets they defeated in the playoffs), I also had to laugh at the much hyped rivalry between San Francisco and LA. Over and over again, I hear the North scoff: "LA is *Silicone* valley." Plastic abs. Dyed Blonde, dumber, more gangsta, less moral, more conservative or such. South, by contrast, sees Bay Aryan white puritan smug smirk streak, "no fun laws," political liberalism masking cultural conservatism. I, as NYC, perhaps still held contempt for both, at least enough not to share many of the Bay Aryans' feeling of superiority over LA.[79]

As I saw it, NYC was once the business capital, the art-world capital, the entertainment world capital, to name but three. This coincided with when it had 3 teams the Yankees, The Giants, and (if you consider Brooklyn to be a part of NYC as Oakland is part of Frisco), The Dodgers. But, as California settled, The Giants and the Beatnik poets went to Northern California, while the Dodgers and TV and Music Industry set up shop in Los Angeles. Hence, the split (which the later rivalry between Hollywood and Silicon Valley would reinforce). Thus, from the perspective of a New Yorker, I saw that much touted SF/LA rivalry, in white culture at least, as overblown, as a battle that occurred *in* NYC. Many Northern Californian (white) people love to scorn the superficial qualities of LA's Hollywood culture, but the New Yorker in me (with its fashion punks and rappers, and Frank O'Hara, Velvet Underground love of glamour) would tend to defend it against the kind of purist (or puritan) sanctimony one can see in aspects of the Robert Duncan vs. the L=A=N=G=U=A=G=E poets, or the suburban punk of Gillman. Neither could equal NYC alone, but if you could combine them, ah!

Now, both LA and SF are places, and can be located on maps, but Hollywood and Silicon Valley cannot be contained by their "host" geographies. The populations

---

[78] There's a debate over whether Anaheim is a part of LA, or Santa Clara a part of San Francisco……

[79] though I'd be more likely to support the Californians who speak of separation from Trumpland if it included separation from Silicon Valley and Hollywood, as much as DC and Wall Street…

may be smaller, but their economy and cultural influence is greater than the Giants winning the World Series 3 out of 5 years. And increasingly San Francisco seems colonized by Silicon Valley (and, together, they colonize Oakland). This point was driven home to me when I still drove into Frisco, circa 2007, and saw, to the right of me, a big billboard advertising the Beatles and, to the right of me, an equally large ad for Yogi Bear. Fearful Symmetry, like abandon all hope ye who enter here in the land of cars that cripple bicyclists.

Yogi Beatles! Watered down remakes---40 years after the original, selling the idea the past is better. No Now Now! And not much here here! Don't buy new local music! Upgrade your classic collection to CD then MP3 (or maybe you can skip the CD phase if you're as far behind as me). What was wrong with cassettes, and video cassettes? The difference between technological progress and social progress; I used to believe in social progress until I realized that mostly it was a thin veil for technological progress that seems like regress to me. Ah, more fodder for the Reagan cowboy nostalgia make America great again. State of the art (more warlike) animated bear and British guys who stole from black American women, but the fine print tells more!

It's Apple Vs. Disney. Hollywood V. Silicon Valley. Los Angeles Angels of Anaheim vs. Palo Alto Giants of Oakland. Two Beasts, two bellies, as they carve up California, America, and even the world economy between them in mock battles, though since, clearly, Silicon Valley is winning this battle (from a 2017 perspective), that it almost makes me feel sorry for, and be nostalgic for the good old days when Hollywood and the major record labels (based in Hollywood) were showing record profits in the 90s and coopting and helping break up local scenes. I say almost, but on a personal level that nostalgia persists....

Still, I tried to assimilate and wear my own little culture shock lightly, as a scientific theory I was testing, and was glad to be proved wrong. After all, whatever pangs of assimilation I had to go through is minor compared to what many of my students from other countries have to go through. I mean, perhaps I just hadn't met the right people yet. It had taken time in Philly and in NYC, and will take time in the Bay Area. Just keep your eyes on the prize, and focus on your job so you can stay... Besides, at the time I told myself I didn't need much of a social life because my job took most of my time....

When I moved the Bay Area, I hoped to put a wider coalition together at least as successfully as I did in Philly, but since I entered the Bay Area, if not exactly "from the upper left hand corner," but as a Distinguished Poet in Residence in an MFA program rather than a complete unknown as in Philly, I knew this would present different challenges.

Being immersed in my job kind of sheltered me a little from the social zeitgeist crumbling around us, and the fact that for many people, it was getting more difficult to survive as an artist. Students could welcome the promise of high-imaginative poetry that marginalized contemporary culture, and I could wear that hat proudly, but even here my students would tell me of the economic difficulties they faced as the loan paybacks were higher now in the 21st century than they were for me in the 20th century, and it seemed that the value of the MFA was even lower than it used to be. The mode of the sublime ingenuous poetry of the leisure classes rather than say working classes began to feel a little like what Obama would call "our nation's ailing infrastructure" or what the advocates of the rising technocracy were deriding as "20th century skills" and I was feeling a little like a town crier, or what some of my friends would call a catastrophist (especially when I published an anti-Bush rant 3 days after 9/11 that scared many 'liberals' away), but I tried to be proactive and practical about it at my job.

The school was not cheap to attend. I taught both undergraduates and graduates, and noticed a demographic split. Many of the undergraduates had contempt for the required English courses, and many were moneyed (one student threatened to have his dad, a big donor to the school, call the dean to protest the fact he received a B, despite his mediocre work and high number of absences---that frankly deserved a lower grade), though there was talk about ways to increase diversity and serve under-served populations. I got especially excited at our deparment meetings when the subject of holding adult learning classes in an abandoned building the school held in Oakland, but that would take a few years....

The graduate creative writing students, by contrast, were not moneyed and were taking out loans to fulfill their passion, and hone their art, to maybe buy a lottery ticket to get a job like mine. I felt I had to find some way for our school to be able to offer more grants, more loans, more work studies, Teaching Assistantships, community service so that their talents wouldn't go to waste and I wouldn't be guilty of helping to fatten bankers at my students' expense! I certainly wasn't going to mimic George W. Bush and say it was their patriotic duty to be a consumer and keep buying grad school.

At the very least, I envisioned starting a magazine as well as a press (and not just use a magazine as a stepping stone for a press) to help my students and create a more inclusive community. In addition, our school really could use more diversity. It wasn't that the other faculty were racist, just the institution (and not just my school)[80]. But, I couldn't quite worry about stuff like that, or push it yet, because I had to make sure I got rehired first, and continue revising and redefining my courses...

---

[80] See Craig Santos Perez, https://craigsantosperez.wordpress.com/2015/10/02/dr-craigs-11-step-program-to-curing-mainly-white-mfa-sickness/

January Term

At several colleges around the country, the month long "intersemester" January term is a perfect opportunity for both teachers and students to stretch out, and spread their wings, beyond the confines of their standard required course load, which, in my case is Shakespeare, Creative Writing, a Great Books class, and the occasional freshman composition, so I'm trying to take full advantage of the school's interdisciplinary shared theme: California. I'm trying to create a well-rounded syllabus for a month-long course based on the recent art and culture of this (Bay Area) geographical region that, if anything, errs on the side of the cautious white moderate, but at least allows for a range of options for budding culture workers, and allows me to learn along with my students since I just recently moved here. The 3 main primary texts I choose are 1) a sophisticated book of Eco-Poetry by Brenda Hillman; 2) a spoken word album by Jello Biafra, and 3) the Black Panther Ten Point Platform, as well as Ishmael Reed's recent book about Oakland.

Although my course is reading and writing centered (rather than centered on community service), I'm putting three different eras in dialogue with each (from 1966 to 2001), and helping to put poetry in dialogue with punk, so called high and so-called low. I may even get a budget to bring Jello Biafra to school since he lives nearby, and runs a record label, and, who knows, maybe we could collaborate (don't hide the selfish motive!). Yes, I see those spoken word albums as poetry as much as Brenda Hillman is even if I never really liked Biafra's singing voice much and, yes, I find Brenda Hillman more fun to be around than Jello, but I can respect him from a distance, for he was/is an activist, and helped create, or at least organize, the (inter)national underground scene of the 80s that supported me and taught me at least as much as a Ph.D. ever did (I may not have made it to 22 without it), whether you call it anarchy or unity in diversity or intercommunalism....

I was just starting to learn the word "intercommunalism" from the Huey Newton reader, so, as a teacher, generally inclined to teach the rhetorical art of analogy in comparison-contrast papers, this month-long course offers ample room for paper topics. You could just write on *Cascadia,* or *No More Cocoons,* or you could get into the "poetry wars" by comparing the two (and figuring out where, if anywhere, you could fit). On the other hand, comparing the 70s/80s (even into the 90s if you really must digress into Gilman) punk scene that Jello "represents" (or is a portal to) to the Panthers who could serve as a synecdoche of to the 60s/70s (and into the 80s) also has many possibilities.

Perhaps comparing *Cascadia* to the Panthers would be less likely to happen. It's probably more ambitious and difficult, but it can get deep into the differences and overlaps between art and activism. Hillman herself is an activist "outside her poetry," but honors a line between them (though it's increasingly included in her poetry), and many of the Panthers were artists and activists. They ran a newspaper and created a revolutionary (if that word can still be positive) school with many pedagogical strategies that I'm convinced would solve much of today's educational crisis if put into practice today.[81]

The Panthers were also an important chapter in Oakland history, all but erased or papered-over in such books as *Oakland: Story of a City*. I certainly wanted to learn about the Panthers, and even though the school was 90% white, many students did too, and what better way to learn about the Panthers than *from* the Panthers. So when I found out that David Hilliard was doing Black Panther Historical tours of Oakland, I knew I had to include it as part of the course.

This was before I knew about The Black House, Marvin X, and the Black Arts Movement-West. Obviously, teaching is the common ground between Panthers, Hillman and Biafra, but of the 3, it was the Panthers who went furthest into community service, a mission our school held sacred, even if the man who founded the school for poor starving children in aristocratic 18th century France would perhaps be rolling over in his grave if he knew how expensive and prohibitory the tuition is, and how much money they spent on the bronze statue of him in the school's entranceway (and many professors joked about it in asides, not that we could do anything about it now).

At the previous years' commencement ceremony, the provost spoke about the importance of community service, saying that "even the poets' in the solitary, sullen, art, have something to contribute." His contempt was so palpable, I'm surprised he didn't call us navel-gazers. So I figured the administration would applaud the community service aspects of this course.

Given the school's history of service to underserved populations, I was thus somewhat surprised that, when I proposed this field trip for the Black Panther tour, the Dean looked at me like I was crazy, immediately mentioning all the possible lawsuits the school might be likely to be liable from if "something happened," even though field trips (and travelling abroad) happened regularly in other courses. It took me awhile to realize that this proposal perhaps marked me as "too radical," but after having the tour nixed, I switched to "safer" ideas like a course on Pop Culture (analyzing Bob Dylan lyrics, using the money to bring in Greil Marcus; even though I disagreed with his baby boomer orthodoxy bias, I learned much from him), and they had no problem with that.

---

[81] Triangular Venn Diagram Graphic Available Upon Request. Perhaps I should assign some of the writings of, and about, the amazing visionary Ericka Huggins, who was largely responsible for the success of the Black Panthers school, to give the course more gender balance; the Panthers, after all, were more than 50% women, and Huggins and Hillman surely have common pedagogical commoinalities. Huggins still lives here, maybe I can introduce them if they don't already know each other.

Nevertheless, my contract was renewed yearly for a few years, and, despite the alienation I felt in Oakland and 'Frisco, in late March 2004, professionally, I was riding at least as high as I was when I left NYC on the eve of 9/11. I had just attended, and read my poetry (and had a blast with Joanna Yas and David Berman, who I had invited to my school to read poetry---the most well attended reading ever at my college!---,and others) at the AWP conference in Chicago where I also got to see many of my NYC friends I hadn't seen in years. My poetry was getting published in anthologies and magazines and my 7th book had just been accepted. Even locally, *The Contra Costa Times* did a cute little puff piece called "Professor Pens *Cliff Notes*," and I could take advantages of summers off to get a little band going.

My girlfriend had finally moved out west, and we were trying to plan a future. After all, I was supposed to be an adult now. Maybe in a few years, things could stabilize to the point where we could have a kid (though with the student loan, home ownership certainly seemed out of the question) and maybe we could get a place with an upright piano, which I still couldn't afford, and finally take advantage of one of the perks of the job: summer's off, for those "research sabbaticals" to work on my art, which now could mean the more expensive art of music as much as writing, and make my creative output even better and thereby help the school recruit more students. But on April 7, 2004, when riding a bicycle in Frisco, I was hit by a car, rendering me permanently crippled (though I didn't know it at the time).

The Crash of 2004

Ah, 2004 was as beautiful as the chance meeting of a car and a bike at the corner of Broderick and Haight. Or, in retrospect, you could say, "in 2004, I was hospitalized for approaching perfection." Berman (Silver Jews) had another song song called "I Remember Me" in which a guy tries to get his previous life (and girlfriend) back after losing it all when being hit by a truck. I could now see my reflection in that, and thought of the myth of the devil at the crossroads, the "Faustian bargain." You sell your soul to the devil (eternal damnation) for the gift of music or some other 'god-like' power of forbidden fruit, Balzac's *Wild Ass's Skin*, etc. Maybe I made a deal with the devil when I didn't die in that accident, and when he (or is it God?) took away my walking, running, jogging, dancing, work-strong legs, it felt kinda like he was taking my soul. But isn't the deal supposed to offer some compensatory gift? Maybe increased empathy or "fertile tears" or something? It was hard not to think this was the car's revenge on me for having lived without it for so long.

The metal beast was now in my leg, as much of my essence as any body "part" not breath, or blood, or food and feces....As I lay bedridden, unable to move, I got word that the same Dean who had nixed my Jan Term Field Trip idea, had written a statement for the tenure committee which included the damning line, "Stroffolino is brilliant and magical in the classroom but lacks a sense of personal grounding." She made no mention of my Panther proposal in her statement, but as I lay in bed wired on Vicodin and subject to erratic mood swings receiving this news, I certainly felt that she was taking advantage of my vulnerable position of being unable to defend myself as she worked to not have me rehired.

And even though 99% of my jobs have been white collar work (though sweeping up the condoms in the porn sections of video store may count as blue collar), part of why the accident traumatized me so severely is because so much of my faith in survival in this society as an adult had been based on the knowledge that no matter what ups and downs my ability to get jobs in the cultural superstructure would be prone to (in the vicissitudes of fashion) that I had the fall-back of a kind of unskilled blue-collar job (like, say, Brandon, who was an on-site building manager at Public Storage. He had to lift a lot of boxes, talk to customers and make the rounds, which helped strengthen his arm muscles for his drumming). But, now, with the disability, that was no longer available.

I know many others are more disabled than I, but not being able to dance (or, frankly, even move) was messing with my mind as much as the pills were. All my life (going back to at least 3 years old when I did that toddler "spinning around 'till you fall" dance that I didn't realize is very similar to what Sufis do!), dancing had been a necessary ingredient for my psychic balance and anger management that allowed me to concentrate on my jobs, or for that "grounding" the Dean said I lacked, or wouldn't admit as a *legitimate* form of grounding (even though I never danced on campus. I saved that for elsewhere before the accident, though I did play the grand piano in the theatre lobby occasionally which I thought they'd like (I *still* couldn't afford one), and I did invite David Berman of The Silver Jews to read his poetry, which I thought they'd like (after it, he didn't even bring an acoustic guitar, and it wasn't like he was much of a dance band)....

Indeed, whatever grounding I was beginning to find in California over the past 3 years felt like quicksand more than ever, as her statement effectively ruined my chances of getting tenure. She never quite defined what "grounding" meant, but given the fact that she claimed that whatever it was, it had no effect on my ability to be "brilliant and magical" in the classroom (unless "magical" was also a barbed put down), it would follow that whatever failing she detected in my personal life (as long as it didn't hurt anybody else) would have no bearing on my employability. After all, she too was member of a marginalized discriminated against population herself who had fought for that right against a catholic church notorious for anti-LGBTQ stances.

Her words stung because I knew there was some truth that I hadn't found the sense of grounding in California that I had in NYC, but I just thought it would take a few more years. It's harder to make new friends in a new town in your 40s than in your 20s or 30s. What on earth did she mean by grounding? Perhaps she had diagnosed as a malady what I considered to be one of my greatest virtues. You could say that I lacked "grounding" in the specialized institution of poetry (and the Euro-Centric "Great Books" canon I was required to teach). Was it my interdisciplinary tendencies that scared them, even though I hardly ever made them public?

And, indeed, my proposal for that class with the Jello Biafra lecture and the Black Panther tour was an attempt at finding that grounding here, a sense of community or even support structure after moving here for a job inadvertently cost me my old east coast support structure and sense of grounding. Sure, I was hired as a poet, with eyes in a fine frenzy rolling, etc., but including the grassroots community activists like the Panthers and the grassroots/radio record activists like Biafra could widen a coalition that would help more than just me find grounding in this land that could be wiped out by an earthquake any second.

Or did she mean that, since it's a Catholic school, I needed to find grounding in the institutions the Catholics call God? When I first got hired, I asked my department chair, who was Jewish, if she had any problems with the school due to being Jewish? She said no, but then added, "that doesn't mean you won't. Because of your last name, they may assume and expect you to act more Catholic." No one ever said anything about this either so I don't think that played a factor, but perhaps that image of the Black Panthers with guns (editing out their allegiance to the constitution) and the mis-information that they "hated whites" had something to do with what she meant by "lacking grounding." Perhaps I was too heavy handed, as if I'm the kind of guy who has to make a big fat mistake and suffer the consequences to learn to be more cautious and moderate even more if there's a next time.

Oh, how I regret, being too weirded out in a haze from Vicodin to try to *fight* the Dean's accusation. I could've sued, but was afraid to risk losing money in it (besides, it might be hard to get hired somewhere else if you're known as someone who sued your previous school). At the very least I could've written a poignant petty poem (which could also be set to music) called "dancing is my grounding, and it's wholesome as unspoken sex (that y'all are doing, right?)." And the words would be better than "Dancing is my grounding, but we can delete that from the text. Dancing is my grounding, but I'll keep it in a box! Dancing is my grounding, like a 21st century fox. Dancing is my grounding, but I'm brilliant in the class/ And forgive, me, if I sometimes need to shake my little ass." Nah, "I don't care about your sex life. So, leave my grounding alone." But now it was "dancing is my grounding, but I can't do it anymore/ And if you give me my job back, I'll join a gospel choir!"

But, instead of writing a letter to the R&T committee to defend myself, I had just passively fell into a drugged-out world. The Vicodin increased mood swings, but being trapped in bed, I couldn't dance out the devil and I'd wake at 4Am crying and calling people in NYC and crying, and then wondering why they never called back. You could say "I pushed people away," but it felt like they were just receding, floating away as I lie, immobile, on spaceship bed. And even though I eventually got off the pain killers, I fear they might have had a lasting effect on my psychic balance, my professional life as culture worker, and my interpersonal relationships. Here's a failed prose-poem I wrote that might do a better job of describing my mental state around that time:

Martin Luther King Day, 2005

Don't you hate it when a revolutionary really knows his Bible, and speaks with the full-force of the moral authority of The Church? Forgive a 40 something riveted to the bed by Martin Luther King oldies, lapping up quote after quote, chewing, grinding. "Another virtuoso performance, right up there with *Howl*," says J. Edgar. Then we hear Nina Simone's tribute and we cry. "For dessert," says J. Edgar, but the tears soon flood him out, so we can hear a faint voice saying, *"do something, do something."* and when someone says "Help!" it means "let me help you." J. Edgar can chalk it up as conceptual art, along with the streets that used to be thriving black business districts until they built highways over them, and named them in honor of MLK. Junior, that is. Or that multi-million dollar memorial made by Chinese slave labor in the mall. Stand-up comics and poets try to use irony against that deadly irony, "and the ladies they roll their eyes," and still a faint voice says *do something do something*, but it's wandered into a poetry party in the venue that used to be a church that let us do punk shows. Oh Martin, we've failed you, but of course I should only speak for myself, though I'm trapped in bed, on Vicodin, unable to walk or wheel myself over to a piano, and so grateful I didn't die in that accident that I can't speak for myself without speaking for all those I've unintentionally oppressed. *Do something*, and Nina Simone can make us cry better because she holds back the tears.

+ + + + + + + +

It wasn't really until after having *too much time* to think while being bedridden in the months following the accident that I began to draw more lines between my "personal history" and this country's political and cultural history. Allegedly, there was no "Great Crash" of 2004; and the anti-Iraq (and Afghanistan) war movements had been fragmented, but it occurred to me that perhaps another event from 2001 was culturally and economically as significant as 9/11 was, at least on the domestic front: the invention of (or more accurately, the market launch of) the iPod, and the beginnings of social media/iPhone culture that would come to dominate the 21st century (or, optimistically, the early 21st century).

If 9/11 was used by proponents of *disaster capitalism* to get people to strengthen and fortify their own personal walls that would be stronger than the oceans that no longer protect us,[82] and be convinced they don't need community as they had before (Stay In Your Homes! Lock Your Doors!), certainly the iPod, along with the

---

[82] Years before Trump's collective walls, though years after the xenophobia of 70s movies that warned of "Killer Bees" coming from Mexico)

entire post-Telecommunications Act of 1996 Culture of the 21st century, helped strengthen the walls by replacing, for many, the more communal, or, in your face, boombox culture, to say nothing of street-corner hip hop or their grandparents' street-corner doo-wop. America had always used walls to conquer, but now they were more privatized, and my Vicodin walls paralleled our culture's iPod walls (though I didn't have an iPod).

It helped create Headphoned Man (and woman), as the iPhone helped create Attention Deficit Disorder woman (and man). Obviously, that was precisely the reason they did it. It was a war on cheap entertainment, and local culture! Thus, throughout the first decade of the 21st century, the iPod and 9/11 post-Patriot Act homeland security worked in tandem to help create what scholars like Scott Timberg call the *culture crash*. I also became aware of social media while bedridden (Friendster at first, but soon MySpace), but little did I know at the time what was going on behind the scenes in Silicon Valley, and how they were planning to transform both the culture and the economy of this country (and the world) in ways that may be ultimately more profound than what the Patriot Act signified.

As I lay bedridden in the spring of 2004, Harvard student Mark Zuckerberg flew to Silicon Valley where he met Napster's Sean Parker, and PayPal's Peter Thiel, who gave Facebook a loan of $500,000. And Jonathan Taplin argues that the real rise of today's digital monopolies began a few months later in:

August of 2004, when Google raised $1.67 billion in its initial public offering. In Decermber of 2004, Google's share of the search engine market was only 35%. Yahoo's was 32% and MSN was at 16%. Today, Google's market share is 88% in the United States and higher in the rest of the world. In 2004 Amazon had net sales revenue of $6.9 billion. In 2015, its net sales revenue was $107 billion, and it now controls 65% of all online new book sales, whether print or digital. In those eleven years, a massive allocation of revenue—perhaps $50 billion per year—has taken place, in which economic value has moved from the creators of content to the owners of monopoly platforms." (*Move Fast And Break Things*, 148, 6).

Meanwhile, Bush continued to deplete the national treasury during this time, and the wealth gap rose (in fact, this was one of Silicon Valley's goals), but it wasn't until 2006, thanks to Mike Malloy, Randi Rhodes, and Thom Hartmann when *Air America* was still around, that I realized that the iPod and Patriot Act could not have effected this cultural transformation, this paradigm shift, without the help of Congress's repeal of Glass Steigal in 1999…but, ultimately, there is no cultural analogue for my little personal Crash of 2004.

Must I Keep Replaying This?

Personally, I groped in 2005 and 2006 to recover from my injury, both physically and psychologically (it took a year to learn to kinda-sorta be able to walk again, and generally needed a cane, and I even wrote a stupid bitter song about the process, "Able without a Cane,").[83] Without my usual anger-management tools, I feared I was becoming bitter. For instance, in 2005, I was driving on the streets I used to bike and walk in the Mission, when I got caught in a traffic jam caused by the army of bicylcists who stage "take back the streets" events on Friday nights. One of them banged his fist on my windshield and said, "Get a Bike!" I like to think of myself as a mild mannered man, but perhaps I lost it, "You know why I'm in a car! Coz a car hit me while I was riding my bike!" It could be you, I didn't say it. Nor did I say, "it's people like you that give bicyclists a bad name, and make cars wanna hit us!" Besides, the woman who hit me wasn't angry or anything, just real stupid....and though I'm all for strict drunk driving laws, it sucks that had she been drunk I would have gotten more money. Stupid driving should be equally punished, not that it will bring my leg back....

I knew I needed to feel that amplified sound of loud guitars coursing through me again, and held out hope that I would recover enough to go out to dance again, and so I took my cane to see an all-female punk band called Las Ultrasonicas from Mexico City sing such songs as "Ven En Mi Boca." While trying to dance, a moshpit formed around me, and I soon learned the hard way that, even with a cane, my legs were too shaky to provide resistance to the other dancers ping-ponging against me. I fell backward, twisting my good leg, and got a few boots and shoes in my face. It hit me that the safest place to be the near the noise (the music) was on stage! And that if I couldn't dance anymore, maybe I can help get others dancing, even if I had to bring a wheelchair, and not just as end in itself, but to help inspire the writer, in solitude, later, with a fluidity of mind, or worded heart or worded collective soul even....

---

[83] My body's been broken since that three year old accident
And the doctors who cost more than a leg
Told me I should lie around and take things much easier
So I tried to be patient and beg
But your promise of happiness heaven and health
Showed no mercy & I waited so long
I wasted away while you got your say
When your next bill comes I'll pay you this song
(chorus)
I'm Damned Coz you don't think what I do is essential
Like your scalpels or whatever you call those utensils
And a perfect painless body shouldn't cost us our souls
But I'll run back to you if you see us as equals
Not that pain is just beautiful or that reruns are sequels
But if you tell me your troubles I won't tell them I know

Ah, a few years earlier one of the poets who came to see a band I was in wrote a review of the show. She wrote how she would have loved to dance but was too shy, and it makes me sad like I, or we, could've done a better job of making her feel less shy, though she's being nice & not blaming us. It's not like she called me the E-word! *Extrovert!* Ah, can I convince her that the reason I danced was *because* I was shy, if shyness is understood as not being able to communicate one's needs and desires, or joys and pains in face-to-face words....rather than mere introversion (some introverts are *very good* hustlers). Now, you can be shy (or "socially uncomfortable") without being introverted, but I, who was both, could always dance my way out of it, out of my fear of the social marketplace (the true meaning of agoraphobia), and meet people, in a way social media does not allow. Now, lacking that social visceral immediacy, I felt that my shyness and introversion was an absolute liability.

I wasn't diagnosed with PTSD until 2006 when I had a relapse and it became evident the doctor's promise that I would be 100% recovered would not come to fruition. As I realized my longing for the "walking city" was now absolutely unrealistic (even if I returned to NYC), my depression (or learned helplessness) rose. I felt the mind/body dualism that I had spent most of my adult life trying to undo becoming reified, like that alien metal now fraying twisted nerves in my leg to hold my bones together. Was this metal's attempt to "make up" for taking the form of a car and destroying my leg in the first place?

Desperately hoping not to be bitter, I tried to play the role of the earnest catastrophist, sublimating my personal sorrow and fatalism into some kind, *any kind,* of social use, but anger became a problem. *What do we mean by anger?* Is it an energy force before we recognize it as anger, like say you wake up with this energy, and if there happens to be a nearby drum or other instrument like say two good legs so you can dance, it's art or expression or even grace, but when you've become a disembodied head trapped in bed with nothing but a pen or paper, it's easy to become the bull in the china shop.

I felt out of the loop in the Bay Area literary scene (especially when the Mills Grad Students who called themselves The New Brutalists scattered due to the necessity of having to pay an overpriced loan back), and I wouldn't be surprised if part of this was due to my mental instability of the Vicodin haze, during which I'm pretty sure I was acting out unreasonably to just about everyone in my life. Unlike in Philly, and NYC, I didn't understand the territory, and, for the first time in my adult professional life, had lost my sense of *context*, and was at a loss how to create a new one since in California (or was it the 21st Century).

Sure, there were many reading series here, but most weren't connected to presses as in NYC. It felt more placeless and impersonal, in contrast to NYC (or was it the 90s?), where editors were candid enough to give feedback, and dialogue. At least in NYC, there was a sense of the local, and a protracted seduction process with editors was permitted. But too often such networking now was criticized as "conflict of interest."[84] Rather, the impersonal etiquette of blind submissions and contests reigned here, and the lack of feedback encourages a culture of isolation and second-guessing (as if that's necessary for good art?)

One exception to this was *Kitchen Sink* magazine. It was more of an Oakland culture magazine, "for people who think too much," with a kind of white generation X sensibility (they loved The Silver Jews). It bore some similarities to the more famous *McSweeney's* and *The Believer* across the Bay, but it was less flippant and smug in its socio-political analyses. They made ample room for poetry and literature, and created a context that would bridge poets and culture critics in contrast to, in my opinion, the more barren poetry journals.

They also had several connections with Mama Buzz Café, and the symbiosis between the magazine and the café (which was also an art gallery and performance space for lit readings and relatively quieter music) worked to the mutual benefit of each, for a few years, before Amazon and the on-line business cut into the magazine's profits forcing it to fold, and Mama Buzz became a casualty of gentrification, which not only priced out the café, but forced many who worked there, and went there, out of Oakland. It wasn't like we didn't try…..how many save a press, a bookstore, a radio station bake sales we had, but to no avail….

Kitchen Sink encouraged my music and cultural criticism, but many other presses that had previously published me had begun to fold, as bookstores were dying, and poetry was more disseminated online. Perhaps California was changing my writing, or I had figured after 6 books of poetry that seemed "excellent scribbling in a period style," to me now, I felt that maybe I earned the right to trade in some "gem-like" successes for more ambitious failures, but my work was more rejected for being "too didactic" or "vulgar." My poetry now seemed useless, pointless, valueless: *hymn to ineffectual beauty*, fiddling while Rome burnt. This was no doubt the PTSD talking…..

Still, if I couldn't use dancing anymore to get out of the (ghetto of the) mind, perhaps I could use music to at least get people to cry, which is a kind of embodiment, no? After all, poetry has never had the power to make me cry, though I may be already crying and reach for a poem, as tears stain the page, but music has. So, when the 9thWard levees broke after Hurricane Katrina (and my friends went missing), and I found myself alternating between debilitating sadness and hopelessness and attempts at pro-active anger, I managed to wheel myself over to

---

[84] College radio went through similar changes: In Philly in the 80s and early 90s, no one would mind if the DJ played his or her own band if it was good (and often they liked the music for the same reason they liked the DJ so it was good), but now (at KALX at least) that would be called "conflict of interest."

the electric piano, with my leg at a 90 degree angle-- my body was like a wounded Aeolian harp, clinking along with melodies that stuttered pain-- out came a slow sad song. Something gnawed at me, I felt like a heretic to music in the "singer songwriter" role, more than even I've been in the "poet" role, but it felt like "the singer songwriter" role was the only choice left….

3 days after 9/11 I had written a stupid rant criticizing Bush (in a "chickens come home to roost" kind of way) which pissed off many poets, at the time. The poem did come off awkward, cold and smug, and I should've revised it, but I let the pressure of the zeitgeist and the "spontaneous overflow of confused thought" reactive mind win out over the "recollection in tranquility," and perhaps if I wanted to express the political and cultural anger I felt burning inside me that a slow sad painful song could couch my bitter acerbic wit in a sad-melody that could make people cry; since I couldn't seem to stop crying, I should at least try to do something with it. Certainly I got to have some social skills suitable to California in 2006? Art as a naked cry for help?

Have you ever had that feeling when you know you look bad but others tell you that you look great, or that something you *hate* doing is called a real talent. That's how I felt about my ability to make others cry. After all, I can do that quite well on my own, or with a girlfriend, I don't need to go to an art event for that. Call me a cold formalist perhaps, but the song I recorded did, for a few months there, have the power to make people cry (or maybe it wasn't the song so much as the way I sang it), if only it didn't hurt my already hurting body:

From *The Lost Years*: 2005

I tried to cry Katrina into art that would *do* something
In a feeble John Prine-esque country-folk waltz
I packaged as a New Orleans Benefit CD (not the Red Cross, dammit).
I raised like $527, a lot for one who sucks at hustlin'.
I saw people cry when I played it on a Casio
Lying on my belly on the floor of Adobe Books
(couldn't get comfortable crosslegged after the accident)

Yet it was kinda sanctimonious
Lacking the spirit of New Orleans
I felt at the Mother-In-Law Lounge just before K-Doe died
And the Krewe du Vieux parade with Brett and Janine
Who were now trapped in an abandoned warehouse[85]
After the flood took their dog
Still, I self-promoted my little song

[85] I bet it's now a luxury market rate condo

More than I self-promoted my previous art
(much to the chagrin of my publishers)
because it didn't seem like a mere self
I was promoting and perhaps it was
Sanctimonious enough for the old white folks on KPFA
Using Katrina as an excuse to dig out
Their old Randy Newman records
As they used Desert Storm as an excuse
To dust off their old Phil Ochs.
KPFA didn't play it....

Was I hung up on trying to convince
The whites to feel some sympathy for black people
Or was I just trying to act like what whites called "my age?"
Like my Tom Waitsy cover of The Coup's "Ride The Fence"
Or strategically using Merle Haggard's "Branded Man"
To convey the same message about the P.I.C
They couldn't hear if Tupac rapped it
Even though at least as many racist whites
Listened to hip hop as that kind of northern country folk
So beloved in Nor-Cal during the height of the hyphy craze...
And soon The Legendary K-O's "George Bush
Don't Care About Black People"
Was getting play in commercial pop stations—
(I love the lineage of that song
sampling a Kanye song
that sampled Jamie Foxx singing
a Ray Charles song
that caused a controversy
for sampling "It Must Be Jesus"...)

KPFA didn't play it, but KPOO did.
I went to KPOO to buy a shirt
And got talking to Terry Collins
About Katrina and told him about the CD
If they would be so kind to mention it.
I didn't expect them to actually play the song
(I was as humble and/or embarrassed
as I was when one of K.Doe's musicians
invited me to play trumpet on stage with them—
in retrospect I deeply regret it
so in awe of the black musicians
or perhaps feeling solidarity
with all the black musicians

who criticized James Brown
when he hired a white musician
or when the Panthers
hired a white lawyer to get Huey out of jail).

But my favorite Bay Area radio jock,
The legendary station manager J.J. On-The-Radio
Said, "we could interview you about the song now."
There's no recording of that. Thank God
And I went back in shame and think
Of what my friends Brett and Janine told me
About a debate brewing in Nawlins next February.
"Should we celebrate Mardi Gras
even amid all the destruction or cancel it?"
Cancelling it would be letting them win, of course,
And however noble in intent my song was,
It don't mean a thing if it ain't got that swing
Or the transformative power of the second line[86]
Or even the funk of the legendary K.O
Sampling Jamie doing Ray—

You can't be truly pro-New Orleans
In Eurocentric words only…so when Yezal got shot
I made sure to go to a nearby traffic triangle
With my trumpet and blast out
When The Saints Go Marchin In (screw my cliché)
As cars flip me the bird or even the bitch
(which almost makes up for my regret
for not jumping up on stage with K Doe)….

+++++++++

The *Bayview* Newspaper referred to Katrina as "Hurricane KKKatrina" and the disaster capitalists were clearly using it to drive out blacks who "drive real estate prices down" and begin reinventing New Orleans as an unaffordable and more curfewed gentrified (white) city. Though Katrina accelerated the process, this would take a few years, but in the meantime many refugees from the New Orleans diaspora were moving to Oakland (Ah, I remember Café Katrina where I saw The New Orleans *Aints* finally win a superbowl; if you can't be in New Orleans, this was the best place to be). And, in some ways, Katrina was providing the script for the gentrification and displacement narrative that Oakland City Planners were

---

[86] I got to join in with one in front of The Make-Out Room, blocking off streets in the Mission to bring a little Mardi Gras back to the city that's now less than 4% black.

busy working on in the name of progress.

In 2006, however, many still believed that Oakland was kind of gentrification proof. Indeed, although Jerry Brown had placed gentrification on the top of his mayoral agenda with his plan to lure 10,000 outsiders to pay higher rents in the downtown area to make it more like what he called the "elegant density" of New York City (but really would make it more like a gated community or suburb), many of the condos he got built remained empty for years. The dot com bubble crash of the early '00s helped prevent it, thankfully, for us, and the fact that Ron Dellums had become mayor placed at least a little check on the greedy plans of the developers and property owners who took a page from what Trump had done to NYC. Nonetheless, the rents were still slowly starting to rise.

And even then, many feared the inevitable, "Starbucks Is Coming....and there's nothing we can do about it," an installation piece at one of the "First Friday" galleries on Telegraph warned (Ben Reisman knows who). I was angry because it seemed so fatalistic. No, it hasn't happened yet, and we can fight! But even though the majority of Oaklanders in poll after poll in *The Oakland Post* have expressed agreement that the median income of the already existing neighborhood should be taken into account when calculating rental prices (rather than the status quo logic underlying "market rate" that dictates people who don't live here yet are more important than people who do), ten years have passed, and we still haven't found a way to organize this grassroots majority into a coherent voice with enough power to back it up to earn a true seat at the table (despite the best efforts of Causa Justa, The Oakland Creative Neighborhoods Coalition, The Oakland Warehouse Coalition, to name but a few).

No, I can't blame anybody without looking at myself, and excuses come pouring in: it's harder to organize today than in 1967 (or, frankly, even 1987) because everything's more expensive. You have to work three jobs. Ah, the longer commute of the priced out.... Busy, inefficient, stressed, depressed. Jailed or surveilled. By comparison the 1970s ball of confusion is a crumb of confusion. Hail the new exurbs. Hail Tracy! (non-ironic). Still, I argued in 2006, as I argue today, that had we made room for the "immediate gratification" of music in public places, like it was at the protest to ban of BBQ (and amplified) music by Lake Merritt, or the street fair put on by the church that had been fined by the city for having choir practice because one of the newbie gentrifiers complained it was too loud (even though the church has been a cultural center of this neighborhood for at least 40 years), it could bring a wider grassroots movement together, but I get carried away....

Ghost Town/ The Creamery

The money I had received from the accident had almost run out, and I got a note that my rent was going up for my one bedroom in downtown Oakland, so I searched for a cheaper new place to live, with roommates again, and even though I was 40 now, I found another live/work warehouse scene very similar to the one I had in Philly almost 20 years before. On one level, this was a sign of how much I had fallen down on my luck (and unlike in my 80s, there was now that stigma of age, "when you're 20 you can think of yourself as young more than poor which, alas, too often means failure"). The place was filthy and grungy (hell, the New York subways were clean by comparison), and I felt so embarrassed when Leslie Scalapino came to the front door to hand me a check from *Poets In Need*; both of us could barely conceal tears; I didn't have the heart to tell her it wouldn't come close to the cost of the surgery. It was also absolutely stupid of me to bring my girlfriend's mom visiting from Atlanta there to see her daughters' artwork in a gallery show, yet on another level living there helped alleviate depression, and give some hope in the future, and the possibility of contributing to a wider community again.

My truncated journey to bring the specialized disciplines of the mind (words) and body (music) together could perhaps be resumed as I still had enough of a poetic reputation to be able to make a little "scratch" (to dig up some old slang) to teach a free-lance, non-accredited, non-institutionalized, creative writing class there. In addition, for the first time in my adult life I was now living in a place with a real piano (and it occurs to that I was roughly the same age that my mom was---40—when she got her first piano), actually, a few of them, even if many of the keys were broken and even melted (don't ask me how; I didn't do it!). And, even better, a ready-made social context that I didn't have to get in the car, or limp to a Bart station too-many-blocks-away to get to, but just 100 feet, or flight of stairs away from my bed: Dance Parties! (or for those who find dancing to be an illegitimate form of grounding, let me say "aerobic workout sessions.")

I must stress this fact polemically for those who are stepping up the crackdown on the existence of such spaces, especially here in Oakland (though I hear it's happening in cities across the country), especially when the dictates of disaster capitalism and gentrification have demonized such "unsafe" and "illegal" spaces more thoroughly after the national media exploited the Ghost Ship Fire Tragedy of 2016. **Live/work artist spaces provide service to the disabled community!** Live/work music spaces provide a civic service to the community! The arts can be an economic engine, a cultural export, for the city's economy! These spaces strive to take up the slack left when the legal economy of the city abandoned its stake in homegrown culture in the 60s and 70s, and again in the 90s. And **Live/work artist spaces provide service to the disabled community,** especially if we can set up mattresses on the dance floor so some of the disabled folk can horizontally dance!

At the multi-media (and multi-roomed) party shows our warehouse held, I could find the non-academic social life I craved. I could play several roles. 1) Dancer when the loud fast bands or DJs played 2) Side-show karaoke piano in the corner between bands, and after the last one around 2AM, or 3) all night ad-hoc jams in the practice room, with some of the best local and touring musicians, as well as 4) go back to my room and chill (or have "quality time") with my girlfriend who hadn't left me yet, even though she never bargained for this filthy place.

From my Ghost Town box seat, I could see enough of our reflection in what was good about *24-Hour Party People*. I'm not even getting into the art shows, belly dancers, rope dancers and installation pieces. I didn't have to look for the "heart of a Saturday Night" anymore. It was the weekdays that were the problem, but with a little tweaking, it could turn into a hub like the Brill Building. I convinced Damon to let Greg Ashley move in and set up his recording studio. Greg was one of the few in the East Bay music scene who had what I (as a "lapsed New Yorker") valorized as a professional (workaholic) attitude, without it killing his soul and genuine love for music. And after he set up the Creamery Recording studio, I could also work as a studio musician (session man) and record some of my own "sonic experiments" with some of Oakland's best musicians.[87]

I had become aware of Greg Ashley first through KALX (via Amy Blaustein of *Blanche Devereaux*). Although Greg's band Gris Gris took the Bay Area by storm, getting international attention for their albums and live shows that rivaled fellow-Bay Aryan Comets On Fire in dance-trance intensity (this was years before the Oh Sees!) while bettering them in darkness, it came with the image price of distorting and reducing the range of Greg's talents and interests. Lumped in on the fringes of the "freak-folk" movement as a "psychedelic *wunderkind*," Greg also wrote songs that were deeper, darker and too heavy for that scene, songs that have a gravitas that Devendra, and even Joanna Newsome, could only dream of.

I met him when he asked me to join him for a version of his college radio hit, "Apple Pie And Genocide" at The Ivy Room, one of the few Bay Area venues that actually had an acoustic piano. Though I didn't really know the song that well, he told me "it's in D-flat minor; just play black keys." I guess it was kind of an audition. My first session work with Greg was on his criminally under-rated *Painted Garden* album (2007). "Pretty Belladonna" was a soulful garage-rock waltz ballad whose melody resembled Cohen's "So Long Marianne" (not that Cohen has any right to sue).

---

[87] The only possible explanation I could ever find for why Greg Ashley is not as well-known, or compensated, for his music as Silver Jews was is not because Greg hasn't produced a body of work at least as interesting and/or important (or can I just say good) as Silver Jews had (or has), but it's because of the institutional diminished returns, and loss of opportunities, available to musicians who prefer to work outside the Hollywood Industry in the 21st century (as David and Greg are), and not because the need, or demand, isn't there (it's not about 'fashion'). Feel free to challenge me on this; it could be a fun comparison-contrast podcast (to be fair, it would probably have to include that Silver Jews side project, Pavement, too)

"Spoon Fisher King," another song I was featured on, shows the depth of sonic textures Greg could combine with a mere 8-track reel-to-reel player in a basement on 34th St.[88] It caught my fingers dancing toward what I love about the Ramsey Lewis Trio more than anything I had recorded. In lesser-skilled hands, Jenny Raven's back-up vocals, Carlos Bermudez's sax and my black key keyboard meandering would have turned into a blurry mess, but Greg was always adept at using percussive sounds to create the illusion of space, even with many overdubs. This minor, self-mocking, song takes up where his earlier *Medicine Fuck Dream*, with its themes of addiction, whether to a girl-as-drug or to a drug-as-girl, left off. Greg's lyrical flair, evident in lines like:

"you were lost like a painted garden starrin in a movie…
if your mind is an orphanage than every child's a junkie…
and now you act like a dollar bill that's waitin' for the powder
you would dance with the weather man who couldn't find the spring…

The lyrics that struck me most, however, were simpler in a way, yet ultimately more difficult: "Give up being a man….Give up being a star." This seemed to have a similar sensibility as David Berman's "anti-performance" attitude, but in a way Greg's work is like a synthesis between the two poles Steve and David represented in The Silver Jews. His band was more Dionysian ("tribal") than Pavement, but he also released solo albums that showcased his poetic sensibilities (even though he didn't graduate from college), and his low-fi studio wizardry were showcased. As a producer, he's the best I worked with, or at least the equal of Steve Albini.

Like Albini, he's not shy about taking sides: analogue over digital, and his low-fi, econo set up makes a lot of a little, though he's moved up to a Tascam 16 track. He understands the power of the acoustic piano much more than more expensive studios like Tiny Telephone: even when he operated out of a tiny bedroom, he always made room for a spinet or upright--and deserves a grand piano.

Albini's Electrical Audio has a better set-up: an acoustic grand with at least four small high-sensitive microphones placed beneath its lid, so I could play live with the band while recording, with the drummer about 15 feet away from me in the same room, without having to worry about "bleed" destroying the "separation." That allows me to be more fluid in playing, yet it doesn't really make Albini's finished product *sound* better. Ashley's got a definite sound and sensibility; he's sometimes saddled with musicians looking for that "distinctive Greg Ashley sound," but his creative restlessness and curiosity toward exploring other forms of music is better served in the studio where he doesn't feel the pressure to be a "star." In my opinion, he's "The best bang for your buck in the Bay." Greg valued local community too much to leave for LA.

---

[88] https://www.youtube.com/watch?v=VpKFcFzlcys

A multi-instumentalist, Greg seems to prefer to work with bands missing a piece or two, or don't quite know what they want, or solo artists, so he can be a more activist hands-on producer, an integral part of the band. Like Albini, he's very direct about what he hears, and he's got Berry Gordy, or at least Phil Spector, ears. During the *Slave To The Weather* sessions, Greg was struggling coming up with a guitar riff. He thought I was getting impatient with him, and apologized, "I'm not really a guitar player." I busted out laughing; I liked his guitar at least as much as Malkmus, but I realized that while Steve's ears usually followed his fingers, Greg's fingers usually followed his ears. Because his ears are so good, he could make stuff work with only one or two takes, and thus found many diamonds in the rough.

Before Greg arrived, The Creamery erred on the side of Dionysian life-transforming transient happening shows. Given the absence of a viable local record label connected to the scene, many of the best live bands placed a low value on recording. In this sense, Greg provided a needed bridge between the "live" and "recorded" aspects of music, and this is part of why the Creamery never felt barren like other studios. It didn't take too long for word to spread to national touring bands either. Some travelled from Japan, Iceland and Germany.[89]

Bay Area Radio

My experience, both in Philly (86-92) as well as in the Bay Area (2006-2011) had shown that the two most necessary ingredients for a thriving music scene are a live/work multi-media performance warehouse (or 11 or 12), depending on the size of the city, and at least one community radio station. At best, they can provide a symbiosis between the transience of the live shows and the permanence of the recorded artifact, to become each other's "house organs" (or 2 or three, analogous to the Mama Buzz/Kitchen Sink nexus).[90] And the Creamery warehouse/ recording studio certainly benefited from some of the local stations, KUSF in particular.

KUSF was a largely white station (like the demographics of its expensive host university), but it helped complement the mostly black KPOO, which, thankfully, still exists. Between KPOO and KUSF, I could usually find everything I needed for my listening fuel (or you could say enjoyment); from morning motivational music, to songs that helped cry me (or rock me) to sleep. Furthermore, KUSF played a lot of the music coming out of the local scene (and was much more devoted to it than

---

[89] I am grateful for getting to work with Greg on Babycakes, Brian Glaze, Sir Lord Von Raven, Inspector Double Negative, The Matinees, Flowers & Bulls, Salinger, Yea-Ming Chen, Zane Allen, Christian Bland ("Black Angels"), King Kahn and Gris Gris, Dreamdate, Convertible, Le Fits, USA for LSD, The Duke and The Duchess, Warm Blood, B.E.M.E The Rapper, and others.
[90] Boots Riley and Stephen Taylor assure me they know how to put this stuff together better in Europe, and if any of you over there are reading this, please get in touch with me, to get it going more here (or, maybe you'd invite me, though I'm a typical American cut off from my heritage who only knows English)…

the 'tamer' college station KALX in Berkeley), including many bands performing at our warehouse, and much of what Greg was recording and producing including my limited edition CD/LP *Single Sided Doubles/In the Sun-Roof Of A Meltdown*.

KUSF may not have quite been as cutting edge and connected to the local scene as WKDU was in the 1980s and into the 90s, but it was certainly much better than KALX, which played some new local music (but often consigned it to a specialty 'ghetto' show). Now a KALX playlist of 2006 might more typically be: Run DMC (20 years old). Frank Sinatra (45 years old), Pavement (15 years old), Greg Ashley (now). Billie Tipton (50 years old), Joanna Newsome (new), and round it off with Etta James or maybe Abba. You get the picture. Not that I entirely blame the DJS, after all many of them felt they had to take up the slack left when commercial radio abandoned a more eclectic approach, but this rendered music more placeless *and* timeless.

Still, I may nostalgically look back to that time when I could still preset my Walkman (yes, this was as late as 2007) to KPOO, KUSF, KALX, PIRATE CAT RADIO 87.9 (all 4 of which I also performed on), a CBS owned AM experimental "Open Source" Radio Station[91] (where I'd hear a Brian Glaze song I played on[92]), and realized how much better Greg Ashley's productions sound on AM Radio (yes, even in 2006). There was also an AM 60s based oldies station, KFRC (even it was a syndicated show originating from a retired Top 40 DJ's house in Florida), and, on the rare occasion that this pieced together menu failed to yield nourishment, I could check out the Democratic Party's attempted answer to right wing talk radio with "Air America." I found it fascinating how Ed Schutz, broadcasting from North Dakota, tried to use Rush Limbaugh's appeal to the "heartland" and "flyover states" against him. And as long as I had a "ready-made' social life at the warehouse, I didn't really need social media.

The "Great Recession" And Obamamania

Sure, living there wasn't idyllically perfect, but it could allow me to kind of get my mojo back, and "make a comeback," even as the global economy was crashing around us, and the Obama campaign was achieving some success in transforming this feeling of collective depression and despair into "hope" (Obamania) just as economists were downsizing this crash, or "meltdown" to a "great recession." Things were bad, and while many "indie-rockers" or many of the poets I knew were playing "music to forget the war by," David Berman had recently disbanded the Silver Jews in order to pursue muckraking about the Washington DC Lobbyist industry's control of America. This project is especially daunting because he targets The Center For Consumer Freedom and Berman And Company, both of

---

[91] http://www.bigtakeover.com/essays/open-source-radio-the-new-weird-americapart-ii
[92] https://www.youtube.com/watch?v=-r5kiZnpQdg

which are run by his father, Richard Berman. Like many of the players in Thomas Frank's *The Wrecking Crew*, Richard Berman has more real power in American society than most of our elected officials, and David heroically refused his father's inheritance to take a stand against K Street. As David writes about him in a statement he made public to Silver Jews fans after breaking up the band in 2009:

He props up fast food/soda/factory farming/childhood obesity and diabetes/drunk driving/secondhand smoke. He attacks animal lovers, ecologists, civil action attorneys, scientists, dieticians, doctors, teachers. His clients include everyone from the makers of Agent Orange to the Tanning Salon Owners of America. He helped ensure the minimum wage did not move a penny from 1997-2007... This winter I decided that the SJs were too small of a force to ever come close to undoing a millionth of all the harm he has caused. To you and everyone you know. Literally, if you eat food or have a job, he is reaching you.... Previously I thought, through songs and poems and drawings I could find and build a refuge away from his world. But there is the matter of Justice."

Take a seemingly benign example. In the 80s and 90s, many of the large companies Richard Berman had been commissioned by had engaged in a very successful campaign of marketing bottled water. If anybody doubts the power of "public relations" (a more benign word for propaganda), look at how Pepsi and Coke managed to convince people that bottled water was indeed healthier than the cheaper public water supplies since the 1980s. As the for-profit bottled water industry grew, public water fountains and restrooms (which many civil rights activists in the 50s and 60s fought hard to integrate) increasingly fell into disrepair and disuse. This simple example of privatization parallels what was happening in education, the healthcare industries and even radio and the music industry in the years since the deregulations of the 80s, so that by the time of *American Water*, American water was increasingly bottled water, and you think what's happening in Flint and Standing Rock is bad, well, you ain't seen nothing yet.[93]

Ah, justice! If, "the SJs were too small of a force to ever come close to undoing a millionth of all the harm he has caused," then what could *I* do as a culture producer in the face of this cultural *meltdown*. The best I could come up with, musically, now that I had some rockin' bands like The Graves Brothers Deluxe to record with, was to set political lyrics about the Healthcare Crisis to "Summertime Blues" or Pere Ubu's "Final Solution" in that novelty Weird-Al, Mad Magazine kind of way (I still think we got a pretty good sound), and get them played as bumper music on Thom Hartmann's show on *Air America*, but surely I could do more, and wanted to help David's righteous struggle in any way I could.
Train and Boat Tour (Forgive me, I Get Carried Away....)

---

[93] After David began sharing more information about his dad's campaigns with me, I found out that his dad was actually the reason why my Dad couldn't unionize at Dana Corporation!

Around 2008 Greg Ashley's indie label, Birdman,[94] was being forced to downsize, due to the tech revolution as well as the Crash of '08. Meanwhile, the SF Music Tech Conference, spearheaded by Brian Zisk was selling (at $272 a pop) musicians innovative new solutions for promoting their work through the new technology, at the same time Obama was selling "hope…." And "change…" Obamamania was very infectious that year, even some usually cynical punks I knew got swept up, "If a great crash (or Great Recession) comes, can a New Deal-like Government Program that puts artists to work on our nation's ailing infrastructure (a big Obama phrase) be far behind." Civic pride seemed to matter then, as one 60-something at the YMCA put it, "if Obama does half of what he says he's going to do, I'll be glad to pay *more taxes* than I'm required to."

As more people were talking about a "we" society (as in Obama's "it's not about me, it's about us"), I tried to think of an alternative to the "diminishing returns" the business-as-usual model of the music industry that was clearly in a crisis (even if the poets didn't think they were in a crisis). There has to be some way that musicians can survive as musicians now that you can't make money selling records anymore. Conventional wisdom (and Warren Buffet) was saying "touring" should be your economical bread and butter, but I had gotten my start in a band that was able to survive (albeit modestly) that refused to tour, and I saw how the new economy was making this kind of introvert radio band less and less possible.

And, in my personal case, my disability put further obstacles in the way of touring (and, yes, I'm aware that musicians more disabled than I, like Vic Chestnut, who toured for years). Besides it was increasingly difficult (especially on the West Coast where cities are more spread out than in the east) to make much money touring, and, many bands, once they reached a certain age, or had kids, just found it not worth it as it seemed in their early 20s when the 'adventure' mattered.

I played on Sir Lord Von Raven's *Please Throw Me Back In The Ocean*, and saw our small indie record label get upset because, even though he managed to get good press (Christgau, etc), he felt frustrated that the band didn't move enough units because it didn't tour, even though he signed the band knowing full well that Eric and Jenny were having their first kid, and thus couldn't tour for at least a year. The label's interested in putting out my album, if I could get a "viable touring band" together, and I'm intrigued. I had just found the best punk rock rhythm section I'd ever worked with: Flipper's bassist and Jello Biafra's drummer. Both these punk acts from were heroes of mine, and rocking out as fiercely as ever, and more than many people half their age, and we quickly developed a chemistry in which Rachel, the bassist would lead, and my voice could follow.[95]

---

[94] The label was founded by David Katznelson who had signed Flaming Lips and other major acts to Warners, before returning to his local-scene roots he honed as a DJ at KUSF back in the 80s.
[95] She was also a member of two of the great all-female punk bands of the 80s/90s, Fright

Rachel brought out a previously latent vocal prowess out in me, as I improvised on expansive structures, embracing phonemes, and the *Death of a Lady's Man* book. I had finally found the band, the sound, that I'd been looking for since the Silver Jews shattered a decade earlier; a trickle *up* band. It's body music, plain and simple, but not at the expense of mind ("you're so bored coz you're boring.") It's got soul. After playing with them, I simply couldn't settle for mediocrity anymore.[96] The challenge of getting to work with these musicians again when they get back from their tours, spurred me on. Ah, if only I had found them 5 years earlier when I still had two strong legs and wouldn't have to lean on a piano, but could kick it away to sing (not that I'd ever be Iggy or Prince, probably more like Mark E. Smith kinda pacing like a professor!)

I got thinking that there's got to be some middle ground, for people like us----for the introvert musician, for the disabled musician, for the musician who doesn't want to be away from his or her kid. For the West Coast musicians having to traverse great distances between cities, wasting fuel and money on inflated gasoline prices! Then it hit me! Obama's speaking of high speed rail! Ah, the railroad. I love the rails, even the slow trains. I'm from a railroad town. What more signifies America's frayed infrastructure, the rust belt, the heartland, than the railroad? Have you ever seen Johnny Cash's 45-minute infomercial for *Amtrak* from 1975 called "Ridin' The Rails?" Remember the days Love Train, Peace Train, Friendship Train, Freedom Train, Soul Train (for some reason Love Truck, Peace Truck, or Soul Truck just never caught on).

Imagine we put together a package tour of, say, local Oakland musicians, that would travel on a train from Oakland to Boston, on the northern route, and then return west on a southern route, stopping at every town that will have them (us) along the way. Because the bands can sleep on the train, and you could indeed bring the family (without sounding as bland as yacht rock or John Hiatt)-as a way to help brand our local music scene a little, to give us a fighting chance against all the trickle down bands with "industry muscle," especially since Big Tech was making it more of a necessity to tour......).

Such tours (other cities can have them too) can help restore regional cultures, and create a cultural dialogue in hopes of more understanding between "red state" people and "blue state" people in that spirit of "unity" (and purple states) that Obama was preaching. It could help begin a process of national healing, in the spirit of The New Deal (but without the racism).

If the train tour is too ambitious, consider a Mississippi Boat Tour, cutting straight

Wig and Mudwimin.
[96] unless it's fun mediocrity, but if it's fun mediocrity then it isn't mediocrity, in rock and roll at least: https://www.youtube.com/watch?v=dMP7BQN2YBw

down the main vein of the US. The Boat's going from Fargo, Minneapolis, St. Paul, through St. Louis down to New Orleans if not up and back around to Galveston. On the bill, the 'extended family' of musicians and other culture workers (including poets) I met largely through living at Ghost Town, some of whom have families now but still want to, need to, rock. The boat, with a stationary stage, quarters or cabins for the musicians and other artist activists, cheap shows at the port of every town the boat docks at, and higher priced 'cruise tickets' for those who want to do the whole 10-14 day trip. I am sure, if done correctly, this would be a smashing success, and help revitalize the music biz, and culture, in America. It absolutely fills a need the for the consumer and creates new markets. Demand will overtake supply! Rolllin' on The River On The Brother Love American Clear Water Revival Show. Can't get more red white and blue than that? I'm a real anti-Bill Graham!

And for those who keep asking me if I can help get the Silver Jews back together (and they mean Steve and Dave), why not ask the Silver Jews to get involved? After all they did a song called "Party Barge" on their last album without Steve or me. Don't know if we should call it The Party Barge tour---maybe he already used that--or "Proud Mary" or "The Legend of the U.S.S. Titanic." The "Water Don't Give A Damn" Tour. I refuse "USA H20" tour sponsored by Evian, or Aquafina, or Dasani. Like data, water's the oil of the 21st century (unless coffee turns out to be). You may have heard of The Blues Cruise; this would be the "No Imagination In The Blues Cruise."

Forgive me, I got carried away. I'm calmer now. If The Train and/or Boat Tour succeeds, it will make it much easier to follow it up with an all-Oakland one, a variety show (that now will have a national audience because we met them where they live, as a group)—for I still believe that a musician should be able to survive as a musician while largely operating mostly in their own town, just like musicians could back in my grandmother's day during the Great Compression (at the risk of sounding like Citizen Kane harping on the word "Rosebud!"), or like studio and session musicians could in medium sized towns and cities across America before it became more of a necessity to move to either LA or Nashville." END DIGRESSION

In retrospect, it seems like a stupid idea, like a little kid talking to his imaginary friends, just like my podcast dance craze idea, and my list of demands for OCCUPY RADIO. (SEE APPENDIX), but my attempts at selfish altruism easily get tangled up in mass causes (and, once upon a time, Obamania, like Occupy, seemed a movement, even if in retrospect it seems more designed to get people hooked on social media). Luckily, I had my day job to ground me from such utopian flights.

Meanwhile, Back In My Professional Life….

After a couple of semesters of adjuncting at Mills and San Francisco Art Institute, where the late great poet/ art-critic Bill Berkson's hopes to get me hired to replace him were thwarted after he retired and they eliminated his position, I was hired by Laney College. My courses at the woman's college were more focused on gender studies (the students wanted to talk about 90s Grrrl Rock over what was officially in the course description, but we found a way to work it in and it inspired an essay I wrote on PJ Harvey for *The Bigtakeover*), and my courses at the art school were more tailored to art students (at the time, there was a big debate between the students who considered themselves "fine" artists, and those who aspired to be "commercial" artists). I love teaching to both groups, but Laney, located in the heart of downtown Oakland, was the most *cosmopolitan* school, or, as people would more commonly say, the more "diverse" school, using terms that try not to seem to reek of paternalism like "Under-served populations."

Still, I'm enough of a New York Snob to prefer "cosmopolitan."[97] I hadn't taught at a majority non-white school since I left NYC, but Laney made me feel more like part of a community than any school I had worked at. Several of the English Faculty had been Black Panthers, and another had been on the committee that helped design Oakland Unified School District's much maligned Ebonics Program. The district's TV station proudly claimed our sister college's role in the formation of the Black Panther party, and the nation's first Ethnic Studies programs, as part of its legacy, and I was permitted and even encouraged to use texts by The Panthers and The Black Arts Movement, for instance, in the classroom.

Though by professional standards, being an adjunct at a community (or junior) college is certainly a demotion, in many other ways (if we bracket money for a second), I came to feel it's a promotion; for, even if my students come in with many grammar and usage problems (thanks to No Child Left Behind, and underfunded public schools, and the school-to-prison pipeline), I have found their insights into the problems this country's and city's government and culture face are often vastly superior to the ones offered by students I've worked with at the more expensive, and whiter, schools.

Still, it's obvious there are structural disadvantages for our students. Class sizes are too big, the facilities are not kept up, and the students don't have the advantage of dorm living I, and others, have had, often having to spend hours commuting to and from their 2 or 3 jobs. In this sense, the term commuter college is more accurate than community college. It's kind of hard to form a community, or even engage in extra-curricular activities, given this. Plus, there's always the constant threat of even more budget cuts, and some wonder how long this school can last

---

[97] Allegedly white supremecists are now using the word "cosmopolitan" pejoratively

as gentrification has it surrounded, and the Oakland Athletics have targeted the campus its top choice for relocating (while the mayor smiles). But, dammit, this school has some of Oakland's best and brightest young (and older) minds, and talent which could contribute greatly to the city and culture of Oakland, if but the public city planners, and the private sector that pulls their strings, realized it.....

The Panthers demanded education that teaches knowledge of self, and "the true nature of this decadent society," and I aspire to live up to that, while reassuring students that they can disagree with me and it won't affect their grade. I also try to remind students that they are their own best assets, that "strength in numbers" need not be just a motto for a Multi-Billion Dollar sports franchise sponsored by an overpriced HMO. One of the most successful moments in the classroom was when a cosmetology student (who hopes to open up a beauty salon), a visual artist (who drew amazing caricatures of every student in the class), and a culinary student (who doesn't just want to have to resign to a food truck), decided to exchange numbers to pool their resources and find ways to professionally work together, as a way to survive, and resist the oligarchic takeover of a city and country that seems bent on keeping them (us!) down.

Recently I heard Pacifica Economist Richard Wolff (who I usually agree with; he's a champion of worker owned coops) comment on how the exploitation of adjunct teachers is bad for students because the overworked and underpaid adjuncts will inevitably be lesser quality teachers than full-time ones. Unfortunately, some colleges have used that "descriptive assumption" as their "rationale" for doing away with adjuncts, and, instead, increase the course load of full-time teachers (rather than hiring new ones). Sure, I think it would be great if adjuncts were paid on par with full-time professors, and received the same benefits, but I must defend the adjunct against Richard Wolff's assertion that overwork makes us worse teachers.

It gives me a motivational chip on my shoulder: I'm going to be at least as good as the full-time teachers are, even if I have to sacrifice some social life for it (or it gave me an excuse not to have a social life, even if that social life would make it easier to get published), or even perhaps if I have to sacrifice being able to afford an apartment to do it!

So rather than pitting adjuncts against full-time teachers, I personally believe that if we're really interested in putting our students first, the best way to solve the problem will be to reduce the course load of the full-time teachers without docking their pay, in addition to establishing pay equity for adjuncts. I say this because I find that only teaching 2 or 3 courses (no more than 10 credits allowed) as an adjunct allows me to devote *more individual time* to our students, given the current backdrop of overcrowded courses—than teaching 4 to 5 classes does. We need solidarity between adjuncts and full time instructors more than ever. Yes, adjuncts are underpaid and exploited, but full-time teachers are overworked too, and the students suffer, even if the District or University suits can find a way to allocate money to give themselves a pay raise, or to create more middlemen. Nonetheless, I am proud to say I teach here!

Meanwhile, Back In My Disability....
"Just because you can't walk doesn't mean you can't water walk."

Since I couldn't jog around Lake Merritt like I used to, I know I had to attend daily water walking or aerobics at the Downtown Oakland YMCA. I used to religiously avoid the Gym; why pay money to work out in a building, when you can jog, and bike, and swing in the sun…to say nothing of dancing, but now it was a necessity. *Remember, it could be worse; I could've died in the accident.* Luckily, some of the water walking instructors played music that was at least as good as those Mod Bar 13 retro-dance parties, or The Duke Of Windsor who DJed many parties at our warehouse. Kelvin in particular was the classic personality DJ as he played R&B from the 50s, 60s, and 70s, and occasionally 80s---from *before his time*—while cracking jokes, using physical humor as he lead us in a workout regimen. In another era, he'd make a better living as a Foole! (and I mean that as highest compliment). The side of the pool became a stage, and then he'd jump into the pool with his large "audience" his classes attracted, often 30 or 40 people, taking up half the pool much to the chagrin of the swimmers who usually get to lord it over the walkers. The lifeguards had to turn people away.

The vast majority of people in Kelvin's classes were retired, "senior citizens," ranging from 60 to 88, very racially mixed, but mostly women, and seeing Kelvin get them (us) moving in the class, to the beat of "Love Rollercoaster," or Solomon Burke's "Cry To Me," 60s garage rock and, of course, James Brown, it hit me that these older black (and white and Latino) women may be exactly the same women in those videos from Hullaballoo and the like whose videos from the early 60s the younger people at the warehouse watch to learn some moves. These women often knew the moves, and danced (I mean "worked out"---I almost forgot it was an aerobics class) more fiercely than many of the young; it hit me that *funk*'s lyrics was never really stuck in the box of 'youth culture' as punk's lyrics are. Yes, these older (mostly non-white) women's taste in music is very similar to so many of the younger white men and women in the white 'underground' scene (minus the punk and hip hop), and that, yes, here too could be another opportunity for coalition building.

At the YMCA, I was also befriending many of the older men (mostly black) who didn't work out in the pool, but rather upstairs with weights (where they could also check out the younger women). Many held court in the locker room, and taught me much about Oakland history that I wasn't getting from the white people and their media. I met Oba T'Shaka, who was an emeritus chair of San Francisco State's Black Studies Program, and whose achievements with SF's C.O.R.E (Congress of

Racial Equality) in the early 60s while still in his 20s (spearheading for instance the successful "Don't Shop Where You Can't Work" boycott) rival what Malcolm and Martin achieved. Here, too, I saw another opportunity for coalition building, even if it only meant asking him to come speak to my class at Laney College, and share his wisdom and experience with my students.

After all, Prof. T'Shaka had written a book which brilliantly argues that the generation gap in the Black Community in the last 20 to 30 years (which many others have spoken about, see for instance Idris Goodwin's "Old Ladies and Dope Boys") was caused by "The Integration Trap."

In T'Shaka's view, if I understand correctly, the Northern white establishment's push, in the 50s and 60s, toward what they called "integration" (which was really more like "assimilation" than true integration which would require economic *enfranchisement*), ostensibly as a way to foster racial equality, was more likely a plot to divide the black community: economically and geographically, as a few of the "talented tenth" would emigrate to the richer, whiter, neighborhoods in an attempt to "integrate," or "move on up," the neighborhoods they left behind became more impoverished. But it also created an ideological division between older and younger, as corporate culture was inserting itself into the family, or, as Amiri Baraka put it in the 90s, in reference to the corporate push of gangsta rap: "our enemies have created our spokesmen."

The corporate media had managed, just like it had with the majority of white people, to insert itself between mother and child with its electronic babysitter (the rise of TV parallels the rise of "the promise of integration"), tempting kids to feel their culture was inferior to a white suburban Brady Bunch culture, or other examples of white culture, pushing its religion of individualism and materialism on pre-school kids before they're old enough to resist. This mainstream media had been manufacturing "generation gaps" ever since the "creation of the teen" and "youth culture" in the 50s and 60s, but, as Nelson George argues, the black community could remain relatively immune from this, as long as it had some self-determination in institutions like the church; even the Negro Leagues, in hindsight, George argues, had advantages to the de-segregating Major League Baseball industry. The dollar circulated in the black community longer. In Oba T'Shaka's view, the problem with some *gangsta rap* is that it's trying to be *white*.[98] Talking to my students, many of whom are young enough to be his grandkids, about the negative consequences of the philosophy of "integration" and how this caused the generation gap, and offering possible solutions for how we can develop a more democratic community based approach rooted in Afro-centric traditions, he certainly helped my students think of the world in a different way. So, when budget permitted (which, alas, was too rare compared to the more

[98] But he says it much better than me...https://www.youtube.com/watch?v=nxpAhOGaVWI

expensive white schools), I also brought in other guest speakers: ex-Black Panther Newspaper editor, Judy Juanita, KPOO DJ and Stand-up Comic/Actor Donald Lacey, local rapper B.E.M.E. and DJ Pill Kozby, Afro-surrealist D. Scot Miller, Joy "Post-Tramatic Slave Syndrome," De Gruy, Alicia Cabellero-Christiansen of The Community Engagement Center, Khafre Jay and Malik Diamond from Hip Hop For Change and, last but not least, Ishmael Reed (even some of the folks from the YMCA showed up for that).

Perhaps I felt that bringing in guest speakers was important because I was aware that students may look skeptically at me because I'm white, but when these men and women spoke, they're more likely to listen. Bringing in guest speakers also encourages students to see that writing and being a public intellectual (whether academic or not) can be a viable career option, even today, amid the culture crash, dammit (just as Gary Adelstein did for me when he brought John Yau to our school almost 30 years earlier).

Because most of what I taught was critical thinking and argumentative writing (civic discourse), I tried to "beat out" my lyric poetry sensibility and/or training from my own writing and thinking to write more like the kind of assignments I was giving my students. I even took a gig for a local magazine (The Oakbook) writing mostly puff pieces with a cultural bent. I wrote articles on a local improv. theatre, a downtown poetry reading series, a local LPFM radio station, a busker who performed by Lake Merritt, a recording studio, and the SF Music Tech Conference, as well as one on Kelvin from the YMCA, while continuing to write music criticism for The BigTakeover.

I also dashed off a sloppy anti-gentrification manifesto in 2007 for *Art For A Democratic Society* I'm not particularly proud of any of these pieces---maybe a sentence here and there, but, damn, these poet habits were hard to shake; in a way, however, I had fallen between the cracks; too poetic for most cultural critics, but too much into culture criticism for the poets (except for Ishmael Reed, who not only published some of my essays, but also some work from my students, in his *Konch* magazine!).

Even though I hadn't published a book of poetry for a decade, I was offered to teach a multi-genre creative writing class, thankfully. When we got to the poetry section, I decided to assign sonnets. One student challenged me: *if you're going to make us write a sonnet, you should bring one you wrote in too!* This made me realize I was a hypocrite. I hadn't tried to write a sonnet in over 20 years (and clearly, they were juvenilia), and by sonnet I mean a traditional formal English or Italian sonnet, adhering to 10 syllables per line, and the tight rhyme schemes. Screw whether it scans iambically or not (you can always read it iambically for theatrical effect even if it's not).

I decided it was fine to let them be clunky and prosey, but, hell, at least I could say "it's a sonnet." So, I wrote almost 200 of them over a period of a year, and though most of them are aesthetically "clunky," and the thoughts are half-baked, only getting started when the poem reaches the 14th line and has to "click shut like a box," and are certainly no match for Tyehimba Jess's double sonnets, a few of these managed to sneak into into *American Poetry Review, Brooklyn Rail, 1111, Entropy*, and others. So, at least I didn't feel like a hypocrite teaching creative writing anymore, though, once again, I can see why some think *I got it backwards*: while others may teach poetry so they can continue to write poetry, I wrote poetry so I could continue to teach it, not that the classroom is a self-contained unit, but I certainly didn't have money to start a literary or cultural magazine (and, even if I did, I wouldn't want to do it "on my own.")

Meanwhile, Back At The Warehouse

By 2011, during the so-called "recovery" (in which the wealth gap increased exponentially), many of my musician and artistic friends had been priced out of Oakland (one friend moved to LA; you know things are bad, when even LA is cheaper than Oakland), and it was clear that Big Tech was encroaching on Oakland's (and America at large's) culture. I had been invited to sit in with Graphic Artist Aaron Han's band Warm Blood to play at the "First Friday" event by the Rock Paper Scissors Collective. Here's what I wrote at the time:

8:45: we play two songs, then a rent-a-cop with a big "Security Guard" jacket defines us as a "public nuisance," and tries to take the sticks out of a drummer's hand in the middle of a song. Security doesn't consider those who loudly appeal to the other senses to be public nuisances. I know I probably had at least a baker's dozen of people try to sell me Vegan Cupcakes, even after 9PM; so nice to live in a land where second-hand fat is tolerated! Nor did the Security Guards force the people to stop carrying the giant KICKSTARTER.COM banner down 23rd St. If rock and roll is noise pollution, what is a banner for a website that's supposed to make it easier to get money from your friends and "facebookfriends" (one word) so that you can make art or even record loud music?

For others, however, the Kickstarter.Com Sign is no more, but also no less, a public nuisance than the loud rock and roll band. While taking a break between trumpet parts, I heard one person in the audience mockingly yell, "now, don't dance--you might knock over the people with the Kickstarter. Com sign!" The first friday events (according to its costly legal agreement with the city) are a celebration of public space, but the kickstarter.com sign's presence, coupled with the silencing of the band, reveals how the event ends up relegating public space to secondary status and the information ("limited access") highway as primary. Is it really an accident that the decrease of music in public spaces (unless they're large arena-like shows like Outside Lands) parallels the obesity crisis, whether your fat is vegan or not?

I guess we were still punk enough to hurl epithets at them: "You call us noise pollution, your sign is sight pollution!" and such, but it was clear under the Quan administration that gentrification and the more staid and expensive tech culture was taking over the cultural life of the city (despite my earlier complaints about the staid culture of poetry in the Bay Area, at least, in contrast to the techies, they valued *cheap* culture). A new owner took over the warehouse, raising the rents, and Damon (who we subletted from) had to save money by getting rid of the art gallery, and the rehearsal room, and the downstairs dance floor (though 16 people could still live there, and the upstairs stage and dance floor, as well as Greg's Creamery studio remained.

Leonard Cohen Digression

Greg assembled a studio band to re-record Leonard Cohen's *Death Of A Ladies Man* album, over 30 years after its original release in 1977, and asked me to play keyboards and trumpet. Cohen's album was the product a collaboration with Phil Spector suggested by Hollywood Suits in hopes of giving Spector a comeback, and Cohen a crossover. Upon release, Cohen immediately disavowed the album, and today many Leonard Cohen purists consider it far and away his worst album—Cohen at his most embarrassingly unhinged, and adolescent/dirty old man persona, yet it became a kind of "underground classic" for a lot of punks, and "post-punks" even though its sound is more Spector "Wall Of Sound" schmaltz than punk (while recording it Spector called it punk). It was certainly one of David Berman's favorite albums, and Greg helped to trim down what he called the "fat" of Spector's production, while remaining largely faithful to the songs and over all vibe (he wasn't trying to transform the songs like, say, Ruin had).

Cohen's not really dance music; frankly I couldn't even cry to most of it; his catharsis usually felt disembodied (With the exception of "Alexandra Leaving" and "Paper Thin Hotel"), but *Death Of A Ladies Man* had at least one song that was the closest to a "balls-out" dance song Cohen ever got, "Don't Go Home With Your Hard On," and I'd get to be part of a horn tandem with Wallace La Fonte on Tenor Saxophone (the closest to Cynthia Robinson I'd ever got), so this project fascinated me for several reasons.

I was even more interested in Cohen's lesser-known *Death Of A Lady's Man* book of prose poems that I always saw as part of the album; the album and book complement each other as a dying ladies' man and a dying lady's man do. If you want the embarrassing, unhinged and adolescent dirty old man, you'll get it even more in the book than the album, and at times he out languages language poetry. Read it alongside the same years' award winning *Houseboat Days*. Anyway, I loved this book enough that I would pull out the dog-eared copy and read "The Asthmatic" or "It's Probably Spring" at rehearsals with that more groovin' Funkadelic meets Flipper and The Fall like band I was hoping to keep together with two touring veterans of the Bay Area punk scene (Rachel Thoele, and Jon Weiss), even though I couldn't pay them what Flipper or Jello could.

Setting Cohen's words to the minimalist pulse riffs of the bass was opening up new musical opportunities for me, especially as I wanted to let the poets know that I'd be willing to set their poetry to musical arrangements if they wanted that[99], even if I wasn't getting my poetry published, that I hadn't forgotten them! So when Greg asked me to be a part of *his* project, I imagined recording a companion piece, in which Rachel and Jon and I would record more dance trance like extended instrumental improvisations and I'd talk/sing excerpts of the book as either Greg, Barrett Avner or Nick Allen played guitar.

At this time, in the Bay Area there were so many people doing covers of Cohen, even Cohen admitted his cash-cow "Hallelujah" was over-covered, and usually in drabber whitewashed versions than even his originals, as writer Kirk Read noted at the time. There was a male a-capella chorus called *Conspiracy of Beards*, and a female counterpart called *Conspiracy of Venus*. It's amazing how much reverence, or even over-reverence to Cohen there was, and is. Yet I was impressed that when Sylvie Simmons decided to have a book party for her biography of Cohen, *I'm Your Man*, that she choose Greg to put together a one-time ad-hoc live band to play the *Death Of A Ladies' Man* album in its entirety, which had never been done before.

And, as we played beneath the stage on a cool/warm September night surrounded by giant redwoods at the Henry Miller library for her book party on the eve of Cohen's 79th birthday while Sylvie projected childhood films of pre-teen Leonard Cohen skating with his sister on a cold Quebec day, I realized that I was in a situation similar to the Anne Sexton Reading at the Poetry Society of America a decade earlier.[100]

Though Sylvie Simmons was no Leonard Cohen purist (and her insights into both the *Death of A Ladies* man album and book go further than Cohen's other biographers), many of the people gathered at the show were, and clearly Greg knew this, as he presided over this crowd like a drunken punk MC ("First time I heard this album," he told the crowd, "I thought it sucked!" But while Alice Quinn tried to shut us down back at the Poetry Society of America event, Sylvie encouraged this, alongside her own ukulele covers of Cohen. I felt an event like this came closer to bringing "high" and "low" together than any project I'd been a part of in a long time **(end digression).**

---

[99] For instance, I worked on setting poems by Creeley, Coolidge, Kenneth Koch, e.e. cummings, helen adam, edna st. Vincent millay, and others to tunes, including Delia Tramontina's amazing work: https://www.youtube.com/watch?v=fYbdIEvZ9YQ
[100] https://www.youtube.com/watch?v=tlAPIGNpq0I

Save KUSF And Occupy Radio

The scene was dealt another blow, however, that ostensibly had nothing to do with gentrification, when the University of San Francisco sold its radio station KUSF in a complex, and rather shady (illegal), deal with corporate behemoth Entercom which allowed the corporate-for-profit networks make inroads into the non-commercial community "left-of-the-dial" airwaves that were supposed to be protected by the FCC when they stopped enforcing the demands that commercial stations should broadcast from, and serve, the city or town in which they're located. I immediately joined in the fight to save it.[101]

By the time of the death of KUSF in 2011, Bay Area radio was bleak indeed. KALX couldn't take up the slack left by KUSF. If one wanted intellectual and political talk as well as music, the visionary KPOO was the last holdout even though it's harder to get KPOO in Oakland, with its larger African American population, than in San Francisco, which is now only 4% Black; in short, either give KPOO a bigger transmitter, or realize Oakland needs a station like KPOO, too! As the radio has become de-musicized, I find it harder and harder to resist the pull of Pacifica in lieu of that morning motivational music (KPOO's gospel shows can do it for me as much as some of Jesse Luscious' punk-centric shows).

The loss of KUSF hurt the scene (even those who didn't listen), as well as put another nail in the coffin of the viability of radio. And this was precisely one of the points of the telecom act, as it helped usher more of the disaffected radio listeners (who had largely rejected corporate radio, but could be fed by the local 'alternative' emphasis of college and community radio) into the tech driven culture and economy, which, for whatever its benefits,[102] generally traded in a more *eclectic local* emphasis for a more *niche-oriented, but placeless,* and often imported from Hollywood, culture. Even if Pandora was based right here in The New Oakland, it doesn't really have any connection to the scene, though quite a few who worked there are local musicians. I'm not saying tech is categorically bad here, only that the way that it's used is....

After Damon was forced to downsize our warehouse, a few musician lifers and I had this dream that we could start another space in an abandoned warehouse that had once been a pool-hall. This would be at least as good as what Ghost Town/ The Creamery had been before Damon had to half it. Since my other musician and artist friends, like me, had a more capacious vision of the arts (stuff that would straddle the low-art/high art divide, and yes I still could never beat out my love of the sophisticated art that John Yau had been turning me onto for over 30 years,

---

[101] http://bigtakeover.com/essays/open-letter-to-president-privett-on-the-sale-of-kusf-by-the-university-of-san-francisco
[102] SEE APPENDIX; my essay on Albini and Lowery

or the amazing jazz-drumming stylings of James Levi or Donald "Duck" Bailey who was living in Oakland and performing with some of my young friends, as well as the more noisy "industrial" or punk we could never quite beat out of us), we imagined a space that could also bring the underground (and mostly white) young musicians together as well as provide job or internship possibilities for my students at Laney, as well as maybe even be attractive to the older poets and people I met at the YMCA.

To do this, we'd have a plan to go legit. I borrowed money from my ex-girlfriend, and David Berman of the Silver Jews for this cause. I would love nothing more than to tell you that we achieved even a fraction of success, instead (due to gentrification, a corrupt landlord, having the wrong partners, and my own stupidity), it plunged me, and some others, into financial ruin, so by the time Occupy Wall Street got Occupy Oakland going, our plans were thwarted, and I fell into hopelessness again.

I was initially excited by Occupy Wall Street, as were many of the old people at the YMCA, but Occupy Oakland showed no interest in cultivating a relationship with the artist community, or those in the Save KUSF movement, or even my students at Laney, and I always thought that if we had the warehouse space we could have helped forge these alliances.

We could have offered them a place for organizational meetings (and with no cell phones allowed!). Hell, we could've even offered them theme songs, etc. But the occupy folks I knew weren't really reaching out to the Black Community. My (mostly non-white) students at Laney were very skeptical of them, and when I tried to get them to come speak to my students, the occupy people didn't write back.

By their email conversations, it was clear that many of them considered folks like me (and my students) to be "armchair intellectuals," and, once again, I saw the movement's incipient failure in the inability (or refusal) for a coalition between the more extrovert "doer" (camping out on the front lines) and my students who valued using rhetorical and persuasive critical thinking skills in hopes of changing their situations, both individually and collectively. Why, oh why, can't these get together? From where I stood (okay, a chair, but it had no arms!), it was easy to blame the loudest voices of this so-called leaderless movement.

It also seemed they lost their grounding against the finance industry, and turned progressively into "protesting for the right to protest." I remember being very excited when some of the occupiers started a website (which also could allow people to avoid social media); one of the goals of this website was to get everybody to democratically vote on a single-demand that we could all agree on. They were planning a convention for July 4th in Philadelphia with delegates and a platform. I read and studied the list of possible demands with my students, and since we were reading The Black Panther Ten Point Platform, we got angry that some of these 99%ers were using the term "reparations" to refer to *student loan forgiveness*.

We were in favor of student loan forgiveness, but noted that they failed to include the demand for *reparations for slavery*. We saw this as an example of "cultural appropriation" at its worst," so we tried to add this demand to the list in the spirit of democracy.....only to see the website fizzle when it lost some kind of cred because some of the leaderless leaders were saying that the website organizers were trying to act too much like a leader, and, yes, even in terms of self-interest, as a white person I know that if reparations were granted black folks, it would help the poor people and artists (even the poets, as well).

The World Is Not Conclusion (or Making Fun of Tragedy)

As Occupy fizzled, and after government austerity measures cut funding for Laney by the end of 2011, and I wasn't rehired, coupled with some health issues, I became homeless for two years, and my depression and isolation grew.[103] By 2014, Laney rehired me, and I was able to move back into Damon's warehouse, now a shadow of its former self, though Greg's studio was there, and he was still doing amazing work. But in 2016, the gentrifiers and disaster capitalists took advantage of the tragic fire at another warehouse (Ghost Ship), which killed 36 (including two people I knew, Kiyomi Tanouye and Ara Jo), as an excuse to evict, or crack down, on the remaining warehouse living situations in Oakland. City officials, coupled with Mass Media, which made a media circus of the tragedy, argued that they were concerned about "safety," but it was clear they just wanted us out of these warehouses so they could raise the rents. By the end of 2017, Greg's studio at the warehouse was now being advertised on Craigslist as a potential "wine cellar" for those who could pay 4X what we paid. So it's hard to avoid that catastrophist feeling that somehow this Warehouse Fire is also the end of an era, and that things are likely to get worse for the survivors, and for artists and musicians or anybody netting under $40,000 a year looking for affordable housing in this city.

In the absence of music emanating from the warehouse (and not being able to play it anymore), I fear the encroaching pull of the Zeitgeist telling us to be more of a talking head. The combined loss of the warehouse and the radio lead to my lapse into social media addiction (and the increased alienation that causes). Social media may work for some people, but I see it cause more division....And *polemically, I must say this loud, so that others (like my students) who have not had the benefit of either, but have severe reservations about today's technocracy in their brilliant critical thinking papers* may hear, especially as they may wish to join in the anti-gentrification, anti-Hollywood, and anti-Silicon Valley fight, by seeing the common ground: **Social Media Causes More Social Fragmentation** (though I'm not going to argue against a previously marginalized person or viewpoint who feels

---

[103] For a more detailed account of my two as homeless see Life In A Tin Can

THEY can be heard more because of it).

Hell, since Hollywood and The Corporate Music Industry have also been casualties of what Big Tech has done to American culture in the 21st century, maybe even Hollywood will come to realize that it should align itself with these underground, local attempts, to get something going, like the proposed Black Arts District in downtown Oakland.

I'm not saying that there's no longer local music scenes in Oakland (ask Nicholas Taplin), only that after the Ghost Ship Fire, the walls are closing in further and further on it, and certainly, for a disabled person like myself, make it much more difficult to continue to create art. The technocracy and gentrification (which, in the Bay Area, are two names for the same thing) are clearly conspiring to render us more disembodied and alienated talking heads (and, in conjunction with Big Pharma, *medicated* tweeting heads, or, better, digits). Despite everything, I still can't beat that dream for a live/work dorm-like art and activism community, or affordable downtown walking city like my grandma knew out of me, or that dreamed of forming a band that could spend two to three months woodshedding, perhaps while living together (kids are invited), whether in the woods or the city, to hone sounds.... even if the poets may scoff "I lost my center/trying to fight the world."

I stuck it out at the warehouse to the bitter end, and though it's difficult not to feel that Laney College itself may not be around in a few years, I intend to try to stick it out (and hope music will find me again) but, to circle back to Chapter One, perhaps that J.D. Vance guy is right, and I should give up on these big blue state coastal cities, and start again somewhere in "Trumpland" where it's cheaper, but jobs are also harder to find. Will they have me? Will they let me teach what Laney lets me teach? Does asking that make me sound like a blue state snob? *Don't wanna die at 50; don't wanna be homeless!* Or maybe I should leave the country (ah, but remember your culture shock on moving from NYC to Oakland; you think you can adjust to Liberia?). Jackson, Mississippi sounds intriguing, as a mostly black city that has just elected perhaps the most progressive mayor (Chokwe Lumumba) in the country. Would they have me? If nothing else, in the meantime, I can at least take a break from social media by writing this in my car in hopes that some of this writing---which may at times seem like "miserable hysterics"—might actually *do something*....if not the punk hip hop retirement home, at least to prepare for the one/off funeral party. After all, I could've, but didn't, die in that accident, which means I still got a debt to pay.... (*& at this point we could use a little instrumental.... or two....*).

Between Poetry and Prose

You could start with Pennsylvania and Pussycat,
but perhaps that's too wide a space. The walls

close in between words. It's too late for pith
but too early for pushovers! Too late for purple
or punk but too early for pink.

Ponder, if you will, the precious prosaic,
yet process-oriented, prairie between poetry and prose—
Popcorn, poppies, and, ever popular pouting pottery!
Pretty polar bears and potty-mouthed Polish poultry!
In the prologue, if you can't produce a premium porch,
Prefer poignant poker-faced precipitation to prohibitive prelates
As polite primates take precautions against polystyrene
Polygamist politicians pouncing on pro-rated prams!

Possibility! And precedent!
Pristine postures prickle precocious primo-dons
so polka-dotted (polo) pony time pops out of the precious portrait
of a poodle in porridge pouring over the prissy preshrunk porpoise poppers
at the Portuguese proofreaders' prom
that presumes the presence of a proletarian potluck
in this postmodern prism-industrial passage port
with pompous pomegranate polemicists
Polarizing prejudices! Profane professors!
And at the preposterous prep school, private property!
Pressured preludes to pretense projects,
more pre-primitive than Prince or Prine,
promising promotion's post-doc privilege of programmers
while prodigious pragmatic propaganda professionals,
whether pre-martial or post-divorce,
proclaim a proclivity to procrastinate.

The prim priests get their portly portion
and tea-partiers and "progressives" profit profusely
by presciently proposing
the problem that predicts the present
by pre-empting perfect prefaces
to preserve prior prescription prejudices
and prevent pre-war price controls
to poison the Post-Office for the privatized prison pros
to poop the prosaic population proliferation.

In the press release, the polished, pre-recorded
President poses proud at the polls
In a premature polio-ridden precinct.
and pronounces his prophetic proposition,

pranks a positive position on prodigal
premenstrual pornography
and pro-life processed charter cheese.

Pole-vaulting over predecessor privilege
He prevails, possessed by the proposal for more police
But no proactive antipoverty programs,
you pound! You pounce! You try not to prance!

Prearranged points of view get processed
Like potbellied potatoes into papitas fritas
And I prattle we could pray or praise
A pontificating preacher postponing
The postwar powwow with the policy makers'
Practical joke of poverty pollutants
Where profits police the police
With prominent premonitions of our posthumous potential
Where prosody, prehaps, ain't purple
preservatives or preschool poison. Prehaps
(in the pregnant pause of a prairie
far from penis pussy bookend coasts).

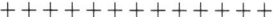

And once upon a time selfishness was altruism & the sacred was a basic need....

APPENDICES

What Can Be Learned From Rwanda About Battling Depression

According to the National Institute of Mental Health, about 14.8 million adult Americans experience clinical depression in any given year -- or about 6.7 percent of the U.S. population over 18.[104] It's possible the number is even higher, but even this is sufficient to show that there's a mental health crisis in the US, despite the fact that the "mental health" industry is one of America's few growth industries in recent years. Or, perhaps, because?

More particularly, many studies have shown that more Americans suffer more intensely from depression during the month of December. The fact that this is the darkest month (and one of the coldest) of the year is often cited as a primary cause for this; some call it Seasonal Affective Disorder (or S.A.D). Some argue that one of the reason Christmas was invented as a holiday placed strategically near the longest night of the year was, in part, to create a social, community, ritual that could lift people's spirits in a, quite literally, dark time. Yet it obviously doesn't work for everyone.

This leads some to wonder: Do the bright lights of Christmas make depression worse than building a ritual around accepting, and even embracing, the dark cold would? Is Christmas similar to the dispersants used to "cover up" the BP Oil Spill in the Gulf of Mexico? Is it possible humans were meant to hibernate in these climates, or at least sleep more, and slow down this time of year? And that the ritual known as Christmas (with New Year's), by pushing people to buy to the prance-tune of that 20th century "Sleigh Ride" standard, and pushing sugar and corn syrup even more than usual to rile people up has actually created a social standard by which a natural, even healthy, response, to the weather is deemed depressive, abnormal, aberrant---and thus add social stigma to reject people and then call them anti-social. To avoid this stigma, many keep their depression hidden during this festive time.

As someone who has been diagnosed with a form of clinical depression, I have seen firsthand how depression is often treated by the mental health industry in general similarly to the way America's ritual of Christmas treats seasonal affective disorder, and have come to some understanding about why current "conventional wisdom" proffered by the mental health establishment is ineffective.

In the US, the two main forms of mental health treatment our mental health system offers are medication and talk therapy, with generally talk therapy being considered the better option that moves beyond the symptom based approach of western medicine, and studies have shown that the white middle class generally has the privilege of talk therapy (not necessarily as a replacement to pills, it could be a supplement) that is not afforded the poorer classes. As one of my students puts it, "a psychiatrist can earn $150 for 3 15

---

[104] http://www.nimh.nih.gov/statistics/1MDD_ADULT.shtml

minute medication visits compared with $90 for a 45 minute talk-therapy session (NY Times 03/06/11, "Health Policy").

With this economic incentive, no wonder medication is preferred by many HMOS. Now, while the verdict is still in on whether the legal pill epidemic (which parallels the illegal opiod epidemic being used to justify a new war on drugs, which like the old war on drugs, may lead to a further increase of drug use) has actually contributed to better mental health—or at least a more behavior-regulated populace, in ways that the talking cure could not achieve on its own, the talking cure remains the favored means of those who can afford it.

Nonetheless, I know many for whom the talking cure hasn't worked (and I always found that talking about my problems more often tended to make them worse), but rather than blaming individual psychologists (certainly some are better than others, or their style meshes better with a particular analysand better), perhaps it's the institution itself that needs some changing. I was thus especially happy to read this quote by an unnamed Rwandan about "western mental health workers." This quote not only offers a diagnosis of what is wrong with the mental health industry, but also suggests an alternative, which could be very helpful here, if we can apply some of this wisdom to America's secular, individualistic, commercial society and an industry still largely based on Freudian models (to say nothing of pharmaceuticals):

"We had a lot of trouble with western mental health workers who came here immediately after the genocide and we had to ask some of them to leave. They came and their practice did not involve being outside in the sun where you begin to feel better. There was no music or drumming to get your blood flowing again. There was no sense that everyone had taken the day off so that the entire community could come together to try to lift you up and bring you back to joy. There was no acknowledgement of the depression as something invasive and external that could actually be cast out again. Instead they would take people one at a time into these dingy little rooms and have them sit around for an hour or so and talk about bad things that had happened to them. We had to ask them to leave." ~ A Rwandan talking to a western writer, Andrew Solomon, about his experience with western mental health and depression. [105]

Many Americans got a taste of the hell of the genocide in Rwanda from the movie Hotel Rwanda. This genocide is a direct result of colonization, or the European attempt to control the population of Rwanda, and other countries in Africa. The most brutal, dramatic manifestations of the genocide may have subsided, but these "western mental health workers," however well-intentioned, are not significantly different from the "Christian missionaries" who beheld "the white man's burden" in Africa and attempted to "enlighten" them into Western ways. Less generously, it's a form of cultural imperialism based on a spurious notion of Western cultural superiority that can be seen in every area

---

[105] From The Moth podcast, 'Notes on an Exorcism'.
http://themoth.org/posts/stories/notes-on-an-exorcismhttp://themoth.org/stories

of our culture. Although not every Rwandan agrees with this quote (and some have claimed great benefits from Western Healthcare methods), I'd like to learn more about these healing practices.[106] They have enough of their own problems after the genocide, and obviously have no interest in trying to colonize America and impose their own cultural rituals here, but reading this statement makes me wish they would!

At the very least, I wish to make the authority of this perspective more permissible and part of a serious discussion on the American mental health crisis. Mental health is understood not in isolation from physical health; being out in the sun makes you feel better. Music and drumming get your blood flowing again, and the spirit flows through the blood. Nor is mental health understood in isolation from the community: "There is no acknowledgement of the depression as something invasive & external that could actually be cast out."

The Western Psychiatric industry makes a little room for "environmental factors."
It even sometimes acknowledges that a sick society produces sick individuals, but it rarely proposes healthy collective outdoor rituals with drumming as a way to address this societal crisis. Neither does American secular culture in general encourage this. The "music industry" in America is usually viewed as entertainment (and it either involves alcohol or drugs, whether legal or not). Even more innovative programs such as "expressive arts therapy" that make an effort to combine the power of music with the paradigm of mental healing often lack that collective, holistic, outdoor, ritual that this Rwandan speaker prefers, and that should at least be considered a legitimate health-care option here.

If the Western mental health professionals in Rwanda can be viewed as a "kinder, gentler" form of "brain police," this policing is running rampant in America. We too are being colonized by such professionals. When the mental health industry became dominant in America during the 20th century, for many the "mental health worker" replaced the traditional role of the "spiritual leader;" the individual in the dingy room that is based on what Freud called "the talking cure" is somewhat similar to the Catholic Confessional. Many believe it's an improvement on that confessional, and on the metaphysics of the church with its "original sin" and sometimes strict and unjust moral codes. Freud's "Copernican revolution" is still, in the official reality, viewed as a sign of progress.

---

[106] NOTE: It may seem to some that I am arguing from a reductive essentialist perspective, or cultural metaphysics, in this piece, so I must make it clear that the Rwandan man I quote should not be emblematic of any quintessentially "uncorrupted" African way of thinking and being if contrasted to a Euro-American way, even though he uses the plural pronoun "we," and even if I mean that this viewpoint is clearly superior. I certainly don't mean to imply that what's best in Africa is anti-modern—to do so would also be a form of cultural imperialism. So I caution against any such overgeneralizations from my anecdote—for I am aware that many Africans are fighting not against modernity, but against its false conflation with (or use by) neo-colonialism.

But whatever the failings of the traditional church to combat what is now called "depression," Joy De Gruy makes an important point when she writes, ""If we were to take the combined number of individuals successfully treated using the recognized theories of Freud, Adler, Jung, Erickson, Bandura and others, would it equal the numbers if those who were able to restore their health through their faith? (pg. 202/3). And some churches make much more room for the kind of healing activities the Rwandans describe.

The gospel music that has characterized the Black Church since Thomas Dorsey brought it in almost a century ago (roughly contemporary to Freud) has been one way to bring this Rwandan wisdom in to the largely dominant secular society, but it need not be restricted to the church. What the Rwandan is speaking in favor of cannot really be understood in terms of the specialization of disciplines and professions as well understand them: The Psychiatric Industry, The Church, and The Music (and Culture) industry, need to be combined, to see their common roots. We need a ritual that serves all three of these purposes in order to have any hope of getting out of our contemporary cultural malaise, and truly address health issues at the root.

Since so many of our rituals, like Christmas, that are designed to stave off depression actually make it worse, we may need a ritual that allows people to scream out their depression, or what that official commercial holiday calls our depression. Perhaps, for starts, we may translate the psychological term "depression" into the religious term, "the devil." Or perhaps it comes even closer to call depression "the blues." Both seem to be a more dynamic way to understand it: Take the lyrics from any Blues song and replace the word "blues" with depression. Ah, to some it seems a paradox, to sing or play the blues to rid oneself of them, or that (as Dizzy Gillespie put it) that "spirituals were the blues too (you need a psychiatrist to figure that one out)," but one of my favorite Christmas blues performances is James Brown singing "Santa Claus, Santa Claus, Please, Please, Please, Don't Make Me Suffer So." (and that by 'blues' we don't just mean the specific (historical?) genre called the blues, but could include hip hop, etc)

Because we're all born into, even baptized, into this individualistic, specialized, fragmented culture, we often have to choose one of these specialized disciplines to work in—if we need to move beyond them. These specialized disciplines, however, can all become "these dingy little rooms:" the office cubicle or heroic artist's studio, the individual coffin buried in private property you must pay for, the private authentic, "real" self, with an "internal" problem that might be part of his salient character, or essence. All of this keeps us divided, fragmented, an alienated from each other. It's grounded in a false consciousness. Can we operate "in" this world without being "of" it; I tried to.

I tried to start from music and drumming, music as drumming, music as drumming and dancing. Of course, I couldn't do it alone. Of course, one doesn't have to do it alone. That won't help; that won't really be music. In contemporary America, however, we call a "singer songwriter" a musician the same we call a psychiatrist a mental health expert—both without drums, and both laboring alone. This might do some good for some people, and I'm not suggesting we ban it from this country. But I do think there are many of us who, like the Rwandans, would like to ask them to leave and stop being so damn paternalistic in speaking for a "norm." We would like the option of "alternative" medicine, even if this "alternative" is ancient wisdom of the oldest culture on earth, a culture that has been threatened by hostile outside forces, been subject to cultural society, and yet still preservers!

What the Rwandans propose is, in this culture, threatening to both the "mental health" industry and the music industry. This is one of the reasons there are so many depressed musicians; however well-known they are, they still are not permitted much of a context in which to present themselves as healers, or at least part of a healing process. The highest most profound purposes and functions that music can have can easily get lost because of an individualistic definition of what "music" is.

In 20th century mass-culture, America never really had a ritual like the ones Rwandans describe, but the rituals of what Nelson George refers to as the "rhythm and blues world" (circa 1950—1975) came close (and there are still local hip hop enclaves to this day, despite what Hollywood wants you to think). The music was closer to, and much more integrally, a part of the culture, and more connected to the "social body." And, today, even with the synthetic, isolated, drum beats, such dance music can still touch the collective soul in a deeper way than other forms of music being pushed.

When I got into music, it was with the mission and purpose that we could at least bring more of this back, to use music as a force to bring people together. Yet, in Hollywood, I was egged on by a "manager" who banished drums and sing-alongs from my "act," to become a terrible heretic to music and to mental health and even a traitor to my body, when I became known as a "singer songwriter." Of all the musical roles, "singer songwriter" is perhaps the stiffest, the most like what the Rwandan describes as the "western mental healthcare professional;" at least it was for me. This doesn't mean that I can't find some pleasure, and health in the singer songwriter (the ability to make one, or many cry, with a heartfelt ballad is nothing to be sneezed at), but I saw firsthand how being cast in this role can be as destructive to mental health as the state-hired health care professionals were. This is not a coincidence.

I am not saying that in order for music to truly have any power we must aspire to exactly what we can still find in contemporary Rwanda; at its best, America produced a music culture that combined elements of African music with elements of European music. "The singer songwriter" is much more a Euro invention of white America, but it can be brought much closer to the African paradigms, and if one feels a deep, authentic, need for drums and dancing to get the blood flowing, we should be able to include it—especially if we're going to be called musicians (but even if we're going to be called mental health workers, teachers, preachers, or other culture workers).

And this is only one aspect of what I learn, and admire, and long for, from this man *in Rwanda. Seriously, I wouldn't mind if this view "colonized" America; it wouldn't be colonization however. The Rwandan isn't telling the colonizing shrinks that they're wrong, they're just asking them to leave. If they continue to speak for us, and tell us what's supposed to better for us (despite the testimony of our senses), I wish they would leave here too…or can they change? Can they understand the damage they do? Can they give us an alternative that doesn't rob of us our heart-beat, especially if they sincerely believe they are trying to help us (and I'm willing to grant they are sincere).*

Underground Classic

*Imagine a life in which just the desserts
Arrive (yes, I know this is supposed to
be an advanced class). Now chisel something
Neurotic from that pre-narcissistic stone.
This is your task (not to have tasks), to think
Of obstacles as easily rid as they really are
In certain moods. Moods certain of uncertainty,
Of the porous walls the actor playing the phantom
Chance topples during the outtake
(of a storm scene by the subway stop)
That becomes an underground classic to pay
The rent of the middlemen I wish
To see myself as now that the autopsy
Proves what the author has died of
("refinery smoke") without proving it dead.
To rest in peace when dead you have to be
A firehouse of activity when alive.
That's probably a law of nature
But prove me wrong. Prove me nothing
But an opinion and I'll come down
From my cross for supper but only if
I can call it breakfast and only if I can
call blood wine and while you're at it
Show me how you watch the tube
Without identifying with the walking
Advertisements, the exclamation
That life truly is for some (who'd rather
play the verb-noun game than the
idea-thing game and maybe they'll get to
the blue-green-yellow, the male-female game
before noon slinks by and notes us).*

What, If Anything, Can David Lowery or Steve Albini Teach Us About The State of The Music (Industry) Today? (2013)

The arguments over free downloading and its effect on musicians and music lovers have, once again, flared up on social media. Judging by the clogged comment boxes on reposts of essays by veteran musicians Steve Albini and David Lowery, it's clear that many are worried about the state of the music industry today. Clearly it has transformed in the last decade—for better or worse? And, if for worse, what can be done to make it better? Despite the immense shift of revenue from the creators of content to the owners of the internet platforms (Google, etc), can independent (non-corporate sponsored) musicians navigate this new technology to our benefit? And, if so, how? Although the arguments tend to get reduced to click bait, the contrasting positions of these two musicians are a good place to start to consider this controversy that doesn't seem to be going away any time soon.

On the one hand, Albini optimistically speaks in defense of fantastic new developments the internet affords both fans and musicians, while others dismiss his arguments as Randian. On the other hand, Lowery pessimistically criticizes these developments and is derisively dismissed as "an old fogey, or someone who won't let go of the past." (Culture Crash, 104). While both men appeal to the lesser-known musician and music appreciator, Albini supports today's status quo, while Lowery searches for alternatives to it. In 1993, it was Lowery who embraced the status quo while Albini argued against it. Revisiting the "indie rock" world of that 1993, as well as the 80s' underground music scene from which both these men emerged, may help illuminate today's debates.

For many, the early 1990s period was/is seen as a golden age—and, in retrospect, perhaps the last golden age-- of grassroots independent American musical culture if compared to the developments of the subsequent two decades. It is during this era when Albini and Lowery achieved their biggest success in pop-culture. Perhaps Albini's biggest success came with producing Nirvana's In Utero, while Lowery's had come as lead singer of "indie rock" band Cracker. These can serve as two contrasting examples of how independent musicians negotiated with the demands of a corporate dominated industry while still maintaining the alternative/street or "college rock" cred they achieved during the 80s (whether through Big Black or Camper Van Beethoven).

Albini, as a producer, could always keep at least one foot out of the coopting corporations ("one foot in the door, the other foot in the gutter/ the sweet smells that you adore, I think I'd rather smother!" as Paul Westerberg would put it). With his recording studio day job, Albini wasn't dependent on the whims of the corporations. If the corporations turned away from indie rock as they largely did by 1998 (with a rare White Stripes exception here and there), Albini could remain grounded in punk's low-fi jam-econo alternative economy and held onto aspects of the DIY aesthetic in a kind of recession-proof field. I remember working with him in 1999 and applauding as he bragged that he could gouge the bands on the corporate labels, and then take that money and charge independent bands less—he represented a kind of heroic Robin Hood figure in this regard.

David Lowery, on the other hand, achieved more mainstream success in his own band's name during the early 90s. In Cracker, his persona as a musician did still partake in some of the quirky, smart-ass, yet cute California laid-back, cow-punk defiance that characterized his 80s band Camper Van Beethoven (whose most famous song, especially after Bowling For Columbine was "Take The Skinheads Bowling") even as he played into that decade's mandate for "larger than life" arena shows.

In both cases, whether fronting Cracker or producing Nirvana, both Lowery and Albini had managed to make the transition from the smaller clubs and college radio scenes of the 1980s to the increasing Winner-Take-All (or All-Or-Nothing) corporate run music economy. The difference between the 80s and 90s, from this perspective, parallels the difference in rock music between the 60s and 70s; Cracker was to CVB what the arena rock band The Faces were to the Small Faces, or Led Zeppelin to The Yardbirds---both aesthetically and in the way they were distributed. Also, from this perspective Cracker, unlike Camper Van Beethoven, isn't strictly speaking "indie rock," but rather (as Wikipedia puts it) alternative rock.

If viewed from the perspective of mainstream culture, the early 90s seemed like a cultural opening (both Big Black and Camper Van Beethoven were non-entities in the era of Madonna/Michael Jackson and the Big Hair Bands), no wonder so many claimed that, in crossing over, WE (the 80s local underground, from punk to hip hop) WON! As Scott Timberg puts it:

The '90s saw the flowering of indie, or 'alternative' rock, and (commercial AOR) radio---which had been locked in a restrictive, repetitive 'classic rock' format enforced by unadventurous programmers for at least two decades—had the chance to open up." (Culture Crash, 95). The corporations had finally seen the light, and now we could have Lollapalooza (just as the baby boomers had Woodstock, which was in many ways just a glorified advertisement for the more expensive, white suburbs and the bigger-is-better society of the spectacle the corporations benefit by).

Yet, for every one celebrating Nirvana's cross-over success and claiming WE WON, there was another one calling Cobain a sell-out, or a victim of forces beyond his control. Amid the debates of this time, Steve Albini published his seminal essay "The Problem With Music" in 1993. In that essay, he urges fellow musicians to avoid signing with a major corporate label—not on any particular moral "sell-out" grounds, but because the label-industry of the time was inefficient, exploited musicians and led to subpar music. He was arguing out of enlightened self-interest.

By contrast, Lowery was enjoying the most successful, biggest selling album of his career (both before and since) released on Richard Branson's Virgin Records (which had been sold to Thorn EMI a year earlier). At the time, Lowery clearly was optimistic about the "free market" and appealed to the post-Nirvana wave of youthful optimism that characterized this time in the lyrics to one of Cracker's biggest hits:

Yeah, we ain't got no government loans
And no one sends a check from home
And get this, we're just doin' what we wanna—
   Cracker, "Get Off This"

Albini and Lowery were both letting their own hedonistic freak flags fly (though Cracker was certainly tamer, and more in line with a conventional rock band formula than Camper Van Beethoven was, and Albini's production of Nirvana was certainly no Rape Man!), and express a cockiness that could stick it to the man! The main difference being that Albini was mostly criticizing the large corporations, while Lowery, who was working for Virgin/EMI, mostly went after the government.

Meanwhile, the grassroots scenes that made both hip hop and punk (or 'indie') so vital in the 80s was being undercut; the ground was crumbling or eroding beneath the well-hyped success stories---thanks to the corporate co-opting and colonizing that narrowed out the range of options (marginalizing "conscious hip hop" as well as the quirkier white indie acts from the select choice cuts it put forth as commodity). While Cracker crossed over, the weirder Monks Of Doom, the other members of Lowery's storied 80s band, Camper Van Beethoven, languished in obscurity; while Dean Wareham's Luna crossed over to an extent, the other 2/3 of Galaxie 500 didn't; while Albini made money off Nirvana and Robert Plant, that didn't mean his own band Shellac crossed over (not that he needed it). The underground, indie, college radio culture, with its more eclectic and democratic playlists that had nourished both Albini and Lowery's career, became decimated as "commercial alternative" stations sprung up. And by 1996, with the passage of the Telecommunications act, which both consolidated corporate ownership of radio, and paved the way for iPOD culture, this window (of opportunity) was shut again, just like the coffins over the corpses of Kurt Cobain and Tupac Shakur.

After the corporations had succeeded in destroying, for many, the viable 'jam econo' strength in numbers scene that Azerrad and others justly mythologize, the Telecommunications Act of 1996, as Timberg puts it, was "a gift to corporate consolidation, and especially to Clear Channel Communications. 'Radio's Big Bully,' as the journalist Eric Boehlert had dubbed the company, swallowed hundreds of stations and standardized their playlists; other consolidations followed suit....now any possibility of a fresh sound on the air was gone. If a song took too long for test audiences to recognize, it was eliminated---so the range of bands that listeners heard narrowed." (95).

Cracker's 1996 album, ironically called The Golden Age, and many others like it as a result bombed when corporate controlled pop came to dominate the late 90s (for instance, the corporations could borrow the image from the "chick rock" phenomena to transition people from Alanis to the Spice Girls to Brittney Spears thus making the pop music of

2000 very similar to the pop music of 1990 as if Nirvana or PJ Harvey, to say nothing of Public Enemy, had never happened).

In this sense, Albini's 1993 essay proved to be all too true, and the optimistic sentiments expressed in Cracker's "Get Off This" seem more and more naïve. Lowery may not have directly needed a government loan to do what he wants to, but he, and other indie and alternative rockers, did need government regulations. College radio, which had played a large part in developing his reputation during the 80s, was created by government intervention. These stations, serving the public interest, were also run on a volunteer economy, often by students who themselves needed government loans to attend college. The corporations wanted control of the entire airwaves. And, once these corporations were deregulated in 1996, there was no room for bands like Cracker, to say nothing of the weirder Camper Van Beethoven.

Considering these lyrics to "Get Off This" in light of Lowery's passionate activism 20 years later against the 21st Century Technopoly may very well reveal the tragic hubris many shared in the early 90s, especially if we contrast what has happened to Lowery to what has happened to Albini in the same two decade period. While Lowery, and many others like him, "have been hit especially hard by the meltdown of the record industry" (Timberg, 88) since 2001, Albini has not suffered---in large part because he didn't put all—or even most—of his eggs in that corporate record industry basket. Lowery's career, by contrast, had already been on the decline before iTunes came along.

Yet, the Telecommunications Act didn't simply kill old models of production, it also, at first, seemed to offer new possibilities that could make up for what was lost for independent musicians. Both Albini and Lowery, in their different ways, embraced these new technological possibilities: "We thought we'd make more money through disintermediation and selling music directly to fans," Lowery claims (Culture Crash, 114) Lowery, however soon found that cutting out the record-label as middle man just created a new, bigger, middleman. "We brought [Facebook] all our fans, and now they're selling them back to us. That's classic exploitative re-intermediation. But we should have seen this coming—the people with the biggest computer servers, the biggest marketing budget, will win." (Timberg 115)

Thus, David Lowery, 20 years after "Get Off This" has changed his tune, and is one of the most vocal proponents of government regulation of the free market. In the process, he has aligned himself with the RIAA labels, those who Albini calls "the administrative parts of the old record business," who seem like the little guy compared to the Telecom Monopolies that have been made possible by the Telecommunications Act of 1996. Albini, by contrast, sees the internet as an extension, a continuation, and even a culmination, of the "old underground" from the 80s in which he, as well as Lowery, cut their teeth. Albini thus maintains his optimism about the internet—in part because he's not interested in making money through selling recordings as Lowery is, and assumes that music listeners have money for the more expensive technological gadgets.

Albini considers the RIAA labels "*the framework of an exploitative system that I have been at odds with my whole life*" (Face The Music), but neither does he argue for the government to regulate them. He can still brag he needs no government loan, and just does what he wants to. He believes the internet has both benefitted fans as well as musicians through the very cutting out of the record label's middleman that Lowery had come to realize he was duped by. "*The internet has facilitated the most direct and efficient, compact relationship ever between band and audience. And I do not mourn the loss of the offices of inefficiencies that died in the process.*" (Face The Music)

By contrast, Lowery shows how the new model hurts both fans and bands. He likens file-sharing and free downloading to "looting" and claims that "*Verizon, AT&T, Charter, etc etc. are charging a toll....to get the free stuff......you need to have a $1,000 dollar laptop, a $500 dollar iPhone or $400 Samsung tablet. It turns out the supposedly "free" stuff really isn't free. In fact it's an expensive way to get "free" music....and none of that money goes to the artists!*"

Both Albini and Lowery make excellent points and both are right from their perspective, and even though they appear to be on opposite sides of the debate over the deregulated free file sharing culture of the internet today, it's reductive to simply argue that Lowery prefers the "old system" while Albini prefers the "new system" especially if we consider the ways in which the pre-internet "indie" or underground world of the 1980s from which both came was opposed to what both refer to as the "old system". (the corporate system that dominated during the 80s and 90s, pre-internet era in which the CD dominated) as they would to the new (tech) system had it been around then.

In his keynote address at the Face The Music symposium in Melbourne, Albini describes why this 80s underground/independent model was better than the old corporate model Lowery seems to want to defend. In the 1980s, "*bands existed outside that label spectrum. The working bands of the type I've always been in, and for those bands everything was always smaller and simpler....*"

This doesn't mean that it was a bed of roses:

"*Local media didn't take bands seriously until there was a national headline about them so you could basically forget about press coverage. And commercial radio was absolutely locked up by the payola-driven system of the pluggers and program directors....So these independent bands had to be resourceful. They'd built their own infrastructure of independent clubs, promoters, fanzines and DJs. They had their own channels of promotion, including the beginnings of the internet culture that is so prevalent today – that being bulletin boards, and newsgroups. These independent bands even made their own record label. Some were collectives and those that weren't were likely to operate on a profit-sharing basis that encouraged efficiency, rather than a recoupable patronage system that encouraged indulgence.*"[107]

[107] Notice how Albini does not, by name at least, mention the important role of college radio in all this.

That's where I cut my teeth, in that independent scene full of punks and noise freaks and drag queens and experimental composers and jabbering street poets. You can thank punk rock for all of that. That's where most of us learned that it was possible to make your own records, to conduct your own business and keep control of your own career....And there was a healthy underground economy of bands making a reasonable income owing to the superior efficiencies of the independent methods. My band, as an example, was returned 50% of the net profit on every title that we released through our record label. I worked it out and that earned us a better per-piece royalty than Michael Jackson, Bruce Springsteen, Prince, Madonna or any other superstar operating concurrently. And we were only one of thousands of such bands." (Face The Music)

Although both Albini and Lowery cut their teeth in this non-corporate pre-internet music economy, neither of them go so far as to use their voices or influences to argue for trying to recreate it, against both the RIAA and Tech profiteers. Albini thinks the internet is at least as good as what was lost, while Lowery seems more interested in reinstating the RIAA's dominance and imposing regulations on tech companies to stop the bleeding. Both, in their differing ways, are fighting for the right of the individual rather than of the scene. Indeed, since they both "developed reputations during the label era," they thus "don't need the same kind of publicity support and investment some labels used to offer." (Culture Crash, 111).

That's the point that needs to be emphasized for the independent musician (of any genre, not just "indie rock") who is trying to develop a reputation today, or for the fan of music who values being part of a contemporary independent music scene at least as vital and self-sustaining as the scene Lowery, Albini, and many others first emerged from. Can people unite today, and be as resourceful, as we were in the 1980s? If so, can Albini or Lowery bring their not inconsiderable clout to this larger cause that could benefit the music culture? Perhaps....but ultimately it's probably more important to look at what they did (then), and not what they say (now)...and, put down our privatized iPod and try to bring the word "independent" back to the collective meaning it had back in the 80s if not the more individualistic one it had corporate-dominated 90s.

I am no fan of what the internet has done to American's music culture, and, by comparison, what Hollywood's Corporate Music Industry did to the underground scenes in the 80s or 90s (unless you were exceptional enough to make a living running a recording studio like Albini) doesn't seem that bad, but just because the independent musician and Hollywood have a shared enemy in the new Technocracy doesn't mean that the enemy of my enemy is necessarily my friend. I, for one, would be willing to work with the old music industry against the current wealth gap promulgated by the technocracy, but only if it can also use its muscle to support local scenes more than it did in the past, and does in the present.

If The Music Branch of Hollywood reallocate some of the funds it spends on PR and lawyers to invest in local scenes, recruiting A&R talent from the local scenes, and, rather than trying to colonize, or otherwise "speak for" local scenes, allow them (us) more autonomy and self-determination, in creating a civic community center (with both physical and virtual component) or 5, that showcases the wealth of local talent, it may be the only thing that could give it a fighting chance in the battle it's losing against Silicon Valley. Sure, Hollywood and the Corporate Music industry wouldn't have risen to the heights it had (whether in the 20s or the 90s) had it not had such success in undercutting and fragmenting local scenes and cultures, but I'm willing to talk to anyone. Oh, Hollywood, I despised you long enough (and I won't deny that I've sometimes been entertained by you, and you've served important social functions), so perhaps we may make a pact. Decentralization (or subsidiarity) is the only thing that can save you, and perhaps that's our only hope.

What Can It Mean To Start A Record Label In The New Tech Economy? (2009)

Since the computer industry has swallowed up both music radio and the retail record business, most "independent" labels and record stores today, like most radio stations, are first and foremost websites. In a social media dominated era where fewer people browse host websites than ever (but rather click on links on facebook), is it possible to create a website/record label that doesn't feel barren and that wouldn't just be an economic disaster?

Perhaps what's needed today is not another "label" per se, but a podcast that thinks like both a record label and a radio station, since radio has historically been less barren, and more two-way, than record labels (record labels were usually dependent on radio). In the radio lexicon, podcasts aren't broadcasts; they're narrowcasts, yet there is nothing intrinsic to podcast technology that demands its current emphasis on the worldwide (placeless) and privatized (individualized) over a basis in local communities. It can utilize the cutting-edge technology, but borrow its mode of production from the local and regional commercial radio stations circa 1947-1967.

Even if Big Tech and Big Music don't want to admit it, many Americans are starving for a local, eclectic culture, even if they don't know it yet (because Big Tech and Hollywood do a good job of indoctrinating kids even before they get to school). With an emphasis on the local, eclectic and collective rather than placeless, niche and individual, Pop Snob's vision is to create a podcast/streaming service, or even "record label" (clearing house) that can bring various currently specialized genres, and segregated demographics, together on a local basis in the spirit of "unity in diversity" and "strength in numbers." Our mission is to bridge the increasingly wide gulf between the vital local (which are usually called underground) live music scenes and existing record labels & radio stations (and services like Pandora) that are local in name only.

The podcast can succeed with a modest-business model where the more expensive e-tech services (peddled at the SF Music Tech Conference) fail because we understand that the podcast must be rooted in a place. We already have an "undisclosed location" to operate from. Because our live/work warehouse is a recording studio as well as a rehearsal and *performance space, we have a larger pool of talent to work with and a built-in audience with unmet needs. This gives us a huge advantage over any 'trickle down' podcast to re-create Oakland as a viable cultural export, or at the very least provide an alternative to the money, and, talent drain from Oakland to cities like LA.*

If you conceive of this website from the point of view of "record label," you could say our first release will be a LOCAL COMPILATION ALBUM, but this new compilation album will not be conceived of as an isolated object; in fact, it's a radio show (podcast) as much as it's a record (of course, they'll be cassettes or vinyl for those inclined). One advantage to conceiving of this label as a streaming podcast is that we can include at least one song by every local band who has submitted one for this comp on the streaming 24/7 flow, which allows it to be more inclusive and democratic than traditional "comps." And, of course, some songs will be more popular than others, but 'sleepers' will be given a chance.

But even if there is a more curated physical object (cassette or vinyl for those so inclined), it doesn't have to be so fetishized, for even the songs that, rightly or wrongly, don't make the comp, will be available for play and sale on the website, and played on the podcasts. This will not just be random (faceless, placeless) radio either, but curated by entertainers who may sing the local weather forecast, and host the events that could also be called "release parties." The first of these events will be a local dance party, with the stated goal of trying to create a new local dance craze that could be a cultural export, like "The Swim" was in 1964.

Despite the conventions of niche marketing, all dance music by definition has one thing in common—a beat that can bring people together more than many community activists. There are only two requirements for participation in this particular inaugural comp: 1) It must be local and 2) It must be a dance song; a dance song that could very well turn into a "Dance Craze." This creates the thematic unity that can accommodate the diversity of Oakland live music, from punk to hip-hop, without forcing any act to change its musical style.

June 19, 2014, to celebrate the 50th anniversary of **"The Swim,"** *Pop Snob records will hold a release dance-party, a multi-media video shoot at our warehouse, and at least one outdoor location.*[108] *This "interdisciplinary" variety show will feature new songs by local bands, and will also be recorded and filmed to coordinate efforts within the fragmented local music culture, and beyond into other specialized, but related, fields. It also provides a perfect opportunity for the many underemployed graduates of the area's many fine colleges in such fields as choreography, fashion, murals, videography, that attend our shows, to show off their skills and beef up their portfolios (i.e. job creation).*

Choreographers will come up with dances, and clothes designers with fashions, that could

---

[108] I was planning ahead 5 years, thinking it would take at least that long...... ;)

also provide thematic unity. Nor will this only be a "youth culture" event, I know quite a few women in their 70s who can do the Hully Gully better than the younger white retro-mods (and you could also think of this event as a weekend-long multi-venue conference, with panel discussions, like academics and Noise Pop do, and these older women are teaching a class on the history of dance moves).

This well publicized event, at first, will utilize a barter (or gift) economy, with no guarantee of economic compensation for anybody involved. But the volunteer economy will last for no more than one year, like the on-the-job training of an internship, and in the meanwhile promises to be at least as fun as the entertainment many of these underemployed cultural workers already pay for.[109] With even this loose coordination of efforts between musicians, dancers, models, fashion designers, painters, comics, activists, DJS, and conceptual artists, we can provide a strong launching pad for the Bay Area's first true collective cultural export since The Humpty Hump. We will even have an on-line voting over what the shared theme of this event should be.

I could say more, but hopefully you get the idea, and it inspires your own creative juices flowing to come up with better ideas. I like the idea of 4 per year, 4 events, 4 "release dates" for a collective release of dozens or, soon, hundreds of shared MP3 singles (or "audio files") played in heavy and light rotation on the podcast (which may grow into a full 24/7 'radio station.')

We will establish firm connections to accredited colleges such as Expressions Studio school, CCA, or Laney, to offer college credit as field work, for helping record and document these events, to help re-establish the original pact live music had with the other non-musical arts and crafts. We don't have to go out of the scene to find commercial cross marketing "tie ins," or mutually beneficial alliances, since many of us wear several hats. Musicians will donate their songs at first to a video that will also serve as an advertisement for a local business. This will be strictly barter arrangement at first; both will benefit. There's at least two equally valid ways of explaining the relationship, depending on the needs of those involved.

For the **musicians**, it's a far cheaper way to create a high quality video for their music (whether they participate in the live event or not), and develop a more loyal, grounded,

---

[109] Since most of the talent is already doing these things anyway, and being unfairly compensated, I'm not worried about exploiting anybody, and am more than willing to sign an agreement straight-up , saying that, for this first year, I too need no profit, or to take anything off the top, from what these artists make once the basic infrastructure is set up.
After a year, we can renegotiate; those who worked from the beginning, can have "shares"

We could talk about profit-sharing methods more deeply…By then, perhaps, we will have lured a VC, or even some of that old Hollywood money, who will help us with no strings attached out of a sense of shared self-interest now that it's own existence is threatened by Silicon Valley.

fan base, and general audience beyond just "those who go to shows." For a locally owned **business,** it's free or cheap advertising that could also lend it some street-cred, and a way around trying to compete with the giant corporate chains on their terms.

Economically, the risk is small, yet with perseverance and collective focus, it can result in taking back local culture from the whims of the globalized, syndicated, outside music and tech corporations who have colonized and fragmented us. We trust the musicians to create high-quality songs, and the choreographers and videographers to have quality control in their fields of specialization.

As our use value increases, once we create a critical mass of high quality, innovative, but low budget, videos and installation pieces, it will be much easier to monetize the relationship with other businesses, as well as between the various participants. Collectively, we will set affordable rates for advertising that will publicize other businesses that understand the benefits of our campaign in the spirit of selfish altruism (because you can't really be one without the other).[110] On a 24/7 podcast, there's more room for other kinds of music as well (to those who don't want dance music, but that seems the best place to start, and could create more opportunities for musicians of all genres, as well as other local artists.

Occupy Radio Demands (Atavistic) (2011)
1. Nationally, the primary legislative demand of Occupy Radio is immediate reinstatement of the regulations that forbid outside owners from owning more than 2 radio stations in any given market, as well as other anti-trust regulations abolished by the Telecom Act.
2. Locally, we demand the reclamation by the City of Oakland of at least 2 radio stations from the monopolistic thieves who have robbed us of jobs, a tax-base, a grass-roots culture, economy and even civic pride
3. We demand that the City explicitly prohibit places of business open to the public from playing canned music not made locally without first considering all the options for locally grown live in store or recorded performances.[111]

---

[110] We don't need your LA Palms.
[111] especially those that have received unfair incentives to undersell and buy out locally owned businesses; they will also be forbidden from placing prefab "art"—often not even made in America by slave labor—without considering the local artists who have better things to do than wait for the magic wand of the 1% to discover them.

www.ingramcontent.com/pod-product-compliance
Lightning Source LLC
Chambersburg PA
CBHW050213230526
45470CB00001B/359